California Cannabis Laws

MAUCRSA Edition

Omar Figueroa

California Cannabis Laws: MAUCRSA Edition

ISBN 978   0-9984215-1-3

Disclaimer

This publication has been created to provide you with accurate and authoritative information concerning California cannabis law. It is sold with the understanding that the publisher is not engaged in rendering legal or other professional services. This publication is not a substitute for legal advice of an attorney. If you require legal or other expert advice, you should seek the services of a competent attorney or other professional.

The law is ever changing and sometimes errors happen even with careful attention to detail. Although this publication is designed to aid in the research and practice of cannabis law, it is recommended that you cross check the California Legislature website for any change in the law. The URL for the Legislature's website is: http://leginfo.legislature.ca.gov/faces/codes.xhtml

Also, please keep yourself informed by purchasing the most up-to-date edition of this publication as it comes available.

Colophon

Author: Omar Figueroa, Esq.
Legal and Research Assistant: Tina S. Smith, J.D.
Book design and layout: Jocelyn Bergen. This book is set in the Sabon typeface.
Cover design: Tina S. Smith, J.D.
Published by Lux Law Publishing

Dedication

This MAUCRSA edition of *California Cannabis Laws* is dedicated to Tina Suzanne Smith, J.D. Thank you, Tina, for your dedication, perseverance, and attention to detail.

Preface

California cannabis laws have greatly expanded in the past few years. Not only did California voters "legalize" cannabis for adults 21 and older with the passage of Proposition 64, known as the Adult Use of Marijuana Act (AUMA) in November of 2016, but the Legislature also created a new framework for medical cannabis regulations with several bills comprising the Medical Cannabis Regulation and Safety Act (MCRSA). Adult use and medical cannabis laws were then merged together in 2017 into a comprehensive regulatory scheme to create the Medicinal and Adult-Use Cannabis Regulation and Safety Act (MAUCRSA).

I am a practicing lawyer in California, and I saw an unmet need for a reference volume containing California's cannabis laws. (I compiled my own binder with AB 243, AB 266, SB 643, etc., like many of my colleagues have, and when that task was completed, I realized I needed to organize the contents of the bills by code and code section.) All of the relevant code sections pertaining to cannabis law in California have been arranged into this comprehensive reference work. Moreover, the relevant code sections can be easily found with the annotated table of contents, with detailed section descriptors summarizing the contents of each code section.

Why is such a book necessary in this day of free online access to California's Codes? Because MAUCRSA did not create a legal tabula rasa by repealing all former cannabis laws and establishing a new legal order. Instead, MAUCRSA changed and augmented the existing laws, making California cannabis laws even more byzantine than before.

It was not always this way. Cannabis was legal in California until 1913, when the Poison Act was amended to outlaw "narcotic preparations of hemp or loco-weed." (At that point, it was legal under federal law.) In the 1950's, possession was escalated to a felony with mandatory jail. The madness continued until 1976, when the Legislature decriminalized possession of small quantities of marijuana with the Moscone Act. Nevertheless, the cultivation of a single plant, and the sale or possession for sale of any amount, remained non-reducible felonies under California law for decades.

On November 5, 1996, California voters approved Proposition 215, the Compassionate Use Act (CUA), making California the first state in the United States to legalize the possession and cultivation of medical cannabis by patients and primary caregivers. For the first time in nearly a century, patients were allowed to use medical cannabis for the treatment of "cancer, anorexia, AIDS, chronic pain, spasticity, glaucoma, arthritis, migraine, or any other illness for which marijuana provides relief."

Senate Bill 420 was passed in 2003, and became effective on January 1, 2004, establishing a voluntary program for the issuance of official identification cards to qualified medical cannabis patients and caregivers. SB 420 also purported to establish default limits of no more than eight ounces of dried processed flowers per qualified patient and no more than six mature or 12 immature marijuana plants per qualified patient; these "limits" were subsequently struck down by the California Supreme Court as unconstitutional legislative amendments to Proposition 215, to the extent that they burden an accused's defense. SB 420 also established a medical defense for qualified patients and caregivers who associate "in order collectively or cooperatively to cultivate cannabis for medical purposes." The era of collectives and cooperatives was born.

In 2010, Governor Schwarzenegger signed Senate Bill 1449, which reclassified possession of up to 28.5 grams of marijuana from a no jail misdemeanor punishable by a $100 maximum fine, to an infraction with the same lenient penalties, but without the right to a jury trial afforded to misdemeanor defendants by the California Constitution.

The Medical Marijuana Regulation and Safety Act (with the unfortunate acronym MMRSA) was passed on September 11, 2015, and went into effect on January 1, 2016. It first consisted of three bills: SB 643, AB 266, and AB 243. They established a new regulatory agency, the Bureau of

Medical Marijuana Regulation (BMMR, pronounced "bummer"), created a regulatory framework with a dual licensing system requiring local permits and state licenses, and added a sunset clause to the collective and cooperative defense. Within the next year, more legislation was added, which resulted in numerous changes including a renamed Medical Cannabis Regulation and Safety Act (MCRSA) and Bureau of Medical Cannabis Regulation (BMCR).

On November 8, 2016, the California voters approved the Adult Use of Marijuana Act (AUMA), which officially went into effect the next day. AUMA partially legalized marijuana under state law by adults 21 and older, allowing adults to legally grow, possess, and use small quantities of marijuana for nonmedical purposes. It also reduced the severity of, and penalties for, many cannabis-related offenses, and established a regulatory framework for non-medical adult-use cannabis similar to the MCRSA framework.

Finally, the laws governing medical and recreational cannabis were merged together to create the Medicinal and Adult-Use Cannabis Regulation and Safety act (MAUCRSA). MAUCRSA set forth a comprehensive regulatory framework with different license types overseen by different regulatory agencies. First, cultivation activities are licensed and regulated by CalCannabis Cultivation Licensing within the California Department of Food and Agriculture. Second, manufacturing is licensed and regulated by the Manufactured Cannabis Safety Branch within the Department of Public Health. Finally, distribution, laboratory testing, retail (both storefront and delivery-only), microbusinesses, and cannabis events are overseen by the Bureau of Cannabis Control within the Department of Consumer Affairs.

The goal of this publication is to combine all of the relevant code sections related to cannabis law into a user-friendly guide that can be used by cannabis lawyers, scholars, and entrepreneurs to be able to research the law. We hope you find California Cannabis Laws: MAUCRSA Edition to be an indispensable tool in your legal library.

Because California law is rapidly evolving, we suggest checking for the latest changes, amendments, and updates at the California Legislature's web site: http://leginfo.legislature.ca.gov/faces/codes.xhtml

A Word About Legal Taxonomy

In order to get the most out of this resource, it's helpful to know the legal classification of California's laws. The California Codes are 29 legal codes enacted by the California State Legislature, which together form the general statutory law of California. The California Codes are organized by subject matter, such as the Business and Professions Code, the Health and Safety Code, or the Vehicle Code. Codes are divided into "Titles," which are numbered and cover a broad area of law within that subject matter. Titles are further broken down into numbered "Divisions" which cover a narrow area of law within that Title. Divisions are broken down into "Parts," followed by "Chapters," then "Articles," and finally into individual "Sections." A law is most typically referred to in the California Courts by its Code name and Section number (for example, Health and Safety Code Section 11362.5).

California Cannabis Laws: MAUCRSA Edition - Omar Figueroa

Table of Contents

I. Business and Professions Code Sections

Division 6. BUSINESS RIGHTS
Chapter 3. Trade Names and Designations

Article 3. Farm Names

Medicinal and Adult-Use Cannabis Regulation and Safety Act

Division 10. Cannabis

Chapter 1. General Provisions and Definitions

Chapter 2. Administration

Chapter 3. Enforcement

Chapter 4. Appeals

Chapter 5. Licensing

Chapter 6. Licensed Cultivation Sites

Chapter 6.5. Unique Identifiers and Track and Trace

Chapter 7. Retailers and Distributors

Chapter 8. Distribution and Transport

Chapter 9. Delivery

Chapter 10. Testing Laboratories

Chapter 11. Quality Assurance, Inspection, and Testing

Chapter 12. Packaging and Labeling

Chapter 13. Manufacturers and Cannabis Products

Chapter 14. Protection of Minors

Chapter 15. Advertising and Marketing Restrictions

Chapter 16. Records

Chapter 18. License Fees

Chapter 19. Annual Reports; Performance Audit

Chapter 20. Local Control

Chapter 21. Funding

Chapter 22. Cannabis Cooperative Associations

Article 1. Definitions

Article 2. General Provisions

Article 3. Purposes

Article 4. Articles of Incorporation

Article 5. Bylaws

Article 6. Directors and Management

Article 7. Powers

Article 8. Financial Provisions

Article 9. Members

Article 10. Marketing Contracts

Article 11. Reorganization of Corporations Organized Pursuant to Other Laws

II. Civil Code Sections

§ 1550.5 [Brief History of California Cannabis Legislation, including Proposition 215, MCRSA, AUMA, and MAUCRSA; Enforceability of Contracts for Commercial Cannabis Activity Conducted in Compliance

III. Evidence Code Sections

IV. Fish and Game Code Sections

V. Food and Agricultural Code Sections

VI. Government Code Sections

VII. Health and Safety Code Sections

VIII. Labor Code Sections

IX. Penal Code Sections

X. Revenue and Taxation Code Sections

XI. Vehicle Code Sections

XII. Water Code Sections

XIII. Regulatory Agencies

I. Business and Professions Code Sections

Business and Professions Code § 27

(Amended by Stats. 2016, Ch. 489, Sec. 1., Effective January 1, 2017.)

(a) Each entity specified in subdivisions (c), (d), and (e) shall provide on the Internet information regarding the status of every license issued by that entity in accordance with the California Public Records Act (Chapter 3.5 (commencing with Section 6250) of Division 7 of Title 1 of the Government Code) and the Information Practices Act of 1977 (Chapter 1 (commencing with Section 1798) of Title 1.8 of Part 4 of Division 3 of the Civil Code). The public information to be provided on the Internet shall include information on suspensions and revocations of licenses issued by the entity and other related enforcement action, including accusations filed pursuant to the Administrative Procedure Act (Chapter 3.5 (commencing with Section 11340) of Part 1 of Division 3 of Title 2 of the Government Code) taken by the entity relative to persons, businesses, or facilities subject to licensure or regulation by the entity. The information may not include personal information, including home telephone number, date of birth, or social security number. Each entity shall disclose a licensee's address of record. However, each entity shall allow a licensee to provide a post office box number or other alternate address, instead of his or her home address, as the address of record. This section shall not preclude an entity from also requiring a licensee, who has provided a post office box number or other alternative mailing address as his or her address of record, to provide a physical business address or residence address only for the entity's internal administrative use and not for disclosure as the licensee's address of record or disclosure on the Internet.

(b) In providing information on the Internet, each entity specified in subdivisions (c) and (d) shall comply with the Department of Consumer Affairs' guidelines for access to public records.

(c) Each of the following entities within the Department of Consumer Affairs shall comply with the requirements of this section:

> (1) The Board for Professional Engineers, Land Surveyors, and Geologists shall disclose information on its registrants and licensees.

(2) The Bureau of Automotive Repair shall disclose information on its licensees, including auto repair dealers, smog stations, lamp and brake stations, smog check technicians, and smog inspection certification stations.

(3) The Bureau of Electronic and Appliance Repair, Home Furnishings, and Thermal Insulation shall disclose information on its licensees and registrants, including major appliance repair dealers, combination dealers (electronic and appliance), electronic repair dealers, service contract sellers, and service contract administrators.

(4) The Cemetery and Funeral Bureau shall disclose information on its licensees, including cemetery brokers, cemetery salespersons, cemetery managers, crematory managers, cemetery authorities, crematories, cremated remains disposers, embalmers, funeral establishments, and funeral directors.

(5) The Professional Fiduciaries Bureau shall disclose information on its licensees.

(6) The Contractors' State License Board shall disclose information on its licensees and registrants in accordance with Chapter 9 (commencing with Section 7000) of Division 3. In addition to information related to licenses as specified in subdivision (a), the board shall also disclose information provided to the board by the Labor Commissioner pursuant to Section 98.9 of the Labor Code.

(7) The Bureau for Private Postsecondary Education shall disclose information on private postsecondary institutions under its jurisdiction, including disclosure of notices to comply issued pursuant to Section 94935 of the Education Code.

(8) The California Board of Accountancy shall disclose information on its licensees and registrants.

(9) The California Architects Board shall disclose information on its licensees, including architects and landscape architects.

(10) The State Athletic Commission shall disclose information on its licensees and registrants.

(11) The State Board of Barbering and Cosmetology shall disclose information on its licensees.

(12) The State Board of Guide Dogs for the Blind shall disclose information on its licensees and registrants.

(13) The Acupuncture Board shall disclose information on its licensees.

(14) The Board of Behavioral Sciences shall disclose information on its licensees, including licensed marriage and family therapists, licensed clinical social workers, licensed educational psychologists, and licensed professional clinical counselors.

(15) The Dental Board of California shall disclose information on its licensees.

(16) The State Board of Optometry shall disclose information on its licensees and registrants.

(17) The Board of Psychology shall disclose information on its licensees, including psychologists, psychological assistants, and registered psychologists.

(d) The State Board of Chiropractic Examiners shall disclose information on its licensees.

(e) The Structural Pest Control Board shall disclose information on its licensees, including applicators, field representatives, and operators in the areas of fumigation, general pest and wood destroying pests and organisms, and wood roof cleaning and treatment.

(f) The Bureau of Medical Cannabis Regulation shall disclose information on its licensees.

(g) "Internet" for the purposes of this section has the meaning set forth in paragraph (6) of subdivision (f) of Section 17538.

Business and Professions Code § 101

(MCRSA- SB 837, Effective June 27, 2016.)

The department is comprised of the following:

(a) The Dental Board of California.

(b) The Medical Board of California.

(c) The State Board of Optometry.

(d) The California State Board of Pharmacy.

(e) The Veterinary Medical Board.

(f) The California Board of Accountancy.

(g) The California Architects Board.

(h) The Bureau of Barbering and Cosmetology.

(i) The Board for Professional Engineers and Land Surveyors.

(j) The Contractors' State License Board.

(k) The Bureau for Private Postsecondary Education.

(l) The Bureau of Electronic and Appliance Repair, Home Furnishings, and Thermal Insulation.

(m) The Board of Registered Nursing.

(n) The Board of Behavioral Sciences.

(o) The State Athletic Commission.

(p) The Cemetery and Funeral Bureau.

(q) The State Board of Guide Dogs for the Blind.

(r) The Bureau of Security and Investigative Services.

(s) The Court Reporters Board of California.

(t) The Board of Vocational Nursing and Psychiatric Technicians.

(u) The Landscape Architects Technical Committee.

(v) The Division of Investigation.

(w) The Bureau of Automotive Repair.

(x) The Respiratory Care Board of California.

(y) The Acupuncture Board.

(z) The Board of Psychology.

(aa) The California Board of Podiatric Medicine.

(ab) The Physical Therapy Board of California.

(ac) The Arbitration Review Program.

(ad) The Physician Assistant Committee.

(ae) The Speech-Language Pathology and Audiology Board.

(af) The California Board of Occupational Therapy.

(ag) The Osteopathic Medical Board of California.

(ah) The Naturopathic Medicine Committee.

(ai) The Dental Hygiene Committee of California.

(aj) The Professional Fiduciaries Bureau.

(ak) The State Board of Chiropractic Examiners.

(al) The Bureau of Real Estate.

(am) The Bureau of Real Estate Appraisers.

(an) The Structural Pest Control Board.

(ao) The Bureau of Medical Cannabis Regulation.

(ap) Any other boards, offices, or officers subject to its jurisdiction by law.

Business and Professions Code § 144

(MCRSA- SB 837, Effective June 27, 2016.)

(a) Notwithstanding any other law, an agency designated in subdivision (b) shall require an applicant to furnish to the agency a full set of fingerprints for purposes of conducting criminal history record checks. Any agency designated in subdivision (b) may obtain and receive, at its discretion, criminal history information from the Department of Justice and the United States Federal Bureau of Investigation.

(b) Subdivision (a) applies to the following:

(1) California Board of Accountancy.

(2) State Athletic Commission.

(3) Board of Behavioral Sciences.

(4) Court Reporters Board of California.

(5) State Board of Guide Dogs for the Blind.

(6) California State Board of Pharmacy.

(7) Board of Registered Nursing.

(8) Veterinary Medical Board.

(9) Board of Vocational Nursing and Psychiatric Technicians.

(10) Respiratory Care Board of California.

(11) Physical Therapy Board of California.

(12) Physician Assistant Committee of the Medical Board of California.

(13) Speech-Language Pathology and Audiology and Hearing Aid Dispenser Board.

(14) Medical Board of California.

(15) State Board of Optometry.

(16) Acupuncture Board.

(17) Cemetery and Funeral Bureau.

(18) Bureau of Security and Investigative Services.

(19) Division of Investigation.

(20) Board of Psychology.

(21) California Board of Occupational Therapy.

(22) Structural Pest Control Board.

(23) Contractors' State License Board.

(24) Naturopathic Medicine Committee.

(25) Professional Fiduciaries Bureau.

(26) Board for Professional Engineers, Land Surveyors, and Geologists.

(27) Bureau of Medical Cannabis Regulation.

(c) For purposes of paragraph (26) of subdivision (b), the term "applicant" shall be limited to an initial applicant who has never been registered or licensed by the board or to an applicant for a new licensure or registration category.

Business and Professions Code § 205.1

(MCRSA- SB 837, Effective June 27, 2016.)

Notwithstanding subdivision (a) of Section 205, the Medical Cannabis Regulation and Safety Act Fund is a special fund within the Professions and Vocations Fund, and is subject to subdivision (b) of Section 205.

Business and Professions Code § 2220.05

(Amended by Stats. 2016, Ch. 840, Sec. 1. Effective January 1, 2017.)

(a) In order to ensure that its resources are maximized for the protection of the public, the Medical Board of California shall prioritize its investigative and prosecutorial resources to ensure that physicians and surgeons representing the greatest threat of harm are identified and disciplined expeditiously. Cases involving any of the following allegations shall be handled on a priority basis, as follows, with the highest priority being given to cases in the first paragraph:

(1) Gross negligence, incompetence, or repeated negligent acts that involve death or serious bodily injury to one or more patients, such that the physician and surgeon represents a danger to the public.

(2) Drug or alcohol abuse by a physician and surgeon involving death or serious bodily injury to a patient.

(3) Repeated acts of clearly excessive prescribing, furnishing, or administering of controlled substances, or repeated acts of prescribing, dispensing, or furnishing of controlled substances without a good faith prior examination of the patient and medical reason therefor. However, in no event shall a physician and surgeon prescribing, furnishing, or administering controlled substances for intractable pain consistent with lawful prescribing, including, but not limited to, Sections 725, 2241.5, and 2241.6 of this code and Sections 11159.2 and 124961 of

the Health and Safety Code, be prosecuted for excessive prescribing and prompt review of the applicability of these provisions shall be made in any complaint that may implicate these provisions.

(4) Repeated acts of clearly excessive recommending of cannabis to patients for medical purposes, or repeated acts of recommending cannabis to patients for medical purposes without a good faith prior examination of the patient and a medical reason for the recommendation.

(5) Sexual misconduct with one or more patients during a course of treatment or an examination.

(6) Practicing medicine while under the influence of drugs or alcohol.

(7) Repeated acts of clearly excessive prescribing, furnishing, or administering psychotropic medications to a minor without a good faith prior examination of the patient and medical reason therefor.

(b) The board may by regulation prioritize cases involving an allegation of conduct that is not described in subdivision (a). Those cases prioritized by regulation shall not be assigned a priority equal to or higher than the priorities established in subdivision (a).

(c) The Medical Board of California shall indicate in its annual report mandated by Section 2312 the number of temporary restraining orders, interim suspension orders, and disciplinary actions that are taken in each priority category specified in subdivisions (a) and (b).

Business and Professions Code § 2241.5

(MCRSA- SB 643, Effective January 1, 2016.)

(a) A physician and surgeon may prescribe for, or dispense or administer to, a person under his or her treatment for a medical condition dangerous drugs or prescription controlled substances for the treatment of pain or a condition causing pain, including, but not limited to, intractable pain.

(b) No physician and surgeon shall be subject to disciplinary action for prescribing, dispensing, or administering dangerous drugs or prescription controlled substances in accordance with this section.

(c) This section shall not affect the power of the board to take any action described in Section 2227 against a physician and surgeon who does any of the following:

(1) Violates subdivision (b), (c), or (d) of Section 2234 regarding gross negligence, repeated negligent acts, or incompetence.

(2) Violates Section 2241 regarding treatment of an addict.

(3) Violates Section 2242 or 2525.3 regarding performing an appropriate prior examination and the existence of a medical indication for prescribing, dispensing, or furnishing dangerous drugs or recommending medical cannabis.

(4) Violates Section 2242.1 regarding prescribing on the Internet.

(5) Fails to keep complete and accurate records of purchases and disposals of substances listed in the California Uniform Controlled Substances Act (Division 10 (commencing with Section 11000) of the Health and Safety Code) or controlled substances scheduled in the federal Comprehensive Drug Abuse Prevention and Control Act of 1970 (21 U.S.C. Sec. 801 et seq.), or pursuant to the federal Comprehensive Drug Abuse Prevention and Control Act of 1970. A physician and surgeon shall keep records of his or her purchases and disposals of these controlled substances or dangerous drugs, including the date of purchase, the date and records of the sale or disposal of the drugs by the physician and surgeon, the name and address of the person receiving the drugs, and the reason for the disposal or the dispensing of the drugs to the person, and shall otherwise comply with all state recordkeeping requirements for controlled substances.

(6) Writes false or fictitious prescriptions for controlled substances listed in the California Uniform Controlled Substances Act or scheduled in the federal Comprehensive Drug Abuse Prevention and Control Act of 1970.

(7) Prescribes, administers, or dispenses in violation of this chapter, or in violation of Chapter 4 (commencing with Section 11150) or Chapter 5 (commencing with Section 11210) of Division 10 of the Health and Safety Code.

(d) A physician and surgeon shall exercise reasonable care in determining whether a particular patient or condition, or the complexity of a patient's treatment, including, but not limited to, a current or recent pattern of drug abuse, requires consultation with, or referral to, a more qualified specialist.

(e) Nothing in this section shall prohibit the governing body of a hospital from taking disciplinary actions against a physician and surgeon pursuant to Sections 809.05, 809.4, and 809.5.

Business and Professions Code § 2242.1

(MCRSA- SB 643, Effective January 1, 2016.)

(a) No person or entity may prescribe, dispense, or furnish, or cause to be prescribed, dispensed, or furnished, dangerous drugs or dangerous devices, as defined in Section 4022, on the Internet for delivery to any person in this state, without an appropriate prior examination and medical indication, except as authorized by Section 2242.

(b) Notwithstanding any other provision of law, a violation of this section may subject the person or entity that has committed the violation to either a fine of up to twenty-five thousand dollars ($25,000) per occurrence pursuant to a citation issued by the board or a civil penalty of twenty-five thousand dollars ($25,000) per occurrence.

(c) The Attorney General may bring an action to enforce this section and to collect the fines or civil penalties authorized by subdivision (b).

(d) For notifications made on and after January 1, 2002, the Franchise Tax Board, upon notification by the Attorney General or the board of a final judgment in an action brought under this section, shall subtract the amount of the fine or awarded civil penalties from any tax refunds or lottery winnings due to the person who is a defendant in the action using the offset authority under Section 12419.5 of the Government Code, as delegated by the Controller, and the processes as established by the Franchise Tax Board for this purpose. That amount shall be forwarded to the board for deposit in the Contingent Fund of the Medical Board of California.

(e) If the person or entity that is the subject of an action brought pursuant to this section is not a resident of this state, a violation of this section shall, if applicable, be reported to the person's or entity's appropriate professional licensing authority.

(f) Nothing in this section shall prohibit the board from commencing a disciplinary action against a physician and surgeon pursuant to Section 2242 or 2525.3.

Business and Professions Code § 2525

(MCRSA- SB 643, Effective January 1, 2016.)

(a) It is unlawful for a physician and surgeon who recommends cannabis to a patient for a medical purpose to accept, solicit, or offer any form of remuneration from or to a facility issued a state license pursuant to Chapter 3.5 (commencing with Section 19300) of Division 8, if the physician and surgeon or his or her immediate family have a financial interest in that facility.

(b) For the purposes of this section, "financial interest" shall have the same meaning as in Section 650.01.

(c) A violation of this section shall be a misdemeanor punishable by up to one year in county jail and a fine of up to five thousand dollars ($5,000) or by civil penalties of up to five thousand dollars ($5,000) and shall constitute unprofessional conduct.

Business and Professions Code § 2525.1

(MCRSA- SB 643, Effective January 1, 2016.)

The Medical Board of California shall consult with the California Marijuana Research Program, known as the Center for Medicinal Cannabis Research, authorized pursuant to Section 11362.9 of the Health and Safety Code, on developing and adopting medical guidelines for the appropriate administration and use of medical cannabis.

Business and Professions Code § 2525.2

(MCRSA- SB 643, Effective January 1, 2016.)

An individual who possesses a license in good standing to practice medicine or osteopathy issued by the Medical Board of California or the Osteopathic Medical Board of California shall not recommend medical cannabis to a patient, unless that person is the patient's attending physician, as defined by subdivision (a) of Section 11362.7 of the Health and Safety Code.

Business and Professions Code § 2525.3

(MCRSA- SB 643, Effective January 1, 2016.)

Recommending medical cannabis to a patient for a medical purpose without an appropriate prior examination and a medical indication constitutes unprofessional conduct.

Business and Professions Code § 2525.4

(MCRSA- SB 643, Effective January 1, 2016.)

It is unprofessional conduct for any attending physician recommending medical cannabis to be employed by, or enter into any other agreement with, any person or entity dispensing medical cannabis.

Business and Professions Code § 2525.5

(MCRSA- SB 643, Effective January 1, 2016.)

(a) A person shall not distribute any form of advertising for physician recommendations for medical cannabis in California unless the advertisement bears the following notice to consumers:

NOTICE TO CONSUMERS: The Compassionate Use Act of 1996 ensures that seriously ill Californians have the right to obtain and use cannabis for medical purposes where medical use is deemed appropriate and has been recommended by a physician who has determined that the person's health would benefit from the use of medical cannabis. Recommendations must come from an attending physician as defined in Section 11362.7 of the Health and Safety Code. Cannabis is a Schedule I drug according to the federal Controlled Substances Act. Activity related to cannabis use is subject to federal prosecution, regardless of the protections provided by state law.

(b) Advertising for attending physician recommendations for medical cannabis shall meet all of the requirements in Section 651. Price advertising shall not be fraudulent, deceitful, or misleading, including statements or advertisements of bait, discounts, premiums, gifts, or statements of a similar nature.

Article 3. Farm Names

Business and Professions Code § 14460

(Added by Stats. 1941, Ch. 59.)

"Farm," as used in this article, includes ranch, estate and villa.

Business and Professions Code 14461

(Amended by Stats. 1999, Ch. 1000, Sec. 6. Effective January 1, 2000.)

Any farm owner or lessee in this state may register the name of his or her farm with the Secretary of State, and the Secretary of State shall issue a certificate setting forth the name and location of the farm and the name of the owner upon payment of the fee as set forth in subdivision (g) of Section 12193 of the Government Code.

Business and Professions Code § 14462

(Added by Stats. 1941, Ch. 59.)

Any person selling or marketing the products grown on a farm may use the name of the farm as a trade-mark on the products of the farm, in the same manner as provided for other trade-marks, and subject to the same rights and duties, as provided in this code.

Business and Professions Code § 14463

(Added by Stats. 1941, Ch. 59.)

Registration under this article shall have the same effect as the registration of a trade-mark.

Business and Professions Code § 14464

(Added by Stats. 1941, Ch. 59.)

When any name has been registered as the name of any farm, that name shall not be registered as the name of any other farm in this State, unless designating words have been prefixed or added thereto. The Secretary of State shall register such name only for the person entitled thereto.

Business and Professions Code § 14465

(Added by Stats. 1941, Ch. 59.)

Any person who registers as his own, any name already in use in this State, knowing that the name is already adopted as the name of a farm, or makes use of the name when regularly registered and in use by any other person entitled thereto under this article is guilty of a misdemeanor.

Medicinal and Adult-Use Cannabis Regulation and Safety Act (MAUCRSA)

Division 10. Cannabis

Chapter 1. General Provisions and Definitions

Business and Professions Code § 26000

(MAUCRSA, Effective June 27, 2017.)

(a) This division shall be known, and may be cited, as the Medicinal and Adult-Use Cannabis Regulation and Safety Act.

(b) The purpose and intent of this division is to establish a comprehensive system to control and regulate the cultivation, distribution, transport, storage, manufacturing, processing, and sale of both of the following:

(1) Medicinal cannabis and medicinal cannabis products for patients with valid physician's recommendations.

(2) Adult-use cannabis and adult-use cannabis products for adults 21 years of age and over.

(c) In the furtherance of subdivision (b), this division sets forth the power and duties of the state agencies responsible for controlling and regulating the commercial medicinal and adult-use cannabis industry.

(d) The Legislature may, by majority vote, enact laws to implement this division, provided those laws are consistent with the purposes and intent of the Control, Regulate and Tax Adult Use of Marijuana Act.

Business and Professions Code § 26001

(Amended by AB 133, Effective September 16, 2017.)

For purposes of this division, the following definitions shall apply:

(a) "A-license" means a state license issued under this division for cannabis or cannabis products that are intended for adults who are 21 years of age and older and who do not possess a physician's recommendation.

(b) "A-licensee" means any person holding a license under this division for cannabis or cannabis products that are intended for adults who are 21 years of age and older and who do not possess a physician's recommendation.

(c) "Applicant" means an owner applying for a state license pursuant to this division.

(d) "Batch" means a specific quantity of homogeneous cannabis or cannabis product that is one of the following types:

(1) Harvest batch. "Harvest batch" means a specifically identified quantity of dried flower or trim, leaves, and other cannabis plant matter that is uniform in strain, harvested at the same time, and, if applicable, cultivated using the same pesticides and other agricultural chemicals, and harvested at the same time.

(2) Manufactured cannabis batch. "Manufactured cannabis batch" means either of the following:

(A) An amount of cannabis concentrate or extract that is produced in one production cycle using the same extraction methods and standard operating procedures.

(B) An amount of a type of manufactured cannabis produced in one production cycle using the same formulation and standard operating procedures.

(e) "Bureau" means the Bureau of Cannabis Control within the Department of Consumer Affairs, formerly named the Bureau of Marijuana Control, the Bureau of Medical Cannabis Regulation, and the Bureau of Medical Marijuana Regulation.

(f) "Cannabis" means all parts of the plant Cannabis sativa Linnaeus, Cannabis indica, or Cannabis ruderalis, whether growing or not; the seeds thereof; the resin, whether crude or purified, extracted from any part of the plant; and every compound, manufacture, salt, derivative, mixture, or preparation of the plant, its seeds, or resin. "Cannabis" also means the separated resin, whether crude or purified, obtained from cannabis. "Cannabis" does not include the mature stalks of the plant, fiber produced from the stalks, oil or cake made from the seeds of the plant, any other compound, manufacture, salt, derivative, mixture, or preparation of the mature stalks (except the resin extracted therefrom), fiber, oil, or cake, or the sterilized seed of the plant which is incapable of germination. For the purpose of this division, "cannabis" does not mean "industrial hemp" as defined by Section 11018.5 of the Health and Safety Code.

(g) "Cannabis accessories" has the same meaning as in Section 11018.2 of the Health and Safety Code.

(h) "Cannabis concentrate" means cannabis that has undergone a process to concentrate one or more active cannabinoids, thereby increasing the product's potency. Resin from granular trichomes from a cannabis plant is a concentrate for purposes of this division. A cannabis concentrate is not considered food, as defined by Section 109935 of the Health and Safety Code, or a drug, as defined by Section 109925 of the Health and Safety Code.

(i) "Cannabis products" has the same meaning as in Section 11018.1 of the Health and Safety Code.

(j) "Child resistant" means designed or constructed to be significantly difficult for children under five years of age to open, and not difficult for normal adults to use properly.

(k) "Commercial cannabis activity" includes the cultivation, possession, manufacture, distribution, processing, storing, laboratory testing, packaging, labeling, transportation, delivery or sale of cannabis and cannabis products as provided for in this division.

(l) "Cultivation" means any activity involving the planting, growing, harvesting, drying, curing, grading, or trimming of cannabis.

(m) "Cultivation site" means a location where cannabis is planted, grown, harvested, dried, cured, graded, or trimmed, or a location where any combination of those activities occurs.

(n) "Customer" means a natural person 21 years of age or older or a natural person 18 years of age or older who possesses a physician's recommendation, or a primary caregiver.

(o) "Day care center" has the same meaning as in Section 1596.76 of the Health and Safety Code.

(p) "Delivery" means the commercial transfer of cannabis or cannabis products to a customer. "Delivery" also includes the use by a retailer of any technology platform.

(q) "Director" means the Director of Consumer Affairs.

(r) "Distribution" means the procurement, sale, and transport of cannabis and cannabis products between licensees.

(s) "Dried flower" means all dead cannabis that has been harvested, dried, cured, or otherwise processed, excluding leaves and stems.

(t) "Edible cannabis product" means cannabis product that is intended to be used, in whole or in part, for human consumption, including, but not limited to, chewing gum, but excluding products set forth in Division 15 (commencing with Section 32501) of the Food and Agricultural Code. An edible cannabis product is not considered food, as defined by Section 109935 of the Health and Safety Code, or a drug, as defined by Section 109925 of the Health and Safety Code.

(u) "Fund" means the Cannabis Control Fund established pursuant to Section 26210.

(v) "Kind" means applicable type or designation regarding a particular cannabis variant or cannabis product type, including, but not limited to, strain name or other grower trademark, or growing area designation.

(w) "Labeling" means any label or other written, printed, or graphic matter upon a cannabis product, upon its container or wrapper, or that accompanies any cannabis product.

(x) "Labor peace agreement" means an agreement between a licensee and any bona fide labor organization that, at a minimum, protects the state's proprietary interests by prohibiting labor organizations and members from engaging in picketing, work stoppages, boycotts, and any other economic interference with the applicant's business. This agreement means that the applicant has agreed not to disrupt efforts by the bona fide labor organization to communicate with, and attempt to organize and represent, the applicant's employees. The agreement shall provide a bona fide labor organization access at reasonable times to areas in which the applicant's employees work, for the purpose of meeting with employees to discuss their right to representation, employment rights under state law, and terms and conditions of employment. This type of agreement shall not mandate a particular method of election or certification of the bona fide labor organization.

(y) "License" means a state license issued under this division, and includes both an A-license and an M-license, as well as a testing laboratory license.

(z) "Licensee" means any person holding a license under this division, regardless of whether the license held is an A-license or an M-license, and includes the holder of a testing laboratory license.

(aa) "Licensing authority" means the state agency responsible for the issuance, renewal, or reinstatement of the license, or the state agency authorized to take disciplinary action against the licensee.

(ab) "Live plants" means living cannabis flowers and plants, including seeds, immature plants, and vegetative stage plants.

(ac) "Local jurisdiction" means a city, county, or city and county.

(ad) "Lot" means a batch or a specifically identified portion of a batch.

(ae) "M-license" means a state license issued under this division for commercial cannabis activity involving medicinal cannabis.

(af) "M-licensee" means any person holding a license under this division for commercial cannabis activity involving medicinal cannabis.

(ag) "Manufacture" means to compound, blend, extract, infuse, or otherwise make or prepare a cannabis product.

(ah) "Manufacturer" means a licensee that conducts the production, preparation, propagation, or compounding of cannabis or cannabis products either directly or indirectly or by extraction methods, or independently by means of chemical synthesis, or by a combination of extraction and chemical synthesis at a fixed location that packages or repackages cannabis or cannabis products or labels or relabels its container.

(ai) "Medicinal cannabis" or "medicinal cannabis product" means cannabis or a cannabis product, respectively, intended to be sold for use pursuant to the Compassionate Use Act of 1996 (Proposition 215), found at Section 11362.5 of the Health and Safety Code, by a medicinal cannabis patient in California who possesses a physician's recommendation.

(aj) "Nursery" means a licensee that produces only clones, immature plants, seeds, and other agricultural products used specifically for the propagation and cultivation of cannabis.

(ak) "Operation" means any act for which licensure is required under the provisions of this division, or any commercial transfer of cannabis or cannabis products.

(al) "Owner" means any of the following:

> (1) A person with an aggregate ownership interest of 20 percent or more in the person applying for a license or a licensee, unless the interest is solely a security, lien, or encumbrance.

> (2) The chief executive officer of a nonprofit or other entity.

> (3) A member of the board of directors of a nonprofit.

> (4) An individual who will be participating in the direction, control, or management of the person applying for a license.

(am) "Package" means any container or receptacle used for holding cannabis or cannabis products.

(an) "Person" includes any individual, firm, partnership, joint venture, association, corporation, limited liability company, estate, trust, business trust, receiver, syndicate, or any other group or combination acting as a unit, and the plural as well as the singular.

(ao) "Physician's recommendation" means a recommendation by a physician and surgeon that a patient use cannabis provided in accordance with the Compassionate Use Act of 1996 (Proposition 215), found at Section 11362.5 of the Health and Safety Code.

(ap) "Premises" means the designated structure or structures and land specified in the application that is owned, leased, or otherwise held under the control of the applicant or licensee where the commercial cannabis activity will be or is conducted. The premises shall be a contiguous area and shall only be occupied by one licensee.

(aq) "Primary caregiver" has the same meaning as in Section 11362.7 of the Health and Safety Code.

(ar) "Purchaser" means the customer who is engaged in a transaction with a licensee for purposes of obtaining cannabis or cannabis products.

(as) "Sell," "sale," and "to sell" include any transaction whereby, for any consideration, title to cannabis or cannabis products is transferred from one person to another, and includes the delivery of cannabis or cannabis products pursuant to an order placed for the purchase of the same and soliciting or receiving an order for the same, but does not include the return of cannabis or cannabis products by a licensee to the licensee from whom the cannabis or cannabis product was purchased.

(at) "Testing laboratory" means a laboratory, facility, or entity in the state that offers or performs tests of cannabis or cannabis products and that is both of the following:

> (1) Accredited by an accrediting body that is independent from all other persons involved in commercial cannabis activity in the state.

> (2) Licensed by the bureau.

(au) "Unique identifier" means an alphanumeric code or designation used for reference to a specific plant on a licensed premises and any cannabis or cannabis product derived or manufactured from that plant.

(av) "Youth center" has the same meaning as in Section 11353.1 of the Health and Safety Code.

Chapter 2. Administration

Business and Professions Code § 26010

(MAUCRSA, Effective June 27, 2017.)

There is in the Department of Consumer Affairs the Bureau of Cannabis Control, under the supervision and control of the director. The director shall administer and enforce the provisions of this division related to the bureau.

Business and Professions Code § 26010.5

(MAUCRSA, Effective June 27, 2017.)

(a) The Governor shall appoint a chief of the bureau, subject to confirmation by the Senate, at a salary to be fixed and determined by the Director of Consumer Affairs with the approval of the Director of Finance. The chief shall serve under the direction and supervision of the Director of Consumer Affairs and at the pleasure of the Governor.

(b) Every power granted to or duty imposed upon the Director of Consumer Affairs under this division may be exercised or performed in the name of the director by a deputy or assistant director or by the chief, subject to conditions and limitations that the director may prescribe. In addition to every power granted or duty imposed under this division, the director shall have all other powers and duties generally applicable in relation to bureaus that are part of the Department of Consumer Affairs.

(c) The Director of Consumer Affairs may employ and appoint all employees necessary to properly administer the work of the bureau, in accordance with civil service laws and regulations. The Governor may also appoint a deputy chief and an assistant chief counsel to the bureau. These positions shall hold office at the pleasure of the Governor.

(d) The bureau has the power, duty, purpose, responsibility, and jurisdiction to regulate commercial cannabis activity as provided in this division.

(e) The bureau and the director shall succeed to and are vested with all the duties, powers, purposes, responsibilities, and jurisdiction formerly vested in the Bureau of Marijuana Control, also formerly known as the Bureau of Medical Cannabis Regulation and the Bureau of Medical Marijuana Regulation, under the former Medical Cannabis Regulation and Safety Act (former Chapter 3.5 (commencing with Section 19300) of Division 8).

(f) Upon the effective date of this section, whenever "Bureau of Marijuana Control," "Bureau of Medical Cannabis Regulation," or "Bureau of Medical Marijuana Regulation" appears in any statute, regulation, or contract, or in any other code, it shall be construed to refer to the bureau.

(g) Upon the effective date of this section, whenever any reference to the "Medical Cannabis Regulation and Safety Act," "Medical Marijuana Regulation and Safety Act," or former Chapter 3.5 (commencing with Section 19300) of Division 8 appears in any statute, regulation, contract, or in any other code, it shall be construed to refer to this division as it relates to medicinal cannabis and medicinal cannabis products.

Business and Professions Code § 26011

(MAUCRSA, Effective June 27, 2017.)

Neither the chief of the bureau nor any member of the Cannabis Control Appeals Panel established under Section 26040 shall do any of the following:

(a) Receive any commission or profit whatsoever, directly or indirectly, from any person applying for or receiving any license or permit under this division.

(b) Engage or have any interest in the sale or any insurance covering a licensee's business or premises.

(c) Engage or have any interest in the sale of equipment for use upon the premises of a licensee engaged in commercial cannabis activity.

(d) Knowingly solicit any licensee for the purchase of tickets for benefits or contributions for benefits.

(e) Knowingly request any licensee to donate or receive money, or any other thing of value, for the benefit of any person whatsoever.

Business and Professions Code § 26011.5

(MAUCRSA, Effective June 27, 2017.)

The protection of the public shall be the highest priority for all licensing authorities in exercising licensing, regulatory, and disciplinary functions under this division. Whenever the protection of the public is inconsistent with other interests sought to be promoted, the protection of the public shall be paramount.

Business and Professions Code § 26012

(MAUCRSA, Effective June 27, 2017.)

(a) It being a matter of statewide concern, except as otherwise authorized in this division:

(1) The bureau shall have the sole authority to create, issue, deny, renew, discipline, suspend, or revoke licenses for microbusinesses, transportation, storage unrelated to manufacturing activities, distribution, testing, and sale of cannabis and cannabis products within the state.

(2) The Department of Food and Agriculture shall administer the provisions of this division related to and associated with the cultivation of cannabis. The Department of Food and Agriculture shall have the authority to create, issue, deny, and suspend or revoke cultivation licenses for violations of this division.

(3) The State Department of Public Health shall administer the provisions of this division related to and associated with the manufacturing of cannabis products. The State Department of Public Health shall have the authority to create, issue, deny, and suspend or revoke manufacturing licenses for violations of this division.

(b) The licensing authorities shall have the authority to collect fees in connection with activities they regulate concerning cannabis. The licensing authorities may create licenses in addition to those identified in this division that the licensing authorities deem necessary to effectuate their duties under this division.

(c) For the performance of its duties, each licensing authority has the power conferred by Sections 11180 to 11191, inclusive, of the Government Code.

(d) Licensing authorities shall begin issuing licenses under this division by January 1, 2018.

Business and Professions Code § 26013

(MAUCRSA, Effective June 27, 2017.)

(a) Licensing authorities shall make and prescribe reasonable rules and regulations as may be necessary to implement, administer and enforce their respective duties under this division in accordance with Chapter 3.5 (commencing with Section 11340) of Part 1 of Division 3 of Title 2 of the Government Code. Those rules and regulations shall be consistent with the purposes and intent of the Control, Regulate and Tax Adult Use of Marijuana Act.

(b) (1) Each licensing authority may adopt emergency regulations to implement this division.

(2) Each licensing authority may readopt any emergency regulation authorized by this section that is the same as, or substantially equivalent to, an emergency regulation previously adopted as authorized by this section. Any such readoption shall be limited to one time for each regulation.

(3) Notwithstanding any other law, the initial adoption of emergency regulations and the readoption of emergency regulations authorized by this section shall be deemed an emergency and necessary for the immediate preservation of the public peace, health, safety, or general welfare. The initial emergency regulations and the readopted emergency regulations authorized by this section shall be each submitted to the Office of Administrative Law for filing with the Secretary of State and shall remain in effect for no more than 180 days, by which time final regulations may be adopted.

(c) Regulations issued under this division shall be necessary to achieve the purposes of this division, based on best available evidence, and shall mandate only commercially feasible procedures, technology, or other requirements, and shall not unreasonably restrain or inhibit the development of alternative procedures or technology to achieve the same substantive requirements, nor shall such regulations make compliance so onerous that the operation under a cannabis license is not worthy of being carried out in practice by a reasonably prudent businessperson.

Business and Professions Code § 26013.5

(MAUCRSA, Effective June 27, 2017.)

Notice of any action of a licensing authority required by this division to be given may be signed and given by the director of the licensing authority or an authorized employee of the licensing authority and may be made personally or in the manner prescribed by Section 1013 of the Code of Civil Procedure, or in the manner prescribed by Section 124 of this code.

Business and Professions Code § 26014

(MAUCRSA, Effective June 27, 2017.)

(a) The bureau shall convene an advisory committee to advise the licensing authorities on the development of standards and regulations pursuant to this division, including best practices and guidelines that protect public health and safety while ensuring a regulated environment for commercial cannabis activity that does not impose such barriers so as to perpetuate, rather than reduce and eliminate, the illicit market for cannabis.

(b) The advisory committee members shall include, but not be limited to, representatives of the cannabis industry, including medicinal cannabis, representatives of labor organizations, appropriate state and local agencies, persons who work directly with racially, ethnically, and economically diverse populations, public health experts, and other subject matter experts, including representatives from the Department of Alcoholic Beverage Control, with expertise in regulating commercial activity for adult-use intoxicating substances. The advisory committee members shall be determined by the director.

(c) Commencing on January 1, 2019, the advisory committee shall publish an annual public report describing its activities including, but not limited to, the recommendations the advisory committee made to the licensing authorities during the immediately preceding calendar year and whether those recommendations were implemented by the licensing authorities.

Business and Professions Code § 26015

(AUMA, Effective November 9, 2016.)

A licensing authority may make or cause to be made such investigation as it deems necessary to carry out its duties under this division.

Business and Professions Code § 26016

(AUMA, Effective November 9, 2016.)

For any hearing held pursuant to this division, except a hearing held under Chapter 4, a licensing authority may delegate the power to hear and decide to an administrative law judge. Any hearing before an administrative law judge shall be pursuant to the procedures, rules, and limitations prescribed in Chapter 5 (commencing with Section 11500) of Part 1 of Division 3 of Title 2 of the Government Code.

Business and Professions Code § 26017

(AUMA, Effective November 9, 2016.)

In any hearing before a licensing authority pursuant to this division, the licensing authority may pay any person appearing as a witness at the hearing at the request of the licensing authority pursuant to a subpoena, his or her actual, necessary, and reasonable travel, food, and lodging expenses, not to exceed the amount authorized for state employees.

Business and Professions Code § 26018

(AUMA, Effective November 9, 2016.)

A licensing authority may on its own motion at any time before a penalty assessment is placed into effect, and without any further proceedings, review the penalty, but such review shall be limited to its reduction.

Chapter 3. Enforcement

Business and Professions Code § 26030

(MAUCRSA, Effective June 27, 2017.)

Grounds for disciplinary action include, but are not limited to, all of the following:

(a) Failure to comply with the provisions of this division or any rule or regulation adopted pursuant to this division.

(b) Conduct that constitutes grounds for denial of licensure pursuant to Chapter 2 (commencing with Section 480) of Division 1.5 or discipline of a license pursuant to Chapter 3 (commencing with Section 490) of Division 1.5.

(c) Any other grounds contained in regulations adopted by a licensing authority pursuant to this division.

(d) Failure to comply with any state law including, but not limited to, the payment of taxes as required under the Revenue and Taxation Code, except as provided for in this division or other California law.

(e) Knowing violations of any state or local law, ordinance, or regulation conferring worker protections or legal rights on the employees of a licensee.

(f) Failure to comply with the requirement of a local ordinance regulating commercial cannabis activity.

(g) The intentional and knowing sale of cannabis or cannabis products by an A-licensee to a person under 21 years of age.

(h) The intentional and knowing sale of medicinal cannabis or medicinal cannabis products by an M-licensee to a person without a physician's recommendation.

(i) Failure to maintain safe conditions for inspection by a licensing authority.

(j) Failure to comply with any operating procedure submitted to the licensing authority pursuant to subdivision (b) of Section 26051.5.

(k) Failure to comply with license conditions established pursuant to subdivision (b) of Section 26060.1.

Business and Professions Code § 26031

(MAUCRSA, Effective June 27, 2017.)

(a) Each licensing authority may suspend, revoke, place on probation with terms and conditions, or otherwise discipline licenses issued by that licensing authority and fine a licensee, after proper notice and hearing to the licensee, if the licensee is found to have committed any of the acts or omissions constituting grounds for disciplinary action. The disciplinary proceedings under this chapter shall be conducted in accordance with Chapter 5 (commencing with Section 11500) of Part 1 of Division 3 of Title 2 of the Government Code, and the director of each licensing authority shall have all the powers granted therein.

(b) A licensing authority may suspend or revoke a license when a local agency has notified the licensing authority that a licensee within its jurisdiction is in violation of state rules and regulations relating to commercial cannabis activities, and the licensing authority, through an investigation, has determined that the violation is grounds for suspension or revocation of the license.

(c) Each licensing authority may take disciplinary action against a licensee for any violation of this division when the violation was committed by the licensee's officers, directors, owners, agents, or employees while acting on behalf of the licensee or engaged in commercial cannabis activity.

(d) A licensing authority may recover the costs of investigation and enforcement of a disciplinary proceeding pursuant to Section 125.3 of this code.

(e) Upon suspension or revocation of a license, the licensing authority shall inform the bureau. The bureau shall then inform all other licensing authorities. Upon any other enforcement action against a licensee, the licensing authority shall notify all other licensing authorities.

Business and Professions Code § 26032

(MAUCRSA, Effective June 27, 2017.)

(a) The actions of a licensee, its employees, and its agents are not unlawful under state law and shall not be an offense subject to arrest, prosecution, or other sanction under state law, or be subject to a civil fine or be a basis for seizure or forfeiture of assets under state law if they are all of the following:

(1) Permitted pursuant to a state license.

(2) Permitted pursuant to a local authorization, license, or permit issued by the local jurisdiction, if any.

(3) Conducted in accordance with the requirements of this division and regulations adopted pursuant to this division.

(b) The actions of a person who, in good faith, allows his or her property to be used by a licensee, its employees, and its agents, as permitted pursuant to a state license and, if required by the applicable local ordinances, a local license or permit, are not unlawful under state law and shall not be an offense subject to arrest, prosecution, or other sanction under state law, or be subject to a civil fine or be a basis for seizure or forfeiture of assets under state law.

Business and Professions Code § 26033

(MAUCRSA, Effective June 27, 2017.)

(a) A qualified patient, as defined in Section 11362.7 of the Health and Safety Code, who cultivates, possesses, stores, manufactures, or transports cannabis exclusively for his or her personal medical use but who does not provide, donate, sell, or distribute cannabis to any other person is not thereby engaged in commercial cannabis activity and is therefore exempt from the licensure requirements of this division.

(b) A primary caregiver who cultivates, possesses, stores, manufactures, transports, donates, or provides cannabis exclusively for the personal medical purposes of no more than five specified qualified patients for whom he or she is the primary caregiver within the meaning of Section 11362.7 of the Health and Safety Code, but who does not receive remuneration for these activities except for compensation in full compliance with subdivision (c) of Section 11362.765 of the Health and Safety Code, is exempt from the licensure requirements of this division.

Business and Professions Code § 26034

(MAUCRSA, Effective June 27, 2017.)

All accusations against licensees shall be filed by the licensing authority within five years after the performance of the act or omission alleged as the ground for disciplinary action; provided, however, that the foregoing provision shall not constitute a defense to an accusation alleging fraud or misrepresentation as a ground for disciplinary action. The cause for disciplinary action in that case shall not be deemed to have accrued until discovery, by the licensing authority, of the facts constituting the fraud or misrepresentation, and, in that case, the accusation shall be filed within five years after that discovery.

Business and Professions Code § 26035

(AUMA, Effective November 9, 2016.)

The director shall designate the persons employed by the Department of

Consumer Affairs for purposes of the administration and enforcement of this division. The director shall ensure that a sufficient number of employees are qualified peace officers for purposes of enforcing this division.

Business and Professions Code § 26036

(AUMA, Effective November 9, 2016.)

Nothing in this division shall be interpreted to supersede or limit state agencies from exercising their existing enforcement authority, including, but not limited to, under the Fish and Game Code, the Food and Agricultural Code, the Government Code, the Health and Safety Code, the Public Resources Code, the Water Code, or the application of those laws.

Business and Professions Code § 26037

(AUMA, Effective November 9, 2016.)

(a) The actions of a licensee, its employees, and its agents that are:

(1) permitted under a license issued under this division and any applicable local ordinances; and

(2) conducted in accordance with the requirements of this division and regulations adopted pursuant to this division, are not unlawful under state law and shall not be an offense subject to arrest, prosecution, or other sanction under state law, or be subject to a civil fine or be a basis for seizure or forfeiture of assets under state law.

(b) The actions of a person who, in good faith, allows his or her property to be used by a licensee, its employees, and its agents, as permitted pursuant to a state license and any applicable local ordinances, are not unlawful under state law and shall not be an offense subject to arrest, prosecution, or other sanction under state law, or be subject to a civil fine or be a basis for seizure or forfeiture of assets under state law.

Business and Professions Code § 26038

(MAUCRSA, Effective June 27, 2017.)

(a) A person engaging in commercial cannabis activity without a license required by this division shall be subject to civil penalties of up to three times the amount of the license fee for each violation, and the court may order the destruction of cannabis associated with that violation in accordance with Section 11479 of the Health and Safety Code. Each day of operation shall constitute a separate violation of this section. All civil penalties imposed and collected pursuant to this section by a licensing authority shall be deposited into the General Fund except as provided in subdivision (b). A violator shall be responsible for the cost of the destruction of cannabis associated with his or her violation.

(b) If an action for civil penalties is brought against a person pursuant to this division by the Attorney General on behalf of the people, the penalty collected shall be deposited into the General Fund. If the action is brought by a district attorney or county counsel, the penalty shall first be used to reimburse the district attorney or county counsel for the costs of bringing the action for civil penalties, with the remainder, if any, to be deposited into the General Fund. If the action is brought by a city attorney or city prosecutor, the penalty collected shall first be used to reimburse the city attorney or city prosecutor for the costs of bringing the action for civil penalties, with the remainder, if any, to be deposited into the General Fund.

(c) Notwithstanding subdivision (a), criminal penalties shall continue to apply to an unlicensed person engaging in commercial cannabis activity in violation of this division.

Chapter 4. Appeals

Business and Professions Code § 26040

(Amended by AB 133, Effective September 16, 2017.)

(a) (1) There is established in state government a Cannabis Control Appeals Panel which shall consist of the following members:

   (A) One member appointed by the Senate Committee on Rules.

   (B) One member appointed by the Speaker of the Assembly.

   (C) Three members appointed by the Governor and subject to confirmation by a majority vote of all of the members elected to the Senate.

(2) Each member, at the time of his or her initial appointment, shall be a resident of a different county from the one in which either of the other members resides. Members of the panel shall receive an annual salary as provided for by Chapter 6 (commencing with Section 11550) of Part 1 of Division 3 of Title 2 of the Government Code.

(b) The members of the panel appointed pursuant to subparagraph (C) of paragraph (1) of subdivision (a) may be removed from office by the Governor, and the Legislature shall have the power, by a majority vote of all members elected to each house, to remove any member of the panel from office for dereliction of duty, corruption, or incompetency.

(c) A concurrent resolution for the removal of any member of the panel may be introduced in the Legislature only if 5 Members of the Senate, or 10 Members of the Assembly, join as authors.

Business and Professions Code § 26041

(AUMA, Effective November 9, 2016.)

All personnel of the panel shall be appointed, employed, directed, and controlled by the panel consistent with state civil service requirements. The director shall furnish the equipment, supplies, and housing necessary for the authorized activities of the panel and shall perform such other mechanics of administration as the panel and the director may agree upon.

Business and Professions Code § 26042

(AUMA, Effective November 9, 2016.)

The panel shall adopt procedures for appeals similar to the procedures used in Articles 3 and 4 in Chapter 1.5 in Division 9 of the Business and Professions Code. Such procedures shall be adopted in accordance with the Administrative Procedure Act (Government Code, Title 2, Division 3, section 11340 et seq.).

Business and Professions Code § 26043

(MAUCRSA, Effective June 27, 2017.)

(a) After proceedings pursuant to Section 26031 or 26058 or Chapter 2 (commencing with Section 480) or Chapter 3 (commencing with Section 490) of Division 1.5, any person aggrieved by the decision of a licensing authority denying the person's application for any license, denying the person's renewal of any license, placing any license on probation, imposing any condition on any license, imposing any fine on any license, assessing any penalty on any license, or canceling, suspending, revoking, or otherwise disciplining any license as provided for under this division, may appeal the licensing authority's written decision to the panel.

(b) The panel shall review the decision subject to such limitations as may be imposed by the Legislature. In such cases, the panel shall not receive evidence in addition to that considered by the licensing authority.

(c) Review by the panel of a decision of a licensing authority shall be limited to the following questions:

(1) Whether the licensing authority has proceeded without or in excess of its jurisdiction.

(2) Whether the licensing authority has proceeded in the manner required by law.

(3) Whether the decision is supported by the findings.

(4) Whether the findings are supported by substantial evidence in the light of the whole record.

Business and Professions Code § 26044

(MAUCRSA, Effective June 27, 2017.)

(a) In appeals where the panel finds that there is relevant evidence which, in the exercise of reasonable diligence, could not have been produced or which was improperly excluded at the hearing before the licensing authority, it may enter an order remanding the matter to the licensing authority for reconsideration in the light of that evidence.

(b) Except as provided in subdivision (a), in all appeals, the panel shall enter an order either affirming or reversing the decision of the licensing authority. When the order reverses the decision of the licensing authority, the panel may direct the reconsideration of the matter in the light of its order and may direct the licensing authority to take such further action as is specially enjoined upon it by law, but the order shall not limit or control in any way the discretion vested by law in the licensing authority.

Business and Professions Code § 26045

(MAUCRSA, Effective June 27, 2017.)

(a) No court of this state, except the Supreme Court and the courts of appeal to the extent specified in this chapter, shall have jurisdiction to review, affirm, reverse, correct, or annul any order, rule, or decision of a licensing authority or to suspend, stay, or delay the operation or execution thereof, or to restrain, enjoin, or interfere with a licensing authority in the performance of its duties, but a writ of mandate shall lie from the Supreme Court or the courts of appeal in any proper case.

(b) Any person affected by a final order of the panel, including a licensing authority, may apply to the Supreme Court or to the court of appeal for the appellate district in which the proceeding arose, for a writ of review of that final order.

(c) The application for writ of review shall be made within 30 days after filing of the final order.

(d) The provisions of the Code of Civil Procedure relating to writs of review shall, insofar as applicable, apply to proceedings in the courts as provided by this chapter. A copy of every pleading filed pursuant to this chapter shall be served on the panel, the licensing authority, and on each party who entered an appearance before the panel.

(e) No decision of a licensing authority that has been appealed to the panel and no final order of the panel shall become effective during the period in which application may be made for a writ of review, as provided by subdivision (c).

(f) The filing of a petition for, or the pendency of, a writ of review shall not of itself stay or suspend the operation of any order, rule, or decision of a licensing authority, but the court before which the petition is filed may stay or suspend, in whole or in part, the operation of the order, rule, or decision of the licensing authority subject to review, upon the terms and conditions which it by order directs.

Business and Professions Code § 26046

(MAUCRSA, Effective June 27, 2017.)

(a) The review by the court shall not extend further than to determine, based on the whole record of the licensing authority as certified by the panel, whether:

(1) The licensing authority has proceeded without or in excess of its jurisdiction.

(2) The licensing authority has proceeded in the manner required by law.

(3) The decision of the licensing authority is supported by the findings.

(4) The findings in the licensing authority's decision are supported by substantial evidence in the light of the whole record.

(5) There is relevant evidence which, in the exercise of reasonable diligence, could not have been produced or which was improperly excluded at the hearing before the licensing authority.

(b) Nothing in this chapter shall permit the court to hold a trial de novo, to take evidence, or to exercise its independent judgment on the evidence.

Business and Professions Code § 26047

(MAUCRSA, Effective June 27, 2017.)

The findings and conclusions of the licensing authority on questions of fact are conclusive and final and are not subject to review. Those questions of fact shall include ultimate facts and the findings and conclusions of the licensing authority. The panel, the licensing authority, and each party to the action or proceeding before the panel shall have the right to appear in the review proceeding. Following the hearing, the court shall enter judgment either affirming or reversing the decision of the licensing authority, or the court may remand the case for further proceedings before or reconsideration by the licensing authority.

Chapter 5. Licensing

Business and Professions Code § 26050

(MAUCRSA, Effective June 27, 2017.)

(a) The license classification pursuant to this division shall, at a minimum, be as follows:

(1) Type 1—Cultivation; Specialty outdoor; Small.

(2) Type 1A—Cultivation; Specialty indoor; Small.

(3) Type 1B—Cultivation; Specialty mixed-light; Small.

(4) Type 1C—Cultivation; Specialty cottage; Small.

(5) Type 2—Cultivation; Outdoor; Small.

(6) Type 2A—Cultivation; Indoor; Small.

(7) Type 2B—Cultivation; Mixed-light; Small.

(8) Type 3—Cultivation; Outdoor; Medium.

(9) Type 3A—Cultivation; Indoor; Medium.

(10) Type 3B—Cultivation; Mixed-light; Medium.

(11) Type 4—Cultivation; Nursery.

(12) Type 5—Cultivation; Outdoor; Large.

(13) Type 5A—Cultivation; Indoor; Large.

(14) Type 5B—Cultivation; Mixed-light; Large.

(15) Type 6—Manufacturer 1.

(16) Type 7—Manufacturer 2.

(17) Type 8—Testing laboratory.

(18) Type 10—Retailer.

(19) Type 11—Distributor.

(20) Type 12—Microbusiness.

(b) With the exception of testing laboratory licenses, which may be used to test cannabis and cannabis products regardless of whether they are intended for use by individuals who possesses a physician's recommendation, all licenses issued under this division shall bear a clear designation indicating whether the license is for commercial adult-use cannabis activity as distinct from commercial medicinal cannabis activity by prominently affixing an "A" or "M," respectively. Examples of such a designation include, but are not limited to, "A-Type 1" or "M-Type 1." Except as specifically specified in this division, the requirements for A-licenses and M-licenses shall be the same. For testing laboratories, the bureau shall create a license that indicates a testing laboratory may test both adult-use and medicinal cannabis.

(c) A license issued pursuant to this division shall be valid for 12 months from the date of issuance. The license may be renewed annually.

(d) Each licensing authority shall establish procedures for the issuance and renewal of licenses.

Business and Professions Code § 26050.1

(MAUCRSA, Effective June 27, 2017.)

(a) Notwithstanding subdivision (c) of Section 26050, until January 1, 2019, a licensing authority may, in its sole discretion, issue a temporary license if the applicant submits all of the following:

(1) A written request to the licensing authority in a manner prescribed by the licensing authority.

(2) A copy of a valid license, permit, or other authorization, issued by a local jurisdiction, that enables the applicant to conduct commercial cannabis activity at the location requested for the temporary license.

(3) The temporary license application fee, if any, required by the licensing authority.

(b) Temporary licenses issued pursuant to this section are subject to the following conditions:

(1) Except as provided for in paragraph (4) below, the temporary license shall be valid for a period of 120 days and may be extended for additional 90-day periods at the discretion of the licensing authority. Temporary licenses shall only be eligible for an extension of the expiration date if the applicant has submitted a complete application for licensure pursuant to regulations adopted under this division.

(2) A temporary license is a conditional license and authorizes the holder thereof to engage in commercial cannabis activity as would be permitted under the privileges of the license for which the applicant has

submitted an application to the licensing authority.

(3) Refusal by the licensing authority to issue or extend a temporary license shall not entitle the applicant to a hearing or appeal of the decision. Chapter 2 (commencing with Section 480) of Division 1.5 and Chapter 4 (commencing with Section 26040) of this division shall not apply to temporary licenses.

(4) A temporary license does not obligate the licensing authority to issue a nontemporary license nor does the temporary license create a vested right in the holder to either an extension of the temporary license or to the granting of a subsequent nontemporary license.

(c) This section shall remain in effect only until January 1, 2019, and as of that date is repealed.

Business and Professions Code § 26051

(MAUCRSA, Effective June 27, 2017.)

(a) The Cartwright Act, the Unfair Practices Act, the Unfair Competition Law, and the other provisions of Part 2 (commencing with Section 16600) of Division 7 apply to all licensees regulated under this division.

(b) It shall be unlawful for any person to monopolize, or attempt to monopolize, or to combine or conspire with any person or persons, to monopolize any part of the trade or commerce related to cannabis. The Attorney General shall have the sole authority to enforce the provisions of this subdivision.

(c) In determining whether to grant, deny, or renew a license for a retail license, microbusiness license, or a license issued under Section 26070.5, the bureau shall consider if an excessive concentration exists in the area where the licensee will operate. For purposes of this section "excessive concentration" applies when either of the following conditions exist:

(1) The ratio of a licensee to population in the census tract or census division in which the applicant premises are located exceeds the ratio of licensees to population in the county in which the applicant premises are located, unless denial of the application would unduly limit the development of the legal market so as to perpetuate the illegal market for cannabis or cannabis products.

(2) The ratio of retail licenses, microbusiness licenses, or licenses under Section 26070.5 to the population in the census tract, census division, or jurisdiction exceeds that allowable by local ordinance adopted under Section 26200.

Business and Professions Code § 26051.5

(Amended by AB 106, Effective March 13, 2018.)

(a) An applicant for any type of state license issued pursuant to this division shall do all of the following:

(1) Require that each owner of the applicant electronically submit to the Department of Justice fingerprint images and related information required by the Department of Justice for the purpose of obtaining information as to the existence and content of a record of state or federal convictions and arrests, and information as to the existence and content of a record of state or federal convictions and arrests for which the Department of Justice establishes that the person is free on bail or on his or her own recognizance, pending trial or appeal.

(A) Notwithstanding any other law, the Bureau of Cannabis Control, the Department of Food and Agriculture, and the State Department of Public Health may obtain and receive, at their discretion, criminal history information from the Department of Justice and the United States Federal Bureau of Investigation for an applicant for any state license under this division, including any license established by a licensing authority by regulation pursuant to subdivision (b) of Section 26012.

(B) The Department of Justice shall forward to the United States Federal Bureau of Investigation all requests for federal criminal history record information received pursuant to this section. The Department of Justice shall review the information returned from the United States Federal Bureau of Investigation and compile and disseminate a response to the licensing authority.

(C) The Department of Justice shall provide a response to the licensing authority pursuant to paragraph (1) of subdivision (p) of Section 11105 of the Penal Code.

(D) The licensing authority shall request from the Department of

Justice subsequent notification service, as provided pursuant to Section 11105.2 of the Penal Code, for applicants.

(E) The Department of Justice shall charge the applicant a fee sufficient to cover the reasonable cost of processing the requests described in this paragraph.

(2) Provide evidence of the legal right to occupy and use the proposed location and provide a statement from the landowner of real property or that landowner's agent where the commercial cannabis activity will occur, as proof to demonstrate the landowner has acknowledged and consented to permit commercial cannabis activities to be conducted on the property by the tenant applicant.

(3) Provide evidence that the proposed location is in compliance with subdivision (b) of Section 26054.

(4) Provide a statement, signed by the applicant under penalty of perjury, that the information provided is complete, true, and accurate.

(5) (A) For an applicant with 20 or more employees, provide a statement that the applicant will enter into, or demonstrate that it has already entered into, and abide by the terms of a labor peace agreement.

(B) For the purposes of this paragraph, "employee" does not include a supervisor.

(C) For the purposes of this paragraph, "supervisor" means an individual having authority, in the interest of the applicant, to hire, transfer, suspend, lay off, recall, promote, discharge, assign, reward, or discipline other employees, or responsibility to direct them or to adjust their grievances, or effectively to recommend such action, if, in connection with the foregoing, the exercise of that authority is not of a merely routine or clerical nature, but requires the use of independent judgment.

(6) Provide the applicant's valid seller's permit number issued pursuant to Part 1 (commencing with Section 6001) of Division 2 of the Revenue and Taxation Code or indicate that the applicant is currently applying for a seller's permit.

(7) Provide any other information required by the licensing authority.

(8) For an applicant seeking a cultivation license, provide a statement

declaring the applicant is an "agricultural employer," as defined in the Alatorre-Zenovich-Dunlap-Berman Agricultural Labor Relations Act of 1975 (Part 3.5 (commencing with Section 1140) of Division 2 of the Labor Code), to the extent not prohibited by law.

(9) Pay all applicable fees required for licensure by the licensing authority.

(10) Provide proof of a bond to cover the costs of destruction of cannabis or cannabis products if necessitated by a violation of licensing requirements.

(b) An applicant shall also include in the application a detailed description of the applicant's operating procedures for all of the following, as required by the licensing authority:

(1) Cultivation.

(2) Extraction and infusion methods.

(3) The transportation process.

(4) Inventory procedures.

(5) Quality control procedures.

(6) Security protocols.

(7) For applicants seeking licensure to cultivate, the source or sources of water the applicant will use for cultivation, as provided in subdivisions (a) to (c), inclusive, of Section 26060.1. For purposes of this paragraph, "cultivation" as used in Section 26060.1 shall have the same meaning as defined in Section 26001. The Department of Food and Agriculture shall consult with the State Water Resources Control Board and the Department of Fish and Wildlife in the implementation of this paragraph.

(c) The applicant shall also provide a complete detailed diagram of the proposed premises wherein the license privileges will be exercised, with sufficient particularity to enable ready determination of the bounds of the premises, showing all boundaries, dimensions, entrances and exits, interior partitions, walls, rooms, and common or shared entryways, and include a brief statement or description of the principal activity to be conducted therein, and, for licenses permitting cultivation, measurements of the planned canopy, including aggregate square footage and individual square footage of separate cultivation areas, if any, roads, water crossings, points of diversion, water storage, and all other facilities and infrastructure related to the cultivation.

(d) Provide a complete list of every person with a financial interest in the person applying for the license as required by the licensing authority. For purposes of this subdivision, "persons with a financial interest" does not include persons whose only interest in a licensee is an interest in a diversified mutual fund, blind trust, or similar instrument.

Business and Professions Code § 26052

(MAUCRSA, Effective June 27, 2017.)

(a) A licensee shall not perform any of the following acts, or permit any of the following acts to be performed by any employee, agent, or contractor of the licensee:

(1) Make any contract in restraint of trade in violation of Section 16600.

(2) Form a trust or other prohibited organization in restraint of trade in violation of Section 16720.

(3) Make a sale or contract for the sale of cannabis or cannabis products, or to fix a price charged therefor, or discount from, or rebate upon, that price, on the condition, agreement, or understanding that the consumer or purchaser thereof shall not use or deal in the goods, merchandise, machinery, supplies, commodities, or services of a competitor or competitors of the seller, where the effect of that sale, contract, condition, agreement, or understanding may be to substantially lessen competition or tend to create a monopoly in any line of trade or commerce.

(4) Sell any cannabis or cannabis products at less than cost for the purpose of injuring competitors, destroying competition, or misleading or deceiving purchasers or prospective purchasers.

(5) Discriminate between different sections, communities, or cities or portions thereof, or between different locations in those sections, communities, or cities or portions thereof in this state, by selling or furnishing cannabis or cannabis products at a lower price in one

section, community, or city or any portion thereof, or in one location in that section, community, or city or any portion thereof, than in another, for the purpose of injuring competitors or destroying competition.

(6) Sell any cannabis or cannabis products at less than the cost thereof to such vendor, or to give away any article or product for the purpose of injuring competitors or destroying competition.

(b) Any person who, either as director, officer, or agent of any firm or corporation, or as agent of any person, violates the provisions of this chapter, or assists or aids, directly or indirectly, in that violation is responsible therefor equally with the person, firm, or corporation for which that person acts.

(c) Any person or trade association may bring an action to enjoin and restrain any violation of this section for the recovery of damages.

Business and Professions Code § 26053

(Amended by AB 133, Effective September 16, 2017.)

(a) All commercial cannabis activity shall be conducted between licensees, except as otherwise provided in this division.

(b) A person that holds a state testing laboratory license under this division is prohibited from licensure for any other activity, except testing, as authorized under this division. A person that holds a state testing laboratory license shall not employ an individual who is also employed by any other licensee that does not hold a state testing laboratory license.

(c) Except as provided in subdivision (b), a person may apply for and be issued more than one license under this division.

(d) Each applicant or licensee shall apply for, and if approved, shall obtain, a separate license for each location where it engages in commercial cannabis activity.

Business and Professions Code § 26054

(MAUCRSA, Effective June 27, 2017.)

(a) A licensee shall not sell alcoholic beverages or tobacco products on or at any premises licensed under this division.

(b) A premises licensed under this division shall not be located within a 600-foot radius of a school providing instruction in kindergarten or any grades 1 through 12, day care center, or youth center that is in existence at the time the license is issued, unless a licensing authority or a local jurisdiction specifies a different radius. The distance specified in this section shall be measured in the same manner as provided in subdivision (c) of Section 11362.768 of the Health and Safety Code unless otherwise provided by law.

(c) It shall not be a violation of state or local law for a business engaged in the manufacture of cannabis accessories to possess, transport, purchase, or otherwise obtain small amounts of cannabis or cannabis products as necessary to conduct research and development related to the cannabis accessories, provided the cannabis and cannabis products are obtained from a person licensed under this division permitted to provide or deliver the cannabis or cannabis products.

(d) It shall not be a violation of state or local law for an agent of a licensing authority to possess, transport, or obtain cannabis or cannabis products as necessary to conduct activities reasonably related to the duties of the licensing authority.

Business and Professions Code § 26054.2

(MAUCRSA, Effective June 27, 2017; Inoperative December 31, 2019, by its Own Provisions.)

(a) A licensing authority shall give priority in issuing licenses under this division to applicants that can demonstrate to the authority's satisfaction that the applicant operated in compliance with the Compassionate Use Act of 1996 (Section 11362.5 of the Health and Safety Code) and its implementing laws before September 1, 2016.

(b) The licensing authorities shall request that local jurisdictions identify for the licensing authorities potential applicants for licensure based on the applicants' prior operation in the local jurisdiction in compliance with state law, including the Compassionate Use Act of 1996 (Section 11362.5 of the Health and Safety Code) and its implementing laws, and any applicable local laws.

(c) In addition to or in lieu of the information described in subdivision (b), an applicant may furnish other evidence as deemed appropriate by the licensing authority to demonstrate operation in compliance with the Compassionate

Use Act of 1996 (Section 11362.5 of the Health and Safety Code). The licensing authorities may accept such evidence to demonstrate eligibility for the priority provided for in subdivision (a).

(d) This section shall cease to be operative on December 31, 2019, unless otherwise provided by law.

Business and Professions Code § 26055

(Amended by AB 133, Effective September 16, 2017.)

(a) Licensing authorities may issue state licenses only to qualified applicants.

(b) Revocation of a state license issued under this division shall terminate the ability of the licensee to operate pursuant to that license within California until a new license is obtained.

(c) A licensee shall not change or alter the premises in a manner which materially or substantially alters the premises, the usage of the premises, or the mode or character of business operation conducted from the premises, from the plan contained in the diagram on file with the application, unless and until written approval by the licensing authority has been obtained. For purposes of this section, material or substantial physical changes of the premises, or in the usage of the premises, shall include, but not be limited to, a substantial increase or decrease in the total area of the licensed premises previously diagrammed, or any other physical modification resulting in substantial change in the mode or character of business operation.

(d) Licensing authorities shall not approve an application for a state license under this division if approval of the state license will violate the provisions of any local ordinance or regulation adopted in accordance with Section 26200.

(e) An applicant may voluntarily provide proof of a license, permit, or other authorization from the local jurisdiction verifying that the applicant is in compliance with the local jurisdiction. An applicant that voluntarily submits a valid, unexpired license, permit, or other authorization from the local jurisdiction shall be presumed to be in compliance with all local ordinances unless the licensing authority is notified otherwise by the local jurisdiction. The licensing authority shall notify the contact person for the local jurisdiction of any applicant that voluntarily submits a valid, unexpired license, permit, or other authorization from the local jurisdiction.

(f) (1) A local jurisdiction shall provide to the bureau a copy of any ordinance or regulation related to commercial cannabis activity and the name and contact information for the person who will serve as the contact for state licensing authorities regarding commercial cannabis activity within the jurisdiction. If a local jurisdiction does not provide a contact person, the bureau shall assume that the clerk of the legislative body of the local jurisdiction is the contact person.

(2) Whenever there is a change in a local ordinance or regulation adopted pursuant to Section 26200 or a change in the contact person for the jurisdiction, the local jurisdiction shall provide that information to the bureau.

(3) The bureau shall share the information required by this subdivision with the other licensing authorities.

(g) (1) The licensing authority shall deny an application for a license under this division for a commercial cannabis activity that the local jurisdiction has notified the bureau is prohibited in accordance with subdivision (f). The licensing authority shall notify the contact person for the local jurisdiction of each application denied due to the local jurisdictions indication that the commercial cannabis activity for which a license is sought is prohibited by a local ordinance or regulation.

(2) Prior to issuing a state license under this division for any commercial cannabis activity, if an applicant has not provided adequate proof of compliance with local laws pursuant to subdivision (e):

(A) The licensing authority shall notify the contact person for the local jurisdiction of the receipt of an application for commercial cannabis activity within their jurisdiction.

(B) A local jurisdiction may notify the licensing authority that the applicant is not in compliance with a local ordinance or regulation. In this instance, the licensing authority shall deny the application.

(C) A local jurisdiction may notify the licensing authority that the applicant is in compliance with all applicable local ordinances and regulations. In this instance, the licensing authority may proceed with the licensing process.

(D) If the local jurisdiction does not provide notification of compliance or noncompliance with applicable local ordinances or regulations, or otherwise does not provide notification indicating that the completion of the local permitting process is still pending, within 60 business days of receiving the inquiry from a licensing authority submitted pursuant to subparagraph (A), the licensing authority shall make a rebuttable presumption that the applicant is in compliance with all local ordinances and regulations adopted in accordance with Section 26200, except as provided in subparagraphs (E) and (F).

(E) At any time after expiration of the 60-business-day period set forth in subparagraph (D), the local jurisdiction may provide written notification to the licensing authority that the applicant or licensee is not in compliance with a local ordinance or regulation adopted in accordance with Section 26200. Upon receiving this notification, the licensing authority shall not presume that the applicant or licensee has complied with all local ordinances and regulations adopted in accordance with Section 26200, and may commence disciplinary action in accordance with Chapter 3 (commencing with Section 26030). If the licensing authority does not take action against the licensee before the time of the renewal of the license, the license shall not be renewed until and unless the local jurisdiction notifies the licensing authority that the licensee is once again in compliance with local ordinances.

(F) A presumption by a licensing authority pursuant to this paragraph that an applicant has complied with all local ordinances and regulations adopted in accordance with Section 26200 shall not prevent, impair, or preempt the local government from enforcing all applicable local ordinances or regulations against the applicant, nor shall the presumption confer any right, vested or otherwise, upon the applicant to commence or continue operating in any local jurisdiction except in accordance with all local ordinances or regulations.

(3) For purposes of this section, "notification" includes written notification or access by a licensing authority to a local jurisdiction's registry, database, or other platform designated by a local jurisdiction, containing information specified by the licensing authority, on applicants to determine local compliance.

(h) Without limiting any other statutory exemption or categorical exemption, Division 13 (commencing with Section 21000) of the Public Resources Code does not apply to the adoption of an ordinance, rule, or regulation by a local jurisdiction that requires discretionary review and approval of permits, licenses, or other authorizations to engage in commercial cannabis activity.

To qualify for this exemption, the discretionary review in any such law, ordinance, rule, or regulation shall include any applicable environmental review pursuant to Division 13 (commencing with Section 21000) of the Public Resources Code. This subdivision shall become inoperative on July 1, 2019.

(i) A local or state public agency may charge and collect a fee from a person proposing a project pursuant to subdivision (a) of Section 21089 of the Public Resources Code.

Business and Professions Code § 26056

(MAUCRSA, Effective June 27, 2017.)

The requirements of Sections 13143.9, 13145, and 13146 of the Health and Safety Code shall apply to all licensees.

Business and Professions Code § 26057

(MAUCRSA, Effective June 27, 2017.)

(a) The licensing authority shall deny an application if either the applicant, or the premises for which a state license is applied, do not qualify for licensure under this division.

(b) The licensing authority may deny the application for licensure or renewal of a state license if any of the following conditions apply:

(1) Failure or inability to comply with the provisions of this division, any rule or regulation adopted pursuant to this division, or any requirement imposed to protect natural resources, including, but not limited to, protections for instream flow, water quality, and fish and wildlife.

(2) Conduct that constitutes grounds for denial of licensure under Chapter 2 (commencing with Section 480) of Division 1.5, except as otherwise specified in this section and Section 26059.

(3) Failure to provide information required by the licensing authority.

(4) The applicant, owner, or licensee has been convicted of an offense

that is substantially related to the qualifications, functions, or duties of the business or profession for which the application is made, except that if the licensing authority determines that the applicant, owner, or licensee is otherwise suitable to be issued a license, and granting the license would not compromise public safety, the licensing authority shall conduct a thorough review of the nature of the crime, conviction, circumstances, and evidence of rehabilitation of the applicant or owner, and shall evaluate the suitability of the applicant, owner, or licensee to be issued a license based on the evidence found through the review. In determining which offenses are substantially related to the qualifications, functions, or duties of the business or profession for which the application is made, the licensing authority shall include, but not be limited to, the following:

(A) A violent felony conviction, as specified in subdivision (c) of Section 667.5 of the Penal Code.

(B) A serious felony conviction, as specified in subdivision (c) of Section 1192.7 of the Penal Code.

(C) A felony conviction involving fraud, deceit, or embezzlement.

(D) A felony conviction for hiring, employing, or using a minor in transporting, carrying, selling, giving away, preparing for sale, or peddling, any controlled substance to a minor; or selling, offering to sell, furnishing, offering to furnish, administering, or giving any controlled substance to a minor.

(E) A felony conviction for drug trafficking with enhancements pursuant to Section 11370.4 or 11379.8 of the Health and Safety Code.

(5) Except as provided in subparagraphs (D) and (E) of paragraph (4) and notwithstanding Chapter 2 (commencing with Section 480) of Division 1.5, a prior conviction, where the sentence, including any term of probation, incarceration, or supervised release, is completed, for possession of, possession for sale, sale, manufacture, transportation, or cultivation of a controlled substance is not considered substantially related, and shall not be the sole ground for denial of a license. Conviction for any controlled substance felony subsequent to licensure shall be grounds for revocation of a license or denial of the renewal of a

license.

(6) The applicant, or any of its officers, directors, or owners, has been subject to fines, penalties, or otherwise been sanctioned for cultivation or production of a controlled substance on public or private lands pursuant to Section 12025 or 12025.1 of the Fish and Game Code.

(7) The applicant, or any of its officers, directors, or owners, has been sanctioned by a licensing authority or a city, county, or city and county for unauthorized commercial cannabis activities, has had a license suspended or revoked under this division in the three years immediately preceding the date the application is filed with the licensing authority.

(8) Failure to obtain and maintain a valid seller's permit required pursuant to Part 1 (commencing with Section 6001) of Division 2 of the Revenue and Taxation Code.

(9) Any other condition specified in law.

Business and Professions Code § 26058

(MAUCRSA, Effective June 27, 2017.)

Upon the denial of any application for a license, the licensing authority shall notify the applicant in writing. Within 30 days of service of the notice, the applicant may file a written petition for a license with the licensing authority. Upon receipt of a timely filed petition, the licensing authority shall set the petition for hearing. The hearing shall be conducted in accordance with Chapter 5 (commencing with Section 11500) of Part 1 of Division 3 of Title 2 of the Government Code, and the director of each licensing authority shall have all the powers granted therein. Any appeal from a final decision of the licensing authority shall be conducted in accordance with Chapter 4 (commencing with Section 26040).

Business and Professions Code § 26059

(AUMA, Effective November 9, 2016.)

An applicant shall not be denied a state license if the denial is based solely on any of the following:

(a) A conviction or act that is substantially related to the qualifications, functions, or duties of the business or profession for which the application is made for which the applicant or licensee has obtained a certificate of rehabilitation pursuant to Chapter 3.5 (commencing with Section 4852.0l) of Title 6 of Part 3 of the Penal Code.

(b) A conviction that was subsequently dismissed pursuant to Sections 1203.4, l203.4a, or 1203.41 of the Penal Code or any other provision allowing for dismissal of a conviction.

Chapter 6. Licensed Cultivation Sites

Business and Professions Code § 26060

(MAUCRSA, Effective June 27, 2017.)

(a) Regulations issued by the Department of Food and Agriculture governing the licensing of indoor, outdoor, nursery, special cottage, and mixed-light cultivation sites shall apply to licensed cultivators under this division. The Department of Food and Agriculture shall have the authority necessary for the implementation of the regulations it adopts pursuant to this division, including regulations governing the licensing of indoor, outdoor, mixed-light cultivation site, nursery, and special cottage cultivation.

(b) The regulations shall do all of the following:

(1) Provide that weighing or measuring devices used in connection with the sale or distribution of cannabis are required to meet standards equivalent to Division 5 (commencing with Section 12001).

(2) Require that cannabis cultivation by licensees is conducted in accordance with state and local laws.

(3) Establish procedures for the issuance and revocation of unique identifiers for activities associated with a cannabis cultivation license, pursuant to Chapter 6.5 (commencing with Section 26067). All cannabis shall be labeled with the unique identifier issued by the Department of Food and Agriculture.

(4) Prescribe standards, in consultation with the bureau, for the reporting of information as necessary related to unique identifiers pursuant to Chapter 6.5 (commencing with Section 26067).

(c) The Department of Food and Agriculture shall serve as the lead agency for purposes of the California Environmental Quality Act (Division 13 (commencing with Section 21000) of the Public Resources Code) related to the licensing of cannabis cultivation.

(d) The Department of Pesticide Regulation shall develop guidelines for the use of pesticides in the cultivation of cannabis and residue in harvested cannabis.

(e) A cannabis cultivator shall not use any pesticide that has been banned for use in the state.

(f) The regulations promulgated by the Department of Food and Agriculture under this division shall implement the requirements of subdivision(b) of Section 26060.1.

(g) The Department of Pesticide Regulation shall require that the application of pesticides or other pest control in connection with the indoor, outdoor, nursery, specialty cottage, or mixed-light cultivation of cannabis complies with Division 6 (commencing with Section 11401) of the Food and Agricultural Code and its implementing regulations.

Business and Professions Code § 26060.1

(Amended by AB 133, Effective September 16, 2017.)

(a) An application for a license for cultivation issued by the Department of Food and Agriculture shall identify the source of water supply as follows:

(1) (A) If water will be supplied by a retail water supplier, as defined in Section 13575 of the Water Code, the application shall identify the retail water supplier.

(B) Paragraphs (2) and (3) do not apply to any water subject to subparagraph (A) unless the retail water supplier has 10 or fewer customers, the applicant receives 10 percent or more of the water supplied by the retail water supplier, 25 percent or more of the water delivered by the retail water supplier is used for cannabis cultivation, or the applicant and the retail water supplier are affiliates, as defined in Section 2814.20 of Title 23 of the California Code of Regulations.

(2) If the water supply includes a diversion within the meaning of Section 5100 of the Water Code, the application shall identify the point of diversion and the maximum amount to be diverted as follows:

(A) For an application submitted before January 1, 2019, the application shall include a copy of one of the following:

(i) A small irrigation use registration certificate, permit, or license issued pursuant to Part 2 (commencing with Section 1200) of Division 2 of the Water Code that covers the diversion.

(ii) A statement of water diversion and use filed with the State Water Resources Control Board on or before October 31, 2017, that covers the diversion and specifies the amount of water used for cannabis cultivation.

(iii) A pending application for a permit to appropriate water, filed with the State Water Resources Control Board on or before October 31, 2017.

(iv) Documentation submitted to the State Water Resources Control Board on or before January 1, 2019, demonstrating that the diversion is subject to subdivision (a), (c), (d), or (e) of Section 5101 of the Water Code.

(v) Documentation submitted to the State Water Resources Control Board on or before October 31, 2017, demonstrating that the diversion is authorized under a riparian right and that no diversion occurred after January 1, 2010, and before January 1, 2017. The documentation shall be submitted on or accompany a form provided by the State Water Resources Control Board and shall include all of the information outlined in subdivisions (a) to (d), inclusive, and (e) of Section 5103 of the Water Code. The documentation shall also include a general description of the area in which the water will be used in accordance with subdivision (g) of Section 5103 of the Water Code and the year in which the diversion is planned to commence.

(B) For an application submitted after December 31, 2018, the application shall include a copy of one of the following:

(i) A small irrigation use registration certificate, permit, or license issued pursuant to Part 2 (commencing with Section 1200) of Division 2 of the Water Code that covers the diversion.

(ii) A statement of water diversion and use filed with the State Water Resources Control Board that covers the diversion and specifies the amount of water used for cannabis cultivation.

(iii) Documentation submitted to the State Water Resources Control Board demonstrating that the diversion is subject to subdivision (a), (c), (d), or (e) of Section 5101 of the Water Code.

(iv) Documentation submitted to the State Water Resources Control Board demonstrating that the diversion is authorized under a riparian right and that no diversion occurred after January 1, 2010, and in the calendar year in which the application is submitted. The documentation shall be submitted on or accompany a form provided by the State Water Resources Control Board and shall include all of the information outlined in subdivisions (a) to (d), inclusive, and (e) of Section 5103 of the Water Code. The documentation shall also include a general description of the area in which the water will be used in accordance with subdivision (g) of Section 5103 of the Water Code and the year in which the diversion is planned to commence.

(3) If water will be supplied from a groundwater extraction not subject to paragraph (2), the application shall identify the location of the extraction and the maximum amount to be diverted for cannabis cultivation in any year.

(b) The Department of Food and Agriculture shall include in any license for cultivation all of the following:

(1) Conditions requested by the Department of Fish and Wildlife and the State Water Resources Control Board to (A) ensure that individual and cumulative effects of water diversion and discharge associated with cultivation do not affect the instream flows needed for fish spawning, migration, and rearing, and the flows needed to maintain natural flow variability; (B) ensure that cultivation does not negatively impact springs, riparian habitat, wetlands, or aquatic habitat; and (C) otherwise protect fish, wildlife, fish and wildlife habitat, and water quality. The conditions shall include, but not be limited to, the principles, guidelines, and requirements established pursuant to Section 13149 of the Water Code.

(2) Any relevant mitigation requirements the Department of Food and Agriculture identifies as part of its approval of the final environmental documentation for the cannabis cultivation licensing program as requirements that should be included in a license for cultivation. Chapter 3.5 (commencing with Section 11340) of Part 1 of Division 3 of Title 2 of the Government Code does not apply to the identification of these mitigation measures. This paragraph does not reduce any requirements established pursuant to Division 13 (commencing with Section 21000) of the Public Resources Code.

(3) A condition that the license shall not be effective until the licensee has demonstrated compliance with Section 1602 of the Fish and Game Code or receives written verification from the Department of Fish and Wildlife that a streambed alteration agreement is not required.

(c) The Department of Food and Agriculture shall consult with the State Water Resources Control Board and the Department of Fish and Wildlife in the implementation of this section.

(d) Notwithstanding paragraph (1) of subdivision (b), the Department of Food and Agriculture is not responsible for verifying compliance with the conditions requested or imposed by the Department of Fish and Wildlife or the State Water Resources Control Board. The Department of Fish and Wildlife or the State Water Resources Control Board, upon finding and making the final determination of a violation of a condition included pursuant to paragraph (1) of subdivision (b), shall notify the Department of Food and Agriculture, which may take appropriate action with respect to the licensee in accordance with Chapter 3 (commencing with Section 26030).

Business and Professions Code § 26061

(MAUCRSA, Effective June 27, 2017.)

(a) The state cultivator license types to be issued by the Department of Food and Agriculture under this division shall include all of the following:

(1) Type 1, or "specialty outdoor," for outdoor cultivation using no artificial lighting of less than or equal to 5,000 square feet of total canopy size on one premises, or up to 50 mature plants on noncontiguous plots.

(2) Type 1A, or "specialty indoor," for indoor cultivation using

exclusively artificial lighting of between 501 and 5,000 square feet of total canopy size on one premises.

(3) Type 1B, or "specialty mixed-light," for cultivation using a combination of natural and supplemental artificial lighting at a maximum threshold to be determined by the licensing authority, of between 2,501 and 5,000 square feet of total canopy size on one premises.

(4) Type 1C, or "specialty cottage," for cultivation using a combination of natural and supplemental artificial lighting at a maximum threshold to be determined by the licensing authority, of 2,500 square feet or less of total canopy size for mixed-light cultivation, up to 25 mature plants for outdoor cultivation, or 500 square feet or less of total canopy size for indoor cultivation, on one premises.

(5) Type 2, or "small outdoor," for outdoor cultivation using no artificial lighting between 5,001 and 10,000 square feet, inclusive, of total canopy size on one premises.

(6) Type 2A, or "small indoor," for indoor cultivation using exclusively artificial lighting between 5,001 and 10,000 square feet, inclusive, of total canopy size on one premises.

(7) Type 2B, or "small mixed-light," for cultivation using a combination of natural and supplemental artificial lighting at a maximum threshold to be determined by the licensing authority, between 5,001 and 10,000 square feet, inclusive, of total canopy size on one premises.

(8) Type 3, or "outdoor," for outdoor cultivation using no artificial lighting from 10,001 square feet to one acre, inclusive, of total canopy size on one premises. The Department of Food and Agriculture shall limit the number of licenses allowed of this type.

(9) Type 3A, or "indoor," for indoor cultivation using exclusively artificial lighting between 10,001 and 22,000 square feet, inclusive, of total canopy size on one premises. The Department of Food and Agriculture shall limit the number of licenses allowed of this type.

(10) Type 3B, or "mixed-light," for cultivation using a combination of natural and supplemental artificial lighting at a maximum threshold to be determined by the licensing authority, between 10,001 and

22,000 square feet, inclusive, of total canopy size on one premises. The Department of Food and Agriculture shall limit the number of licenses allowed of this type.

(11) Type 4, or "nursery" for cultivation of cannabis solely as a nursery.

(b) Except as otherwise provided by law:

(1) Type 5, or "outdoor," means for outdoor cultivation using no artificial lighting greater than one acre, inclusive, of total canopy size on one premises.

(2) Type 5A, or "indoor," means for indoor cultivation using exclusively artificial lighting greater than 22,000 square feet, inclusive, of total canopy size on one premises.

(3) Type 5B, or "mixed-light," means for cultivation using a combination of natural and supplemental artificial lighting at a maximum threshold to be determined by the licensing authority, greater than 22,000 square feet, inclusive, of total canopy size on one premises.

(c) No Type 5, Type 5A, or Type 5B cultivation licenses may be issued before January 1, 2023.

(d) Commencing on January 1, 2023, a Type 5, Type 5A, or Type 5B licensee may apply for and hold a Type 6 or Type 7 license and apply for and hold a Type 10 license. A Type 5, Type 5A, or Type 5B licensee shall not be eligible to apply for or hold a Type 8, Type 11, or Type 12 license.

Business and Professions Code § 26062

(MAUCRSA, Effective June 27, 2017.)

(a) No later than January 1, 2021, the Department of Food and Agriculture shall establish a program for cannabis that is comparable to the National Organic Program (Section 6517 of the federal Organic Foods Production Act of 1990 (7 U.S.C. Sec. 6501 et seq.)), and the California Organic Food and Farming Act (Chapter 10 (commencing with Section 46000) of Division 17 of the Food and Agricultural Code) and Article 7 (commencing with Section 110810) of Chapter 5 of Part 5 of Division 104 of the Health and Safety Code. The Department of Food and Agriculture shall be the sole determiner of designation and certification.

(b) If at any time preceding or following the establishment of a program by the Department of Food and Agriculture pursuant to subdivision (a), the National Organic Program (Section 6517 of the federal Organic Foods Production Act of 1990 (7 U.S.C. Sec. 6501 et seq.)) authorizes organic designation and certification for cannabis, this section shall become inoperative and, as of January 1, of the following year, is repealed.

Business and Professions Code § 26062.5

(MAUCRSA, Effective June 27, 2017.)

A person shall not represent, sell, or offer for sale any cannabis or cannabis product as organic except in accordance with the National Organic Program (Section 6517 of the federal Organic Foods Production Act of 1990 (7 U.S.C. Sec. 6501 et seq.)), if applicable. A person shall not represent, sell, or offer for sale any cannabis or cannabis product with the designation or certification established by the Department of Food and Agriculture pursuant to subdivision (a) of Section 26062 except in accordance with that subdivision.

Business and Professions Code § 26063

(MAUCRSA, Effective June 27, 2017.)

(a) No later than January 1, 2018, the Department of Food and Agriculture shall establish standards by which a licensed cultivator may designate a county of origin for cannabis. To be eligible for the designation, 100 percent of the cannabis shall be produced within the designated county, as defined by finite political boundaries.

> (1) Cannabis shall not be advertised, marketed, labeled, or sold as grown in a California county when the cannabis was not grown in that county.

> (2) The name of a California county, including any similar name that is likely to mislead consumers as to the origin of the product, shall not be used in the advertising, labeling, marketing, or packaging of cannabis products unless the cannabis contained in the product was grown in that county.

(b) No later than January 1, 2021, the Department of Food and Agriculture shall establish a process by which licensed cultivators may establish appellations of standards, practices, and varietals applicable to cannabis grown in a certain geographical area in California, not otherwise specified in subdivision (a).

Business and Professions Code § 26065

(MAUCRSA, Effective June 27, 2017.)

An employee engaged in the cultivation of cannabis under this division shall be subject to Wage Order No. 4-2001 of the Industrial Welfare Commission.

Business and Professions Code § 26066

(MAUCRSA, Effective June 27, 2017.)

Indoor and outdoor cannabis cultivation by persons and entities licensed under this division shall be conducted in accordance with state and local laws related to land conversion, current building and fire standards, grading, electricity usage, water usage, water quality, woodland and riparian habitat protection, agricultural discharges, and similar matters. State agencies, including, but not limited to, the State Board of Forestry and Fire Protection, the Department of Fish and Wildlife, the State Water Resources Control Board, the California regional water quality control boards, and traditional state law enforcement agencies, shall address environmental impacts of cannabis cultivation and shall coordinate when appropriate with cities and counties and their law enforcement agencies in enforcement efforts.

Chapter 6.5. Unique Identifiers and Track and Trace

Business and Professions Code § 26067

(MAUCRSA, Effective June 27, 2017.)

(a) The department, in consultation with the bureau, shall establish a track and trace program for reporting the movement of cannabis and cannabis products throughout the distribution chain that utilizes a unique identifier pursuant to Section 26069, secure packaging, and is capable of providing information that captures, at a minimum, all of the following:

(1) The licensee receiving the product.

(2) The transaction date.

(3) The cultivator from which the product originates, including the associated unique identifier pursuant to Section 26069.

(b) (1) The department, in consultation with the State Board of Equalization, shall create an electronic database containing the electronic shipping manifests to facilitate the administration of the track and trace program, which shall include, but not be limited to, the following information:

(A) The variety and quantity or weight of products shipped.

(B) The estimated times of departure and arrival.

(C) The variety and quantity or weight of products received.

(D) The actual time of departure and arrival.

(E) A categorization of the product.

(F) The license number and the unique identifier pursuant to Section 26069 issued by the licensing authority for all licensees involved in the shipping process, including, but not limited to, cultivators, manufacturers, distributors, and dispensaries.

(2) (A) The database shall be designed to flag irregularities for all licensing authorities in this division to investigate. All licensing authorities pursuant to this division may access the database and share information related to licensees under this chapter, including social security and individual taxpayer identifications notwithstanding Section 30.

(B) The department shall immediately inform the bureau upon the finding of an irregularity or suspicious finding related to a licensee, applicant, or commercial cannabis activity for investigatory purposes.

(3) Licensing authorities and state and local agencies may, at any time, inspect shipments and request documentation for current inventory.

(4) The bureau shall have 24-hour access to the electronic database administered by the department. The State Board of Equalization shall have read access to the electronic database for the purpose of taxation and regulation of cannabis and cannabis products.

(5) The department shall be authorized to enter into memoranda of understandings with licensing authorities for data sharing purposes, as

deemed necessary by the department.

(6) Information received and contained in records kept by the department or licensing authorities for the purposes of administering this chapter are confidential and shall not be disclosed pursuant to the California Public Records Act (Chapter 3.5 (commencing with Section 6250) of Division 7 of Title 1 of the Government Code), except as necessary for authorized employees of the State of California or any city, county, or city and county to perform official duties pursuant to this division or a local ordinance.

(7) Upon the request of a state or local law enforcement agency, licensing authorities shall allow access to or provide information contained within the database to assist law enforcement in their duties and responsibilities pursuant to this division.

Business and Professions Code § 26068

(MAUCRSA, Effective June 27, 2017.)

(a) The department, in consultation with the bureau and the State Board of Equalization, shall ensure that the track and trace program can also track and trace the amount of the cultivation tax due pursuant to Part 14.5 (commencing with Section 34010) of Division 2 of the Revenue and Taxation Code. The track and trace program shall include an electronic seed to sale software tracking system with data points for the different stages of commercial activity, including, but not limited to, cultivation, harvest, processing, distribution, inventory, and sale.

(b) The department, in consultation with the bureau, shall ensure that licensees under this division are allowed to use third-party applications, programs, and information technology systems to comply with the requirements of the expanded track and trace program described in subdivision (a) to report the movement of cannabis and cannabis products throughout the distribution chain and communicate the information to licensing agencies as required by law.

(c) Any software, database, or other information technology system utilized by the department to implement the expanded track and trace program shall support interoperability with third-party cannabis business software applications and allow all licensee-facing system activities to be performed through a secure application programming interface (API) or comparable technology that is well documented, bi-directional, and accessible to any third-party application that has been validated and has appropriate credentials. The API or comparable technology shall have version control and provide adequate notice of updates to third-party applications. The system should provide a test environment for third-party applications to access that mirrors the production environment.

Business and Professions Code § 26069

(Amended by AB 133, Effective September 16, 2017.)

(a) The department shall establish a Cannabis Cultivation Program to be administered by the secretary. The secretary shall administer this section as it pertains to the cultivation of cannabis. For purposes of this division, cannabis is an agricultural product.

(b) A person or entity shall not cultivate cannabis without first obtaining a state license issued by the department pursuant to this division.

(c) (1) The department, in consultation with, but not limited to, the bureau, shall implement a unique identification program for cannabis. In implementing the program, the department shall consider issues including, but not limited to, water use and environmental impacts. If the State Water Resources Control Board or the Department of Fish and Wildlife finds, based on substantial evidence, that cannabis cultivation is causing significant adverse impacts on the environment in a watershed or other geographic area, the department shall not issue new licenses or increase the total number of plant identifiers within that watershed or area.

(2) (A) The department shall establish a program for the identification of permitted cannabis plants at a cultivation site during the cultivation period. A unique identifier shall be issued for each cannabis plant. The department shall ensure that unique identifiers are issued as quickly as possible to ensure the implementation of this division. The unique identifier shall be attached at the base of each plant or as otherwise required by law or regulation.

(B) Unique identifiers shall only be issued to those persons appropriately licensed by this section.

(C) Information associated with the assigned unique identifier and licensee shall be included in the trace and track program specified in Section 26067.

(D) The department may charge a fee to cover the reasonable costs of issuing the unique identifier and monitoring, tracking, and inspecting each cannabis plant.

(E) The department may promulgate regulations to implement this section.

(3) The department shall take adequate steps to establish protections against fraudulent unique identifiers and limit illegal diversion of unique identifiers to unlicensed persons.

(d) A city, county, or city and county may administer unique identifiers and associated identifying information but a city, county, or city and county's identifiers shall not supplant the department's track and trace program.

(e) (1) This section does not apply to the cultivation of cannabis in accordance with Section 11362.1 of the Health and Safety Code or the Compassionate Use Act.

(2) Subdivision (b) does not apply to persons or entities licensed under subdivision (b) of Section 26070.5.

Business and Professions Code § 26069.1

(MAUCRSA, Effective June 27, 2017.)

The secretary may enter into a cooperative agreement with a county agricultural commissioner or other state or local agency to assist the department in implementing the provisions of this division related to administration, investigation, inspection, fee collection, document management, education and outreach, distribution of individual licenses approved by the secretary, and technical assistance pertaining to the cultivation of cannabis. The department shall pay compensation under a cooperative agreement from fees collected and deposited pursuant to this division and shall provide reimbursement to a county agricultural commissioner, state, or local agency for associated costs. The secretary shall not delegate through a cooperative agreement, or otherwise, its authority to issue cultivation licenses to a county agricultural commissioner, local agency, or another state agency. The secretary shall provide notice of any cooperative agreement entered into pursuant to this section to other relevant state agencies involved in the regulation of cannabis cultivation. No cooperative agreement under this section shall relieve the department of its obligations under paragraph (2) of subdivision (a) of Section 26012 to administer the provisions of this division related to, and associated with, the cultivation of cannabis.

Business and Professions Code § 26069.9

(MAUCRSA, Effective June 27, 2017.)

For purposes of this chapter:

(a) "Department" means the Department of Food and Agriculture.

(b) "Secretary" means the Secretary of Food and Agriculture.

Chapter 7. Retailers and Distributors

Business and Professions Code § 26070

(Amended by AB 133, Effective September 16, 2017.)

Retailers and Distributors.

(a) State licenses to be issued by the bureau related to the sale and distribution of cannabis and cannabis products are as follows:

(1) "Retailer," for the retail sale and delivery of cannabis or cannabis products to customers. A retailer shall have a licensed premises which is a physical location from which commercial cannabis activities are conducted. A retailer's premises may be closed to the public. A retailer may conduct sales exclusively by delivery.

(2) "Distributor," for the distribution of cannabis and cannabis products. A distributor licensee shall be bonded and insured at a minimum level established by the licensing authority.

(3) (A) "Microbusiness," for the cultivation of cannabis on an area less than 10,000 square feet and to act as a licensed distributor, Level 1 manufacturer, and retailer under this division, provided such licensee can demonstrate compliance with all requirements imposed by this division on licensed cultivators, distributors, Level 1 manufacturers, and retailers to the extent the licensee engages in such activities. Microbusiness licenses that authorize cultivation of cannabis shall include the license conditions described in subdivision (b) of Section 26060.1.

(B) In coordination with each other, the licensing authorities shall establish a process by which an applicant for a microbusiness license can demonstrate compliance with all the requirements under this division for the activities that will be conducted under the license.

(C) The bureau may enter into interagency agreements with licensing authorities to implement and enforce the provisions of this division related to microbusinesses. The costs of activities carried out by the licensing authorities as requested by the bureau pursuant to the interagency agreement shall be calculated into the application and licensing fees collected pursuant to this division, and shall provide for reimbursement to state agencies for associated costs as provided for in the interagency agreement.

(b) The bureau shall establish minimum security and transportation safety requirements for the commercial distribution and delivery of cannabis and cannabis products. Except as provided in subdivision (d) of Section 26110, the transportation of cannabis and cannabis products shall only be conducted by persons holding a distributor license under this division or employees of those persons. Transportation safety standards established by the bureau shall include, but not be limited to, minimum standards governing the types of vehicles in which cannabis and cannabis products may be distributed and delivered and minimum qualifications for persons eligible to operate such vehicles.

(c) The driver of a vehicle transporting or transferring cannabis or cannabis products shall be directly employed by a licensee authorized to transport or transfer cannabis or cannabis products.

(d) Notwithstanding any other law, all vehicles transporting cannabis and cannabis products for hire shall be required to have a valid motor carrier permit pursuant to Chapter 2 (commencing with Section 34620) of Division 14.85 of the Vehicle Code. The Department of the California Highway Patrol shall have authority over the safe operation of these vehicles, including, but not limited to, requiring licensees engaged in the transportation of cannabis or cannabis products to participate in the Basic Inspection of Terminals (BIT) program pursuant to Section 34501.12 of the Vehicle Code.

(e) Prior to transporting cannabis or cannabis products, a licensed distributor shall do both of the following:

(1) Complete an electronic shipping manifest as prescribed by the licensing authority. The shipping manifest shall include the unique

identifier, pursuant to Section 26069, issued by the Department of Food and Agriculture for the original cannabis product.

(2) Securely transmit the manifest to the bureau and the licensee that will receive the cannabis product. The bureau shall inform the Department of Food and Agriculture of information pertaining to commercial cannabis activity for the purpose of the track and trace program identified in Section 26067.

(f) During transportation, the licensed distributor shall maintain a physical copy of the shipping manifest and make it available upon request to agents of the Department of Consumer Affairs and law enforcement officers.

(g) The licensee receiving the shipment shall maintain each electronic shipping manifest and shall make it available upon request to the Department of Consumer Affairs and any law enforcement officers.

(h) Upon receipt of the transported shipment, the licensee receiving the shipment shall submit to the licensing authority a record verifying receipt of the shipment and the details of the shipment.

(i) Transporting, or arranging for or facilitating the transport of, cannabis or cannabis products in violation of this chapter is grounds for disciplinary action against the license.

(j) Licensed retailers and microbusinesses, and licensed nonprofits under Section 26070.5, shall implement security measures reasonably designed to prevent unauthorized entrance into areas containing cannabis or cannabis products and theft of cannabis or cannabis products from the premises. These security measures shall include, but not be limited to, all of the following:

(1) Prohibiting individuals from remaining on the licensee's premises if they are not engaging in activity expressly related to the operations of the retailer.

(2) Establishing limited access areas accessible only to authorized personnel.

(3) Other than limited amounts of cannabis used for display purposes, samples, or immediate sale, storing all finished cannabis and cannabis products in a secured and locked room, safe, or vault, and in a manner reasonably designed to prevent diversion, theft, and loss.

(k) A retailer shall notify the licensing authority and the appropriate law enforcement authorities within 24 hours after discovering any of the following:

> (1) Significant discrepancies identified during inventory. The level of significance shall be determined by the bureau.

> (2) Diversion, theft, loss, or any criminal activity pertaining to the operation of the retailer.

> (3) Diversion, theft, loss, or any criminal activity by any agent or employee of the retailer pertaining to the operation of the retailer.

> (4) The loss or unauthorized alteration of records related to cannabis or cannabis products, registered qualifying patients, primary caregivers, or retailer employees or agents.

> (5) Any other breach of security.

(l) Beginning January 1, 2018, a licensee may sell cannabis or cannabis products that have not been tested for a limited and finite time as determined by the bureau. The cannabis or cannabis products must have a label affixed to each package containing the cannabis or cannabis products that clearly states "This product has not been tested as required by the Medicinal and Adult-Use Cannabis Regulation and Safety Act" and must comply with any other requirement as determined by the bureau.

Business and Professions Code § 26070.1

(MAUCRSA, Effective June 27, 2017.)

Cannabis or cannabis products purchased by a customer shall not leave a licensed retail premises unless they are placed in an opaque package.

Business and Professions Code § 26070.5

(MAUCRSA, Effective June 27, 2017.)

(a) The bureau shall, by January 1, 2020, investigate the feasibility of creating one or more classifications of nonprofit licenses under this section. The feasibility determination shall be made in consultation with the relevant licensing agencies and representatives of local jurisdictions which issue temporary licenses pursuant to subdivision (b). The bureau shall consider factors including, but not limited to, the following:

(1) Should nonprofit licensees be exempted from any or all state taxes, licensing fees and regulatory provisions applicable to other licenses in this division?

(2) Should funding incentives be created to encourage others licensed under this division to provide professional services at reduced or no cost to nonprofit licensees?

(3) Should nonprofit licenses be limited to, or prioritize those, entities previously operating on a not-for-profit basis primarily providing whole-plant cannabis and cannabis products and a diversity of cannabis strains and seed stock to low-income persons?

(b) Any local jurisdiction may issue temporary local licenses to nonprofit entities primarily providing whole-plant cannabis and cannabis products and a diversity of cannabis strains and seed stock to low-income persons so long as the local jurisdiction does all of the following:

(1) Confirms the license applicant's status as a nonprofit entity registered with the California Attorney General's Registry of Charitable Trusts and that the applicant is in good standing with all state requirements governing nonprofit entities.

(2) Licenses and regulates any such entity to protect public health and safety, and so as to require compliance with all environmental requirements in this division.

(3) Provides notice to the bureau of any such local licenses issued, including the name and location of any such licensed entity and all local regulations governing the licensed entity's operation.

(4) Certifies to the bureau that any such licensed entity will not generate annual gross revenues in excess of two million dollars ($2,000,000).

(c) Temporary local licenses authorized under subdivision (b) shall expire after 12 months unless renewed by the local jurisdiction.

(d) The bureau may impose reasonable additional requirements on the local licenses authorized under subdivision (b).

(e) (1) No new temporary local licenses shall be issued pursuant to this section after the date the bureau determines that creation of nonprofit licenses under this division is not feasible, or if the bureau determines such licenses are feasible, after the date a licensing agency commences issuing state nonprofit licenses.

(2) If the bureau determines such licenses are feasible, no temporary license issued under subdivision (b) shall be renewed or extended after the date on which a licensing agency commences issuing state nonprofit licenses.

(3) If the bureau determines that creation of nonprofit licenses under this division is not feasible, the bureau shall provide notice of this determination to all local jurisdictions that have issued temporary licenses under subdivision (b). The bureau may, in its discretion, permit any such local jurisdiction to renew or extend on an annual basis any temporary license previously issued under subdivision (b).

Chapter 8. Distribution and Transport

Business and Professions Code § 26080

(MAUCRSA, Effective June 27, 2017.)

(a) This division shall not be construed to authorize or permit a licensee to transport or distribute, or cause to be transported or distributed, cannabis or cannabis products outside the state, unless authorized by federal law.

(b) A local jurisdiction shall not prevent transportation of cannabis or cannabis products on public roads by a licensee transporting cannabis or cannabis products in compliance with this division.

Chapter 9. Delivery

Business and Professions Code § 26090

(Amended by AB 133, Effective September 16, 2017.)

(a) Deliveries, as defined in this division, may only be made by a licensed retailer or microbusiness, or a licensed nonprofit under Section 26070.5.

(b) All employees of a retailer, microbusiness, or nonprofit delivering cannabis or cannabis products shall carry a copy of the licensee's current license and a government-issued identification with a photo of the employee, such as a driver's license. The employee shall present that license and identification upon request to state and local law enforcement, employees of regulatory authorities, and other state and local agencies enforcing this division.

(c) During delivery, the licensee shall maintain a copy of the delivery request and shall make it available upon request of the licensing authority and law enforcement officers. The delivery request documentation shall comply with state and federal law regarding the protection of confidential medical information.

(d) A customer requesting delivery shall maintain a physical or electronic copy of the delivery request and shall make it available upon request by the licensing authority and law enforcement officers.

(e) A local jurisdiction shall not prevent delivery of cannabis or cannabis products on public roads by a licensee acting in compliance with this division and local law as adopted under Section 26200.

Chapter 10. Testing Laboratories

Business and Professions Code § 26100

(MAUCRSA, Effective June 27, 2017.)

(a) Except as otherwise provided by law, cannabis or cannabis products shall not be sold pursuant to a license provided for under this division unless a representative sample of the cannabis or cannabis products has been tested by a licensed testing laboratory.

(b) The bureau shall develop criteria to determine which batches shall be tested. All testing of the samples shall be performed on the final form in which the cannabis or cannabis product will be consumed or used.

(c) Testing of batches to meet the requirements of this division shall only be conducted by a licensed testing laboratory.

(d) For each batch tested, the testing laboratory shall issue a certificate of analysis for selected lots at a frequency determined by the bureau with supporting data, to report both of the following:

(1) Whether the chemical profile of the sample conforms to the labeled content of compounds, including, but not limited to, all of the following, unless limited through regulation by the bureau:

    (A) Tetrahydrocannabinol (THC).

    (B) Tetrahydrocannabinolic Acid (THCA).

    (C) Cannabidiol (CBD).

    (D) Cannabidiolic Acid (CBDA).

    (E) The terpenes required by the bureau in regulation.

    (F) Cannabigerol (CBG).

    (G) Cannabinol (CBN).

    (H) Any other compounds or contaminants required by the bureau.

(2) That the presence of contaminants does not exceed the levels established by the bureau. In establishing the levels, the bureau shall consider the American Herbal Pharmacopoeia monograph, guidelines set by the Department of Pesticide Regulation pursuant to subdivision (d) of Section 26060, and any other relevant sources. For purposes of this paragraph, "contaminants" includes, but is not limited to, all of the following:

    (A) Residual solvent or processing chemicals.

    (B) Foreign material, including, but not limited to, hair, insects, or similar or related adulterant.

    (C) Microbiological impurities as identified by the bureau in regulation.

(e) Standards for residual levels of volatile organic compounds shall be established by the bureau.

(f) The testing laboratory shall conduct all testing required by this section in a manner consistent with general requirements for the competence of testing and calibrations activities, including sampling and using verified methods.

(g) All testing laboratories performing tests pursuant to this section shall obtain and maintain ISO/IEC 17025 accreditation as required by the bureau in regulation.

(h) If a test result falls outside the specifications authorized by law or regulation, the testing laboratory shall follow a standard operating procedure to confirm or refute the original result.

(i) A testing laboratory shall destroy the remains of the sample of medical cannabis or medical cannabis product upon completion of the analysis, as determined by the bureau through regulations.

(j) Any presale inspection, testing transfer, or transportation of cannabis products pursuant to this section shall conform to a specified chain of custody protocol and any other requirements imposed under this division.

(k) This division does not prohibit a licensee from performing testing on the licensee's premises for the purposes of quality assurance of the product in conjunction with reasonable business operations. This division also does not prohibit a licensee from performing testing on the licensee's premises of cannabis or cannabis products obtained from another licensee. Onsite testing by the licensee shall not be certified by the bureau and does not exempt the licensee from the requirements of quality assurance testing at a testing laboratory pursuant to this section.

Business and Professions Code § 26102

(MAUCRSA, Effective June 27, 2017.)

A testing laboratory shall not be licensed by the bureau unless the laboratory meets all of the following:

(a) Complies with any other requirements specified by the bureau.

(b) Notifies the bureau within one business day after the receipt of notice of any kind that its accreditation has been denied, suspended, or revoked.

(c) Has established standard operating procedures that provide for adequate chain of custody controls for samples transferred to the testing laboratory for testing.

Business and Professions Code § 26104

(Amended by AB 133, Effective September 16, 2017.)

(a) A licensed testing laboratory shall, in performing activities concerning cannabis and cannabis products, comply with the requirements and restrictions set forth in applicable law and regulations.

(b) The bureau shall develop procedures to do all of the following:

(1) Ensure that testing of cannabis and cannabis products occurs prior to distribution to retailers, microbusinesses, or nonprofits licensed under Section 26070.5.

(2) Specify how often licensees shall test cannabis and cannabis products, and that the cost of testing cannabis shall be borne by the licensed cultivators and the cost of testing cannabis products shall be borne by the licensed manufacturer, and that the costs of testing cannabis and cannabis products shall be borne by a nonprofit licensed under Section 26070.5.

(3) Require destruction of harvested batches whose testing samples indicate noncompliance with health and safety standards required by the bureau, unless remedial measures can bring the cannabis or cannabis products into compliance with quality assurance standards as specified by law and implemented by the bureau.

(4) Ensure that a testing laboratory employee takes the sample of cannabis or cannabis products from the distributor's premises for testing required by this division and that the testing laboratory employee transports the sample to the testing laboratory.

(c) Except as provided in this division, a testing laboratory shall not acquire or receive cannabis or cannabis products except from a licensee in accordance with this division, and shall not distribute, sell, or dispense cannabis or cannabis products, from the licensed premises from which the cannabis or cannabis products were acquired or received. All transfer or transportation shall be performed pursuant to a specified chain of custody protocol.

(d) A testing laboratory may receive and test samples of cannabis or cannabis products from a qualified patient or primary caregiver only if the qualified patient or primary caregiver presents the qualified patient's valid physician's recommendation for cannabis for medicinal purposes. A testing laboratory shall not certify samples from a qualified patient or primary caregiver for resale or transfer to another party or licensee. All tests performed by a testing laboratory for a qualified patient or primary caregiver shall be recorded with the name of the qualified patient or primary caregiver and the amount of cannabis or cannabis product received.

Business and Professions Code § 26105

(AUMA, Effective November 9, 2016.)

Manufacturing Level 2 licensees shall enact sufficient methods or procedures to capture or otherwise limit risk of explosion, combustion, or any other unreasonably dangerous risk to public safety created by volatile solvents. The Department of Public Health shall establish minimum standards concerning such methods and procedures for Level 2 licensees.

Business and Professions Code § 26106

(MAUCRSA, Effective June 27, 2017.)

Standards for the production, packaging, and labeling of all cannabis products developed by the State Department of Public Health apply to all licensed manufacturers and microbusinesses, and nonprofits licensed under Section 26070.5, unless otherwise specified by the State Department of Public Health.

Chapter 11. Quality Assurance, Inspection, and Testing

Business and Professions Code § 26110

(MAUCRSA, Effective June 27, 2017.)

(a) Cannabis batches are subject to quality assurance and testing prior to sale at a retailer, microbusiness, or nonprofit licensed under Section 26070.5, except for immature cannabis plants and seeds, as provided for in this division.

(b) A licensee that holds a valid distributor license may act as the distributor for the licensee's cannabis and cannabis products.

(c) The distributor shall store, as determined by the bureau, the cannabis batches on the premises of the distributor before testing and continuously until either of the following occurs:

(1) The cannabis batch passes the testing requirements pursuant to this division and is transported to a licensed retailer.

(2) The cannabis batch fails the testing requirements pursuant to this division and is destroyed or transported to a manufacturer for remediation as allowed by the bureau or the Department of Public Health.

(d) The distributor shall arrange for a testing laboratory to obtain a representative sample of each cannabis batch at the distributor's licensed premises. After obtaining the sample, the testing laboratory representative shall maintain custody of the sample and transport it to the testing laboratory.

(e) Upon issuance of a certificate of analysis by the testing laboratory that the cannabis batch has passed the testing requirements pursuant to this division, the distributor shall conduct a quality assurance review before distribution to ensure the labeling and packaging of the cannabis and cannabis products conform to the requirements of this division.

(f) (1) There shall be a quality assurance compliance monitor who is an employee or contractor of the bureau and who shall not hold a license in any category or own or have an ownership interest in a licensee or the premises of a licensee.

(2) The quality assurance compliance monitor shall conduct random quality assurance reviews at a distributor's licensed premises before distribution to ensure the labeling and packaging of the cannabis and cannabis products conform to the requirements of this division.

(3) The quality assurance compliance monitor shall have access to all records and test results required of a licensee by law in order to conduct quality assurance analysis and to confirm test results. All records of inspection and verification by the quality assurance compliance monitor shall be provided to the bureau. Failure to comply shall be noted by the quality assurance compliance monitor for further investigation. Violations shall be reported to the bureau. The quality assurance compliance monitor shall also verify the tax payments collected and paid under Sections 34011 and 34012 of the Revenue and Tax Code are accurate. The monitor shall also have access to

the inputs and assumptions in the track and trace system and shall be able to verify the accuracy of those and that they are commensurate with the tax payments.

(g) After testing, all cannabis and cannabis products fit for sale may be transported only from the distributor's premises to the premises of a licensed retailer, microbusiness, or nonprofit.

(h) A licensee is not required to sell cannabis or cannabis products to a distributor and may directly contract for sale with a licensee authorized to sell cannabis and cannabis products to purchasers.

(i) A distributor performing services pursuant to this section may collect a fee from the licensee for the services provided. The fee may include, but is not limited to, the costs incurred for laboratory testing. A distributor may also collect applicable state or local taxes and fees.

(j) This section does not prohibit a licensee from performing testing on the licensee's premises for the purposes of quality assurance of the product in conjunction with reasonable business operations. The testing conducted on the licensee's premises by the licensee does not meet the testing requirements pursuant to this division.

Chapter 12. Packaging and Labeling

Business and Professions Code § 26120

(MAUCRSA, Effective June 27, 2017.)

(a) Prior to delivery or sale at a retailer, cannabis and cannabis products shall be labeled and placed in a resealable, tamper-evident, child-resistant package and shall include a unique identifier for the purposes of identifying and tracking cannabis and cannabis products.

(b) Packages and labels shall not be made to be attractive to children.

(c) All cannabis and cannabis product labels and inserts shall include the following information prominently displayed in a clear and legible fashion in accordance with the requirements, including font size, prescribed by the bureau or the State Department of Public Health:

    (1) The following statements, in bold print:

(A) For cannabis: "GOVERNMENT WARNING: THIS PACKAGE CONTAINS CANNABIS, A SCHEDULE I CONTROLLED SUBSTANCE. KEEP OUT OF REACH OF CHILDREN AND ANIMALS. CANNABIS MAY ONLY BE POSSESSED OR CONSUMED BY PERSONS 21 YEARS OF AGE OR OLDER UNLESS THE PERSON IS A QUALIFIED PATIENT. CANNABIS USE WHILE PREGNANT OR BREASTFEEDING MAY BE HARMFUL. CONSUMPTION OF CANNABIS IMPAIRS YOUR ABILITY TO DRIVE AND OPERATE MACHINERY. PLEASE USE EXTREME CAUTION."

(B) For cannabis products: "GOVERNMENT WARNING: THIS PRODUCT CONTAINS CANNABIS, A SCHEDULE I CONTROLLED SUBSTANCE. KEEP OUT OF REACH OF CHILDREN AND ANIMALS. CANNABIS PRODUCTS MAY ONLY BE POSSESSED OR CONSUMED BY PERSONS 21 YEARS OF AGE OR OLDER UNLESS THE PERSON IS A QUALIFIED PATIENT. THE INTOXICATING EFFECTS OF CANNABIS PRODUCTS MAY BE DELAYED UP TO TWO HOURS. CANNABIS USE WHILE PREGNANT OR BREASTFEEDING MAY BE HARMFUL. CONSUMPTION OF CANNABIS PRODUCTS IMPAIRS YOUR ABILITY TO DRIVE AND OPERATE MACHINERY. PLEASE USE EXTREME CAUTION."

(2) For packages containing only dried flower, the net weight of cannabis in the package.

(3) Identification of the source and date of cultivation, the type of cannabis or cannabis product and the date of manufacturing and packaging.

(4) The appellation of origin, if any.

(5) List of pharmacologically active ingredients, including, but not limited to, tetrahydrocannabinol (THC), cannabidiol (CBD), and other cannabinoid content, the THC and other cannabinoid amount in milligrams per serving, servings per package, and the THC and other cannabinoid amount in milligrams for the package total.

(6) A warning if nuts or other known allergens are used.

(7) Information associated with the unique identifier issued by the

Department of Food and Agriculture.

(8) For a medicinal cannabis product sold at a retailer, the statement "FOR MEDICAL USE ONLY."

(9) Any other requirement set by the bureau or the State Department of Public Health.

(d) Only generic food names may be used to describe the ingredients in edible cannabis products.

(e) In the event the Attorney General determines that cannabis is no longer a Schedule I controlled substance under federal law, the label prescribed in subdivision (c) shall no longer require a statement that cannabis is a Schedule I controlled substance.

Business and Professions Code § 26121

(MAUCRSA, Effective June 27, 2017.)

(a) A cannabis product is misbranded if it is any of the following:

(1) Manufactured, packed, or held in this state in a manufacturing premises not duly licensed as provided in this division.

(2) Its labeling is false or misleading in any particular.

(3) Its labeling or packaging does not conform to the requirements of Section 26120 or any other labeling or packaging requirement established pursuant to this division.

(b) It is unlawful for any person to manufacture, sell, deliver, hold, or offer for sale a cannabis product that is misbranded.

(c) It is unlawful for any person to misbrand a cannabis product.

(d) It is unlawful for any person to receive in commerce a cannabis product that is misbranded or to deliver or offer for delivery any such cannabis product.

Chapter 13. Manufacturers and Cannabis Products

Business and Professions Code § 26130

(Amended by AB 133, Effective September 16, 2017.)

(a) The State Department of Public Health shall promulgate regulations governing the licensing of cannabis manufacturers and standards for the manufacturing, packaging, and labeling of all manufactured cannabis products. Licenses to be issued are as follows:

(1) "Manufacturing Level 1," for sites that manufacture cannabis products using nonvolatile solvents, or no solvents.

(2) "Manufacturing Level 2," for sites that manufacture cannabis products using volatile solvents.

(b) For purposes of this section, "volatile solvents" shall have the same meaning as in paragraph (3) of subdivision (b) of Section 11362.3 of the Health and Safety Code, unless otherwise provided by law or regulation.

(c) Edible cannabis products shall be:

(1) Not designed to be appealing to children or easily confused with commercially sold candy or foods that do not contain cannabis.

(2) Produced and sold with a standardized concentration of cannabinoids not to exceed 10 milligrams tetrahydrocannabinol (THC) per serving.

(3) Delineated or scored into standardized serving sizes if the cannabis product contains more than one serving and is an edible cannabis product in solid form.

(4) Homogenized to ensure uniform disbursement of cannabinoids throughout the product.

(5) Manufactured and sold under sanitation standards established by the State Department of Public Health, in consultation with the bureau, that are similar to the standards for preparation, storage, handling, and sale of food products.

(6) Provided to customers with sufficient information to enable the informed consumption of the product, including the potential effects of the cannabis product and directions as to how to consume the cannabis product, as necessary.

(7) Marked with a universal symbol, as determined by the State Department of Public Health through regulation.

(d) Cannabis, including concentrated cannabis, included in a cannabis product manufactured in compliance with law is not considered an adulterant under state law.

Business and Professions Code § 26131

(MAUCRSA, Effective June 27, 2017.)

(a) A cannabis product is adulterated if it is any of the following:

(1) It has been produced, prepared, packed, or held under unsanitary conditions in which it may have become contaminated with filth or in which it may have been rendered injurious.

(2) It consists in whole or in part of any filthy, putrid, or decomposed substance.

(3) It bears or contains any poisonous or deleterious substance that may render it injurious to users under the conditions of use suggested in the labeling or under conditions as are customary or usual.

(4) It bears or contains a substance that is restricted or limited under this division or regulations promulgated pursuant to this division and the level of substance in the product exceeds the limits specified pursuant to this division or in regulation.

(5) Its concentrations differ from, or its purity or quality is below, that which it is represented to possess.

(6) The methods, facilities, or controls used for its manufacture, packing, or holding do not conform to, or are not operated or administered in conformity with, practices established by regulations adopted under this division to ensure that the cannabis product meets the requirements of this division as to safety and has the concentrations it purports to have and meets the quality and purity characteristics that

it purports or is represented to possess.

(7) Its container is composed, in whole or in part, of any poisonous or deleterious substance that may render the contents injurious to health.

(8) It is an edible cannabis product and a substance has been mixed or packed with it after testing by a testing laboratory so as to reduce its quality or concentration or if any substance has been substituted, wholly or in part, for the edible cannabis product.

(b) It is unlawful for a person to manufacture, sell, deliver, hold, or offer for sale a cannabis product that is adulterated.

(c) It is unlawful for a person to adulterate a cannabis product.

(d) It is unlawful for a person to receive in commerce a cannabis product that is adulterated or to deliver or proffer for delivery any such cannabis product.

Business and Professions Code § 26132

(MAUCRSA, Effective June 27, 2017.)

(a) When the State Department of Public Health has evidence that a cannabis product is adulterated or misbranded, the department shall notify the manufacturer.

(b) The State Department of Public Health may order a manufacturer to immediately cease distribution of a cannabis product and recall the product if the department determines both of the following:

(1) The manufacture, distribution, or sale of the cannabis product creates or poses an immediate and serious threat to human life or health.

(2) Other procedures available to the State Department of Public Health to remedy or prevent the occurrence of the situation would result in an unreasonable delay.

(c) The State Department of Public Health shall provide the manufacturer an opportunity for an informal proceeding on the matter, as determined by the department, within five days, on the actions required by the order and on why the product should not be recalled. Following the proceeding, the order shall be affirmed, modified, or set aside as determined appropriate by the

State Department of Public Health.

(d) The State Department of Public Health's powers set forth in this section expressly include the power to order movement, segregation, isolation, or destruction of cannabis products, as well as the power to hold those products in place.

(e) If the State Department of Public Health determines it is necessary, it may issue the mandatory recall order and may use all appropriate measures to obtain reimbursement from the manufacturer for any and all costs associated with these orders. All funds obtained by the State Department of Public Health from these efforts shall be deposited into a fee account specific to the State Department of Public Health, to be established in the Cannabis Control Fund, and will be available for use by the department upon appropriation by the Legislature.

(f) It is unlawful for any person to move or allow to be moved a cannabis product subject to an order issued pursuant to this section unless that person has first obtained written authorization from the State Department of Public Health.

Business and Professions Code § 26133

(MAUCRSA, Effective June 27, 2017.)

(a) If the State Department of Public Health finds or has probable cause to believe that a cannabis product is adulterated or misbranded within the meaning of this division or the sale of the cannabis product would be in violation of this division, the department shall affix to the cannabis product, or component thereof, a tag or other appropriate marking. The State Department of Public Health shall give notice that the cannabis product is, or is suspected of being, adulterated or misbranded, or the sale of the cannabis would be in violation of this division and has been embargoed and that no person shall remove or dispose of the cannabis product by sale or otherwise until permission for removal or disposal is given by the State Department of Public Health or a court.

(b) It is unlawful for a person to remove, sell, or dispose of a detained or embargoed cannabis product without written permission of the State Department of Public Health or a court. A violation of this subdivision is punishable by a fine of not more than ten thousand dollars ($10,000).

(c) If the adulteration or misbranding can be corrected by proper labeling or additional processing of the cannabis product and all of the provisions of this division can be complied with, the licensee or owner may request the State Department of Public Health to remove the tag or other marking. If, under the supervision of the State Department of Public Health, the adulteration or misbranding has been corrected, the department may remove the tag or other marking.

(d) If the State Department of Public Health finds that a cannabis product that is embargoed is not adulterated or misbranded, or that its sale is not otherwise in violation of this division, the State Department of Public Health may remove the tag or other marking.

(e) The cannabis product may be destroyed by the owner pursuant to a corrective action plan approved by the State Department of Public Health and under the supervision of the department. The cannabis product shall be destroyed at the expense of the licensee or owner.

(f) A proceeding for condemnation of a cannabis product under this section shall be subject to appropriate notice to, and the opportunity for a hearing with regard to, the person affected in accordance with Section 26016.

(g) Upon a finding by the administrative law judge that the cannabis product is adulterated or misbranded, or that its sale is otherwise in violation of this division, the administrative law judge may direct the cannabis product to be destroyed at the expense of the licensee or owner. The administrative law judge may also direct a licensee or owner of the affected cannabis product to pay fees and reasonable costs, including the costs of storage and testing, incurred by the bureau or the State Department of Public Health in investigating and prosecuting the action taken pursuant to this section.

(h) When, under the supervision of the State Department of Public Health, the adulteration or misbranding has been corrected by proper labeling or additional processing of the cannabis and cannabis product and when all provisions of this division have been complied with, and after costs, fees, and expenses have been paid, the State Department of Public Health may release the embargo and remove the tag or other marking.

(i) The State Department of Public Health may condemn a cannabis product under provisions of this division. The cannabis product shall be destroyed at the expense of the licensee or owner.

Business and Professions Code § 26134

(MAUCRSA, Effective June 27, 2017.)

(a) The State Department of Public Health may issue a citation, which may contain an order of abatement and an order to pay an administrative fine assessed by the department if the licensee is in violation of this division or any regulation adopted pursuant to it.

(1) Citations shall be in writing and shall describe with particularity the nature of the violation, including specific reference to the law determined to have been violated.

(2) If appropriate, the citation shall contain an order of abatement fixing a reasonable time for abatement of the violation.

(3) The administrative fine assessed by the State Department of Public Health shall not exceed five thousand dollars ($5,000) for each violation, unless a different fine amount is expressly provided by this division. In assessing a fine, the department shall give due consideration to the appropriateness of the amount of the fine with respect to factors such as the gravity of the violation, the good faith of the licensee, and the history of previous violations.

(4) A citation issued or a fine assessed pursuant to this section shall notify the licensee that if the licensee desires a hearing to contest the finding of a violation, that hearing shall be requested by written notice to the State Department of Public Health within 30 days of the date of issuance of the citation or fine. If a hearing is not requested pursuant to this section, payment of any fine shall not constitute an admission of the violation charged. Hearings shall be held pursuant to Chapter 5 (commencing with Section 11500) of Part 1 of Division 3 of Title 2 of the Government Code.

(5) Failure of a licensee to pay a fine within 30 days of the date of assessment of the fine, unless assessment of the fine or the citation is being appealed, may result in further legal action being taken by the State Department of Public Health. If a licensee does not contest a citation or pay the fine, the full amount of the fine shall be added to the fee for renewal of the license. A license shall not be renewed without payment of the renewal fee, including the amount of the fine.

(6) A citation may be issued without the assessment of an administrative fine.

(7) The State Department of Public Health may limit the assessment of administrative fines to only particular violations of this division and establish any other requirement for implementation of the citation system by regulation.

(b) Notwithstanding any other law, if a fine is paid to satisfy an assessment based on the finding of a violation, payment of the fine shall be represented as satisfactory resolution of the matter for purposes of public disclosure.

Business and Professions Code § 26135

(MAUCRSA, Effective June 27, 2017.)

A peace officer, including a peace officer within the State Department of Public Health or the bureau, may seize cannabis and cannabis products in any of the following circumstances:

(a) The cannabis or cannabis product is subject to recall or embargo by any licensing authority.

(b) The cannabis or cannabis product is subject to destruction pursuant to this division.

(c) The cannabis or cannabis product is seized related to an investigation or disciplinary action for violation of this division.

Chapter 14. Protection of Minors

Business and Professions Code § 26140

(Amended by AB 133, Effective September 16, 2017.)

(a) An A-licensee shall not:

(1) Sell cannabis or cannabis products to persons under 21 years of age.

(2) Allow any person under 21 years of age on its premises, unless the A-licensee holds an M-license and the licensed premises for the A-license and M-license are the same.

(3) Employ or retain persons under 21 years of age.

(4) Sell or transfer cannabis or cannabis products unless the person

to whom the cannabis or cannabis product is to be sold first presents documentation which reasonably appears to be a valid government-issued identification card showing that the person is 21 years of age or older.

(b) Persons under 21 years of age may be used by peace officers in the enforcement of this division and to apprehend licensees, or employees or agents of licensees, or other persons who sell or furnish cannabis to minors. Notwithstanding any provision of law, any person under 21 years of age who purchases or attempts to purchase any cannabis while under the direction of a peace officer is immune from prosecution for that purchase or attempt to purchase cannabis. Guidelines with respect to the use of persons under 21 years of age as decoys shall be adopted and published by the bureau in accordance with the rulemaking portion of the Administrative Procedure Act (Chapter 3.5 (commencing with Section 11340) of Part 1 of Division 3 of Title 2 of the Government Code).

(c) Notwithstanding subdivision (a), an M-licensee may:

(1) Allow on the premises any person 18 years of age or older who possesses a valid government-issued identification card, and either a valid county-issued identification card under Section 11362.712 of the Health and Safety Code or a valid physician's recommendation for himself or herself or for a person for whom he or she is a primary caregiver.

(2) Allow any person 21 years of age or older on its premises if the M-licensee holds an A-license and the licensed premises for the M-license and A-license are the same.

(3) Sell cannabis, cannabis products, and cannabis accessories to a person 18 years of age or older who possesses a valid government-issued identification card and either a valid county-issued identification card under Section 11362.712 of the Health and Safety Code or a valid physician's recommendation for himself or herself or for a person for whom he or she is a primary caregiver.

(4) The bureau may establish requirements for the purchase of cannabis, cannabis products, or cannabis accessories by a primary caregiver for a patient to ensure that the status of a person as a primary caregiver is verified.

Chapter 15. Advertising and Marketing Restrictions

Business and Professions Code § 26150

(MAUCRSA, Effective June 27, 2017.)

For purposes of this chapter:

(a) "Advertise" means the publication or dissemination of an advertisement.

(b) "Advertisement" includes any written or verbal statement, illustration, or depiction which is calculated to induce sales of cannabis or cannabis products, including any written, printed, graphic, or other material, billboard, sign, or other outdoor display, public transit card, other periodical literature, publication, or in a radio or television broadcast, or in any other media; except that such term shall not include:

> (1) Any label affixed to any cannabis or cannabis products, or any individual covering, carton, or other wrapper of that container that constitutes a part of the labeling under provisions of this division.

> (2) Any editorial or other reading material, such as a news release, in any periodical or publication or newspaper for the publication of which no money or valuable consideration is paid or promised, directly or indirectly, by any licensee, and which is not written by or at the direction of the licensee.

(c) "Advertising sign" is any sign, poster, display, billboard, or any other stationary or permanently affixed advertisement promoting the sale of cannabis or cannabis products which are not cultivated, manufactured, distributed, or sold on the same lot.

(d) "Health-related statement" means any statement related to health, and includes statements of a curative or therapeutic nature that, expressly or by implication, suggest a relationship between the consumption of cannabis or cannabis products and health benefits, or effects on health.

(e) "Market" or "Marketing" means any act or process of promoting or selling cannabis or cannabis products, including, but not limited to, sponsorship of sporting events, point-of-sale advertising, and development of products specifically designed to appeal to certain demographics.

Business and Professions Code § 26151

(MAUCRSA, Effective June 27, 2017.)

(a) (1) All advertisements and marketing shall accurately and legibly identify the licensee responsible for its content, by adding, at a minimum, the licensee's license number.

(2) A technology platform shall not display an advertisement by a licensee on an Internet Web page unless the advertisement displays the license number of the licensee.

(3) An outdoor advertising company subject to the Outdoor Advertising Act (Chapter 2 (commencing with Section 5200) of Division 3) shall not display an advertisement by a licensee unless the advertisement displays the license number of the licensee.

(b) Any advertising or marketing placed in broadcast, cable, radio, print, and digital communications shall only be displayed where at least 71.6 percent of the audience is reasonably expected to be 21 years of age or older, as determined by reliable, up-to-date audience composition data.

(c) Any advertising or marketing involving direct, individualized communication or dialogue controlled by the licensee shall utilize a method of age affirmation to verify that the recipient is 21 years of age or older before engaging in that communication or dialogue controlled by the licensee. For purposes of this section, that method of age affirmation may include user confirmation, birth date disclosure, or other similar registration method.

(d) All advertising shall be truthful and appropriately substantiated.

Business and Professions Code § 26152

(MAUCRSA, Effective June 27, 2017.)

A licensee shall not do any of the following:

(a) Advertise or market in a manner that is false or untrue in any material particular, or that, irrespective of falsity, directly, or by ambiguity, omission, or inference, or by the addition of irrelevant, scientific, or technical matter, tends to create a misleading impression.

(b) Publish or disseminate advertising or marketing containing any statement concerning a brand or product that is inconsistent with any statement on the labeling thereof.

(c) Publish or disseminate advertising or marketing containing any statement, design, device, or representation which tends to create the impression that the cannabis originated in a particular place or region, unless the label of the advertised product bears an appellation of origin, and such appellation of origin appears in the advertisement.

(d) Advertise or market on a billboard or similar advertising device located on an Interstate Highway or on a State Highway which crosses the California border.

(e) Advertise or market cannabis or cannabis products in a manner intended to encourage persons under 21 years of age to consume cannabis or cannabis products.

(f) Publish or disseminate advertising or marketing that is attractive to children.

(g) Advertise or market cannabis or cannabis products on an advertising sign within 1,000 feet of a day care center, school providing instruction in kindergarten or any grades 1 through 12, playground, or youth center.

Business and Professions Code § 26153

(MAUCRSA, Effective June 27, 2017.)

A licensee shall not give away any amount of cannabis or cannabis products, or any cannabis accessories, as part of a business promotion or other commercial activity.

Business and Professions Code § 26154

(MAUCRSA, Effective June 27, 2017.)

A licensee shall not include on the label of any cannabis or cannabis product or publish or disseminate advertising or marketing containing any health-related statement that is untrue in any particular manner or tends to create a misleading impression as to the effects on health of cannabis consumption.

Business and Professions Code § 26155

(MAUCRSA, Effective June 27, 2017.)

(a) The provisions of subdivision (g) of Section 26152 shall not apply to the placement of advertising signs inside a licensed premises and which are not visible by normal unaided vision from a public place, provided that such advertising signs do not advertise cannabis or cannabis products in a manner intended to encourage persons under 21 years of age to consume cannabis or cannabis products.

(b) This chapter does not apply to any noncommercial speech.

Business and Professions Code § 26156

(MAUCRSA, Effective June 27, 2017.)

The requirements of Section 5272 apply to this division.

Chapter 16. Records

Business and Professions Code § 26160

(MAUCRSA, Effective June 27, 2017.)

(a) A licensee shall keep accurate records of commercial cannabis activity.

(b) All records related to commercial cannabis activity as defined by the licensing authorities shall be maintained for a minimum of seven years.

(c) Licensing authorities may examine the records of a licensee and inspect the premises of a licensee as the licensing authority, or a state or local agency, deems necessary to perform its duties under this division. All inspections and examinations of records shall be conducted during standard business hours of the licensed facility or at any other reasonable time. Licensees shall provide and deliver records to the licensing authority upon request.

(d) Licensees shall keep records identified by the licensing authorities on the premises of the location licensed. The licensing authorities may make any examination of the records of any licensee. Licensees shall also provide and deliver copies of documents to the licensing authority upon request.

(e) A licensee, or its agent or employee, that refuses, impedes, obstructs, or interferes with an inspection of the premises or records of the licensee pursuant to this section, has engaged in a violation of this division.

(f) If a licensee, or an agent or employee of a licensee, fails to maintain or provide the records required pursuant to this section, the licensee shall be subject to a citation and fine of up to thirty thousand dollars ($30,000) per individual violation.

Business and Professions Code § 26161

(MAUCRSA, Effective June 27, 2017.)

(a) Every sale or transport of cannabis or cannabis products from one licensee to another licensee must be recorded on a sales invoice or receipt. Sales invoices and receipts may be maintained electronically and must be filed in such manner as to be readily accessible for examination by employees of the licensing authorities or State Board of Equalization and shall not be commingled with invoices covering other commodities.

(b) Each sales invoice required by subdivision (a) shall include the name and address of the seller and shall include the following information:

(1) Name and address of the purchaser.

(2) Date of sale and invoice number.

(3) Kind, quantity, size, and capacity of packages of cannabis or cannabis products sold.

(4) The cost to the purchaser, together with any discount applied to the price as shown on the invoice.

(5) The place from which transport of the cannabis or cannabis product was made unless transport was made from the premises of the licensee.

(6) Any other information specified by the licensing authority.

Business and Professions Code § 26162

(MAUCRSA, Effective June 27, 2017.)

(a) Information identifying the names of patients, their medical conditions, or the names of their primary caregivers received and contained in records kept by the office or licensing authorities for the purposes of administering this chapter are confidential and shall not be disclosed pursuant to the California Public Records Act (Chapter 3.5 (commencing with Section 6250) of Division 7 of Title 1 of the Government Code), except as necessary for authorized employees of the State of California or any city, county, or city and county to perform official duties pursuant to this chapter, or a local ordinance.

(b) Information identifying the names of patients, their medical conditions, or the names of their primary caregivers received and contained in records kept by the bureau for the purposes of administering this chapter shall be maintained in accordance with Chapter 1 (commencing with Section 123100) of Part 1 of Division 106 of the Health and Safety Code, Part 2.6 (commencing with Section 56) of Division 1 of the Civil Code, and other state and federal laws relating to confidential patient information.

(c) Nothing in this section precludes the following:

(1) Employees of the bureau or any licensing authorities notifying state or local agencies about information submitted to the agency that the employee suspects is falsified or fraudulent.

(2) Notifications from the bureau or any licensing authorities to state or local agencies about apparent violations of this chapter or applicable local ordinance.

(3) Verification of requests by state or local agencies to confirm licenses and certificates issued by the regulatory authorities or other state agency.

(4) Provision of information requested pursuant to a court order or subpoena issued by a court or an administrative agency or local governing body authorized by law to issue subpoenas.

(d) Information shall not be disclosed by any state or local agency beyond what is necessary to achieve the goals of a specific investigation, notification, or the parameters of a specific court order or subpoena.

Business and Professions Code § 26162.5

(MAUCRSA, Effective June 27, 2017.)

Information contained in a physician's recommendation issued in accordance with Article 25 (commencing with Section 2525) of Chapter 5 of Division

2 and received by a licensee, including, but not limited to, the name, address, or social security number of the patient, the patient's medical condition, or the name of the patient's primary caregiver is hereby deemed "medical information" within the meaning of the Confidentiality of Medical Information Act (Part 2.6 (commencing with Section 56) of Division 1 of the Civil Code) and shall not be disclosed by a licensee except as necessary for authorized employees of the State of California or any city, county, or city and county to perform official duties pursuant to this chapter, or a local ordinance.

Chapter 18. License Fees

Business and Professions Code § 26180

(MAUCRSA, Effective June 27, 2017.)

Each licensing authority shall establish a scale of application, licensing, and renewal fees, based upon the cost of enforcing this division, as follows:

(a) Each licensing authority shall charge each licensee a licensure and renewal fee, as applicable. The licensure and renewal fee shall be calculated to cover the costs of administering this division. The licensure fee may vary depending upon the varying costs associated with administering the various regulatory requirements of this division as they relate to the nature and scope of the different licensure activities, including, but not limited to, the track and trace program required pursuant to Section 26067, but shall not exceed the reasonable regulatory costs to the licensing authority.

(b) The total fees assessed pursuant to this division shall be set at an amount that will fairly and proportionately generate sufficient total revenue to fully cover the total costs of administering this division.

(c) All license fees shall be set on a scaled basis by the licensing authority, dependent on the size of the business.

(d) The licensing authority shall deposit all fees collected in a fee account specific to that licensing authority, to be established in the Cannabis Control Fund. Moneys in the licensing authority fee accounts shall be used, upon appropriation by the Legislature, by the designated licensing authority for the administration of this division.

Business and Professions Code § 26180.5

(MAUCRSA, Effective June 27, 2017.)

No later than January 1, 2018, the Secretary of Business, Consumer Services, and Housing or his or her designee shall initiate work with the Legislature, the Department of Consumer Affairs, the Department of Food and Agriculture, the State Department of Public Health, and any other related departments to ensure that there is a safe and viable way to collect cash payments for taxes and fees related to the regulation of cannabis activity throughout the state.

Business and Professions Code § 26181

(MAUCRSA, Effective June 27, 2017.)

The State Water Resources Control Board, the Department of Fish and Wildlife, and other agencies may establish fees to cover the costs of their cannabis programs.

Chapter 19. Annual Reports; Performance Audit

Business and Professions Code § 26190

(MAUCRSA, Effective June 27, 2017.)

Beginning on March 1, 2023, and on or before March 1 of each year thereafter, each licensing authority shall prepare and submit to the Legislature an annual report on the authority's activities, in compliance with Section 9795 of the Government Code, and post the report on the authority's Internet Web site. The report shall include, but not be limited to, the following information for the previous fiscal year:

(a) The amount of funds allocated and spent by the licensing authority for cannabis licensing, enforcement, and administration.

(b) The number of state licenses issued, renewed, denied, suspended, and revoked, by state license category.

(c) The average time for processing state license applications, by state license category.

(d) The number of appeals from the denial of state licenses or other disciplinary actions taken by the licensing authority and the average time spent on these appeals.

(e) The number of complaints submitted by citizens or representatives of cities or counties regarding licensees, provided as both a comprehensive statewide number and by geographical region.

(f) The number and type of enforcement activities conducted by the licensing authorities and by local law enforcement agencies in conjunction with the licensing authorities.

(g) The number, type, and amount of penalties, fines, and other disciplinary actions taken by the licensing authorities.

(h) A detailed list of the petitions for regulatory relief or rulemaking changes received by the licensing authorities from licensees requesting modifications of the enforcement of rules under this division.

(i) (1) For the first publication of the reports, the licensing authorities shall provide a joint report to the Legislature regarding the state of the cannabis market in California. This report shall identify any statutory or regulatory changes necessary to ensure that the implementation of this division does not do any of the following:

(A) Allow unreasonable restraints on competition by creation or maintenance of unlawful monopoly power.

(B) Perpetuate the presence of an illegal market for cannabis or cannabis products in the state or out of the state.

(C) Encourage underage use or adult abuse of cannabis or cannabis products, or illegal diversion of cannabis or cannabis products out of the state.

(D) Result in an excessive concentration of licensees in a given city, county, or both.

(E) Present an unreasonable risk of minors being exposed to cannabis or cannabis products.

(F) Result in violations of any environmental protection laws.

(2) For purposes of this subdivision, "excessive concentration" means when the premises for a retail license, microbusiness license, or a license issued under Section 26070.5 is located in an area where either of the following conditions exist:

(A) The ratio of licensees to population in a census tract or census division exceeds the ratio of licensees to population in the county in which the census tract or census division is located, unless reduction of that ratio would unduly limit the development of the legal market so as to perpetuate the illegal market for cannabis or cannabis products.

(B) The ratio of retail licenses, microbusiness licenses, or licenses under Section 26070.5 to population in the census tract, division, or jurisdiction exceeds that allowable by local ordinance adopted under Section 26200.

Business and Professions Code § 26190.5

(MAUCRSA, Effective June 27, 2017.)

The bureau shall contract with the California Cannabis Research Program, known as the Center for Medicinal Cannabis Research, and formerly known as the California Marijuana Research Program, authorized pursuant to Section 11362.9 of the Health and Safety Code, to develop a study that identifies the impact that cannabis has on motor skills.

Business and Professions Code § 26191

(MAUCRSA, Effective June 27, 2017.)

(a) Commencing January 1, 2019, and by January 1 triennially thereafter, the Office of State Audits and Evaluations within the Department of Finance shall conduct a performance audit of the bureau's activities under this division, and shall report its findings to the bureau and the Legislature by July 1 of that same year. The report shall include, but not be limited to, the following:

(1) The actual costs of the program.

(2) The overall effectiveness of enforcement programs.

(3) Any report submitted pursuant to this section shall be submitted in compliance with Section 9795 of the Government Code.

(b) The Legislature shall provide sufficient funds to the Department of Finance to conduct the triennial audit required by this section.

Chapter 20. Local Control

Business and Professions Code § 26200

(MAUCRSA, Effective June 27, 2017.)

(a) (1) This division shall not be interpreted to supersede or limit the authority of a local jurisdiction to adopt and enforce local ordinances to regulate businesses licensed under this division, including, but not limited to, local zoning and land use requirements, business license requirements, and requirements related to reducing exposure to secondhand smoke, or to completely prohibit the establishment or operation of one or more types of businesses licensed under this division within the local jurisdiction.

(2) This division shall not be interpreted to supersede or limit existing local authority for law enforcement activity, enforcement of local zoning requirements or local ordinances, or enforcement of local license, permit, or other authorization requirements.

(b) This division shall not be interpreted to require a licensing authority to undertake local law enforcement responsibilities, enforce local zoning requirements, or enforce local licensing, permitting, or other authorization requirements.

(c) A local jurisdiction shall notify the bureau upon revocation of any local license, permit, or authorization for a licensee to engage in commercial cannabis activity within the local jurisdiction. Within 10 days of notification, the bureau shall inform the relevant licensing authorities. Within 60 days of being so informed by the bureau, the relevant licensing authorities shall begin the process to determine whether a license issued to the licensee should be suspended or revoked pursuant to Chapter 3 (commencing with Section 26030).

(d) For facilities issued a state license that are located within the incorporated area of a city, the city shall have full power and authority to enforce this division and the regulations promulgated by the bureau or any licensing authority, if delegated by the state. Notwithstanding Sections 101375, 101400, and 101405 of the Health and Safety Code or any contract entered into pursuant thereto, or any other law, the city shall assume complete responsibility for any regulatory function pursuant to this division within the city limits that would otherwise be performed by the county or any county officer or employee, including a county health officer, without liability, cost, or expense to the county.

(e) This division does not prohibit the issuance of a state temporary event license to a licensee authorizing onsite cannabis sales to, and consumption by, persons 21 years of age or older at a county fair or district agricultural association event, provided that the activities, at a minimum, comply with the requirements of paragraphs (1) to (3), inclusive, of subdivision (g), that all participants are licensed under this division, and that the activities are otherwise consistent with regulations promulgated and adopted by the bureau governing state temporary event licenses. These temporary event licenses shall only be issued in local jurisdictions that authorize such events.

(f) This division, or any regulations promulgated thereunder, shall not be deemed to limit the authority or remedies of a city, county, or city and county under any provision of law, including, but not limited to, Section 7 of Article XI of the California Constitution.

(g) Notwithstanding paragraph (1) of subdivision (a) of Section 11362.3 of the Health and Safety Code, a local jurisdiction may allow for the smoking, vaporizing, and ingesting of cannabis or cannabis products on the premises of a retailer or microbusiness licensed under this division if all of the following are met:

>(1) Access to the area where cannabis consumption is allowed is restricted to persons 21 years of age and older.

>(2) Cannabis consumption is not visible from any public place or nonage-restricted area.

>(3) Sale or consumption of alcohol or tobacco is not allowed on the premises.

Business and Professions Code § 26201

(AUMA, Effective November 9, 2016.)

Any standards, requirements, and regulations regarding health and safety, environmental protection, testing, security, food safety, and worker protections established by the state shall be the minimum standards for all licensees under this division statewide. A local jurisdiction may establish additional standards, requirements, and regulations.

Business and Professions Code § 26202

(MAUCRSA, Effective June 27, 2017.)

(a) A local jurisdiction may enforce this division and the regulations promulgated by any licensing authority if delegated the power to do so by the licensing authority.

(b) A licensing authority shall implement the delegation of enforcement authority in subdivision (a) through an agreement between the licensing authority and the local jurisdiction to which enforcement authority is to be delegated.

Chapter 21. Funding

Business and Professions Code § 26210

(MAUCRSA, Effective June 27, 2017.)

(a) The Marijuana Control Fund, formerly known as the Medical Cannabis Regulation and Safety Act Fund and the Medical Marijuana Regulation and Safety Act Fund, is hereby renamed the Cannabis Control Fund. Notwithstanding Section 16305.7 of the Government Code, the fund shall include any interest and dividends earned on moneys in the fund.

(b) Upon the effective date of this section, whenever "Marijuana Control Fund," "Medical Cannabis Regulation and Safety Act Fund," or "Medical Marijuana Regulation and Safety Act Fund" appears in any statute, regulation, or contract, or in any other code, it shall be construed to refer to the Cannabis Control Fund.

(c) Any General Fund or special fund loan that was used to establish and support the regulatory activities of the state licensing entities pursuant to former Section 19351 shall be repaid by the initial proceeds from fees collected pursuant to this division or any rule or regulation adopted pursuant to this division, by January 1, 2022. Should the initial proceeds from fees not be sufficient to repay the loan, moneys from the Cannabis Fines and Penalties Account shall be made available to the bureau, by appropriation of the

Legislature, to repay the loan.

(d) The Medical Cannabis Fines and Penalties Account established in former Section 19351 is hereby renamed the Cannabis Fines and Penalties Account.

Business and Professions Code § 26210.5

(MAUCRSA, Effective June 27, 2017.)

By July 1, 2018, the bureau, in coordination with the Department of General Services, shall establish an office to collect fees and taxes in the County of Humboldt, County of Trinity, or County of Mendocino in order to ensure the safe payment and collection of cash in those counties.

Business and Professions Code § 26211

(MAUCRSA, Effective June 27, 2017.)

(a) Funds for the initial establishment and support of the regulatory activities under this division, including the public information program described in subdivision (c), and for the activities of the State Board of Equalization under Part 14.5 (commencing with Section 34010) of Division 2 of the Revenue and Taxation Code until July 1, 2017, or until the 2017 Budget Act is enacted, whichever occurs later, shall be advanced from the General Fund and shall be repaid by the initial proceeds from fees collected pursuant to this division, any rule or regulation adopted pursuant to this division, or revenues collected from the tax imposed by Sections 34011 and 34012 of the Revenue and Taxation Code, by January 1, 2025.

> (1) Funds advanced pursuant to this subdivision shall be appropriated to the bureau, which shall distribute the moneys to the appropriate licensing authorities, as necessary to implement the provisions of this division, and to the State Board of Equalization, as necessary, to implement the provisions of Part 14.5 (commencing with Section 34010) of Division 2 of the Revenue and Taxation Code.

> (2) Within 45 days of November 9, 2016, the date this section became operative:

>> (A) The Director of Finance shall determine an amount of the initial advance from the General Fund to the Cannabis Control Fund that does not exceed thirty million dollars ($30,000,000);

and

(B) There shall be advanced a sum of five million dollars ($5,000,000) from the General Fund to the State Department of Health Care Services to provide for the public information program described in subdivision (c).

(b) Notwithstanding subdivision (a), the Legislature shall provide sufficient funds to the Cannabis Control Fund to support the activities of the bureau, state licensing authorities under this division, and the State Board of Equalization to support its activities under Part 14.5 (commencing with Section 34010) of Division 2 of the Revenue and Taxation Code. It is anticipated that this funding will be provided annually beginning on July 1, 2017.

(c) The State Department of Health Care Services shall establish and implement a public information program no later than September 1, 2017. This public information program shall, at a minimum, describe the provisions of the Control, Regulate and Tax Adult Use of Marijuana Act of 2016, the scientific basis for restricting access of cannabis and cannabis products to persons under the age of 21 years, describe the penalties for providing access to cannabis and cannabis products to persons under the age of 21 years, provide information regarding the dangers of driving a motor vehicle, boat, vessel, aircraft, or other vehicle used for transportation while impaired from cannabis use, the potential harms of using cannabis while pregnant or breastfeeding, and the potential harms of overusing cannabis or cannabis products.

Chapter 22. Cannabis Cooperative Associations

Article 1. Definitions

Business and Professions Code § 26220

(MAUCRSA, Effective June 27, 2017.)

Unless the context otherwise requires, the definitions in this article govern the construction of this chapter.

Business and Professions Code § 26220.1

(MAUCRSA, Effective June 27, 2017.)

"Association" means any cannabis cooperative that is organized pursuant to this chapter. An association shall be deemed incorporated pursuant to this chapter, or organized pursuant to this chapter and shall be deemed a cultivator of a cannabis product within the meaning of this chapter, if it is functioning under, or is subject to, the provisions of this chapter, irrespective of whether it was originally incorporated pursuant to those provisions or was incorporated under other provisions.

Business and Professions Code § 26220.2

(MAUCRSA, Effective June 27, 2017.)

"Member" includes members of associations without capital stock and holders of common stock in associations that are organized with shares of stock.

Business and Professions Code § 26220.3

(MAUCRSA, Effective June 27, 2017.)

"Cannabis product" includes any cannabis associated with a licensed cultivator.

Article 2. General Provisions

Business and Professions Code § 26222

(MAUCRSA, Effective June 27, 2017.)

The purpose of this chapter is to do all of the following:

(a) Promote, foster, and encourage the intelligent and orderly marketing of cannabis product through cooperation.

(b) Eliminate speculation and waste.

(c) Make the distribution of cannabis product as direct as can be efficiently done.

(d) Stabilize the marketing of cannabis product.

(e) Satisfy the conditions of Section 26052.

Business and Professions Code § 26222.1

(MAUCRSA, Effective June 27, 2017.)

An exemption under law that applies to a cannabis product in the possession, or under the control, of the individual cultivator, shall apply similarly and completely to the cannabis product that is delivered by its cultivator members that are in the possession, or under the control, of the association.

Business and Professions Code § 26222.2

(MAUCRSA, Effective June 27, 2017.)

A person, firm, corporation, or association, that is hereafter organized or doing business in this state, may not use the word "cannabis cooperative" as part of its corporate name or other business name or title for producers' cooperative marketing activities, unless it has complied with this chapter.

Business and Professions Code § 26222.3

(MAUCRSA, Effective June 27, 2017.)

An association that is organized pursuant to this chapter shall not conspire in restraint of trade, or serve as an illegal monopoly, attempt to lessen competition, or to fix prices in violation of law of this state.

Business and Professions Code § 26222.4

(MAUCRSA, Effective June 27, 2017.)

The marketing contracts and agreements between an association that is organized pursuant to this chapter and its members and any agreements authorized in this chapter shall not result in restraint of trade, or violation of law of this state.

Business and Professions Code § 26222.5

(MAUCRSA, Effective June 27, 2017.)

The General Corporation Law (Division 1 (commencing with Section 100) of Title 1 of the Corporations Code) applies to each association that is organized pursuant to this chapter, except where those provisions are in conflict with or inconsistent with the express provisions of this chapter. For the purpose of associations organized without shares of stock, the members shall be deemed to be "shareholders" as the term is used in the General Corporation Law.

Business and Professions Code § 26222.6

(MAUCRSA, Effective June 27, 2017.)

(a) Except as provided in subdivision (c), Chapter 7 (commencing with Section 1500) of Title 10 of Part 3 of the Code of Civil Procedure does not apply to a proprietary interest in an association organized in accordance with this chapter. A proprietary interest that would otherwise escheat to the state pursuant to Chapter 7 (commencing with Section 1500) of Title 10 of Part 3 of the Code of Civil Procedure shall instead become the property of the association.

(b) Notwithstanding subdivision (a), no proprietary interest shall become the property of the association under this section unless all of the following requirements are satisfied:

(1) At least 60 days' prior notice of the proposed transfer of the proprietary interest to the association is given to the affected member by first-class or certified mail to the last address of the member shown on the association's records, and by publication in a newspaper of general circulation in the county in which the member last resided as shown on the association's records. Notice given pursuant to this paragraph constitutes actual notice.

(2) No written notice objecting to the transfer is received by the association from the affected member or, if the member is deceased, from the member's heirs or the executor or executrix of the estate, prior to the date of the proposed transfer.

(c) "Proprietary interest" means and includes any membership, membership certificate, membership share, share certificate, or equity or dividend certificate of any class representing a proprietary interest in, and issued by, the association together with all accrued and unpaid earnings, dividends, and patronage distributions relating thereto.

Article 3. Purposes

Business and Professions Code § 26223

(MAUCRSA, Effective June 27, 2017.)

(a) Three or more natural persons, who are engaged in the cultivation of any cannabis product, may form an association pursuant to this chapter for the purpose of engaging in any activity in connection with any of the following:

> (1) The cultivation, marketing, or selling of the cannabis products of its members.

> (2) The growing, harvesting, curing, drying, trimming, packing, grading, storing, or handling of any product of its members.

> (3) The manufacturing, selling, or supplying to its members of machinery, equipment, or supplies.

> (4) The financing of the activities that are specified by this section.

(b) Members of a cannabis cooperative shall be disclosed to the licensing authority before the application is processed.

(c) Members of a cannabis cooperative formed pursuant to this chapter shall be limited to cultivators who only hold a single Type 1 or Type 2 license.

(d) Collectively, members of a cannabis cooperative shall not grow more than four acres of total canopy size of cultivation throughout the state during the period that the respective licensees are valid.

(e) No member of a cooperative formed pursuant to this section shall be licensed to operate a cannabis business in another state or country.

Article 4. Articles of Incorporation

Business and Professions Code § 26224

(MAUCRSA, Effective June 27, 2017.)

The articles of incorporation of an association shall show that the signers of the articles of incorporation are engaged in the cultivation of cannabis products, and that they propose to incorporate an association pursuant to this chapter, and shall state all of the following:

(a) The name of the association.

(b) The purposes for which it is formed.

(c) The city, county, or city and county where the principal office for the transaction of business of the association is to be located.

(d) The number of directors of the association, which shall not be less than three, and the names and addresses of the persons who are to serve as first directors. If it is desired that the first directors shall serve for terms of different lengths, the term for which each person so named to serve shall also be stated.

(e) If organized without shares of stock, whether the voting power and the property rights and interest of each member are equal or unequal. If voting power and property rights and interest of each member are unequal, the general rule or rules that are applicable to all members by which the voting power and the property rights and interests, respectively, of each member may be and are determined and fixed shall also be stated.

(f) (1) If organized with shares of stock, the number of shares that may be issued and if the shares are to have a par value, the par value of each share, and the aggregate par value of all shares. If the shares are to be without par value, it shall be so stated.

(2) If the shares of stock are to be classified, a description of the classes of shares and a statement of the number of shares of each kind or class and the nature and extent of the preferences, rights, privileges, and restrictions that are granted to or imposed upon the holders of the respective classes of stock. Except as to the matters and things so stated, no distinction shall exist between the classes of stock or the holders of them. One class of stock shall always be known as common stock, and voting power may be restricted to

holders of common stock.

Business and Professions Code § 26224.1

(MAUCRSA, Effective June 27, 2017.)

Articles of incorporation shall be signed, acknowledged, and filed in the manner that is prescribed by the general laws of this state for domestic corporations.

Business and Professions Code § 26224.2

(MAUCRSA, Effective June 27, 2017.)

The articles of incorporation of any association may be amended in the manner and for the purposes which are authorized by the General Corporation Law, Division 1 (commencing with Section 100) of Title 1 of the Corporations Code.

Article 5. Bylaws

Business and Professions Code § 26225

(MAUCRSA, Effective June 27, 2017.)

Each association shall, within 30 days after its incorporation, adopt for its government and management, a code of bylaws, consistent with this chapter. The vote or written assent of shareholders or members that hold at least a majority of the voting power is necessary to adopt the bylaws and is effectual to repeal or amend a bylaw, or to adopt an additional bylaw. The power to repeal and amend the bylaws, and adopt new bylaws, may, by a similar vote, or similar written assent, be delegated to the board of directors, which authority may, by a similar vote, or similar written assent, be revoked.

Business and Professions Code § 26225.1

(MAUCRSA, Effective June 27, 2017.)

The bylaws may prescribe the time, place, and manner of calling and conducting its meetings. Meetings of members or stockholders shall be held at the place as provided in the bylaws, or, if no provision is made, in the city, county, or city and county where the principal place of business is located at a place designated by the board of directors. Meetings of the board of directors may be held at any place within or without the state that is fixed by a quorum of the board of directors unless otherwise provided in the articles of incorporation or bylaws.

Business and Professions Code § 26225.2

(MAUCRSA, Effective June 27, 2017.)

The bylaws may prescribe the number of stockholders, directors, or members that constitutes a quorum.

Business and Professions Code § 26225.3

(MAUCRSA, Effective June 27, 2017.)

The bylaws may prescribe the following:

(a) The right of members or stockholders to vote by proxy or by mail or both, and the conditions, manner, form, and effects of those votes.

(b) The right of members or stockholders to cumulate their votes and the prohibition, if any, of cumulative voting.

Business and Professions Code § 26225.4

(MAUCRSA, Effective June 27, 2017.)

(a) The bylaws may prescribe the qualifications, compensation, duties, and term of office of directors and officers and the time of their election.

(b) The number of directors set forth in the articles of incorporation shall be either a fixed number or a variable number. If a fixed number, it shall not be less than three, and if a variable number, the stated minimum shall not be less than three and the stated maximum shall not be greater than two times the stated minimum minus one.

(c) The number of directors may also be set forth in the bylaws either as a fixed number or as a variable number subject to the same limitations as in subdivision (b). After shares have been issued or members have been admitted, any adoption or amendment of the bylaw provision shall be approved by the outstanding shares as provided in Section 152 of the

Corporations Code.

(d) In the event of an inconsistency between an article provision referred to in subdivision (b) and a bylaw provision referred to in subdivision (c), the provision more recently adopted or amended shall prevail.

(e) If a variable number of directors is set forth in the articles of incorporation or the bylaws, the exact number of directors shall be fixed, within the limits specified, by approval of the board of directors or the shareholders as provided in Section 153 of the Corporations Code in the manner designated in the bylaws.

Business and Professions Code § 26225.5

(MAUCRSA, Effective June 27, 2017.)

The bylaws may prescribe penalties for violations of the bylaws.

Business and Professions Code § 26225.6

(MAUCRSA, Effective June 27, 2017.)

The bylaws may prescribe the amount of entrance, organization, and membership fees, if any, the manner and method of collection of the fees, and the purposes for which they may be used.

Business and Professions Code § 26225.7

(MAUCRSA, Effective June 27, 2017.)

The bylaws may prescribe the amount that each member or stockholder shall be required to pay annually, or from time to time, if at all, to carry on the business of the association, the charge, if any, to be paid by each member or stockholder for services that are rendered by the association to him, the time of payment and the manner of collection, and the marketing contract between the association and its members or stockholders that every member or stockholder may be required to sign.

Business and Professions Code § 26225.8

(MAUCRSA, Effective June 27, 2017.)

The bylaws may prescribe the amount of dividends, if any, that may be declared on the stock or membership capital. To the extent that dividends are payable out of the excess of association income over association expenses attributable to business transacted with or for members, dividends shall not exceed 8 percent per annum.

Business and Professions Code § 26225.9

(MAUCRSA, Effective June 27, 2017.)

The bylaws may prescribe any of the following:

(a) The number and qualification of members or stockholders of the association and the conditions precedent to membership or ownership of common stock.

(b) The method, time, and manner of permitting members to withdraw or the holders of common stock to transfer their stock.

(c) The manner of assignment and transfer of the interest of members, and of the shares of common stock.

(d) The conditions under which, and time when, membership of a member shall cease.

(e) The automatic suspension of the rights of a member when he or she ceases to be eligible to membership in the association.

(f) The mode, manner, and effect of the expulsion of a member.

Business and Professions Code § 26225.95

(MAUCRSA, Effective June 27, 2017.)

(a) The bylaws may prescribe any of the following:

(1) The manner of determining the value of a member's interest and provision for its purchase by the association upon the death or withdrawal of a member or upon the expulsion of a member or forfeiture of his or her membership, or at the option of the association, the purchase at a price fixed by conclusive appraisal by the board of directors.

(2) The conditions and terms for the repurchase by the association

from its stockholders of their stock upon their disqualification as stockholders.

(b) If a member is expelled and the bylaws do not provide any procedure or penalty for expulsion, the board of directors shall equitably and conclusively appraise his or her property interest in the association and shall fix the amount of his or her property interest in money, which shall be paid to him or her within one year after such expulsion.

Article 6. Directors and Management

Business and Professions Code § 26226

(MAUCRSA, Effective June 27, 2017.)

The affairs of the association shall be managed by a board of not less than three directors who are elected by the members or stockholders.

Business and Professions Code § 26226.1

(MAUCRSA, Effective June 27, 2017.)

The bylaws may provide that the territory in which the association has members shall be divided into districts and that directors shall be elected from the several districts. If the bylaws divides the territory into districts for the election of directors, the bylaws shall specify the number of directors to be elected by each district and the manner and method of reapportioning the directors and of redistricting the territory covered by the association.

Business and Professions Code § 26226.2

(MAUCRSA, Effective June 27, 2017.)

The bylaws may provide that primary elections shall be held to nominate directors. If the bylaws provide that the territory in which the association has members shall be divided into districts, the bylaws may also provide that the results of the primary elections in the various districts shall be final and shall be ratified at the annual meeting of the association.

Business and Professions Code § 26226.3

(MAUCRSA, Effective June 27, 2017.)

The bylaws may provide that the territory in which the association has members shall be divided into districts, and that the directors shall be elected by representatives or advisers, who themselves have been elected by the members or stockholders from the several territorial districts. If the bylaws divide the territory into districts for the election of representatives or advisers who elect the directors, the bylaws shall specify the number of representatives or advisers to be elected by each district and the manner and method of reapportioning the representatives or advisers and of redistricting the territory that is covered by the association.

Business and Professions Code § 26226.4

(MAUCRSA, Effective June 27, 2017.)

The bylaws may provide that one or more directors may be chosen by a public official or commission or by the other directors selected by the members. The director shall represent primarily the interest of the general public in the association. The director shall have the same powers and rights as other directors. These directors shall not number more than one-fifth of the entire number of directors.

Business and Professions Code § 26226.5

(MAUCRSA, Effective June 27, 2017.)

The bylaws may provide for an executive committee and may allot to the committee all the functions and powers of the board of directors, subject to the general direction and control of the board.

Business and Professions Code § 26226.6

(MAUCRSA, Effective June 27, 2017.)

An association may provide a fair remuneration for the time that is actually spent by its officers and directors in its service and for the service of the members of its executive committee.

Business and Professions Code § 26226.7

(MAUCRSA, Effective June 27, 2017.)

If a vacancy on the board of directors occurs, except by expiration of term, the remaining members of the board, by a majority vote, shall fill the vacancy, unless the bylaws provide for an election of directors by districts. If the bylaws provide for an election of directors by districts, the vacancy shall be filled either by the election of a director from the district in which the vacancy occurs or by the board of directors calling a special meeting of the members or stockholders in that district to fill the vacancy.

Business and Professions Code § 26226.8

(MAUCRSA, Effective June 27, 2017.)

(a) The directors shall elect a president, one or more vice presidents, a secretary, a treasurer, and such other officers as may be prescribed by the bylaws. Any two or more offices, except those of president and secretary, may be held by the same person.

(b) The treasurer may be a bank or a depository and, as such, shall not be considered as an officer, but as a function of the board of directors. In such case, the secretary shall perform the usual accounting duties of the treasurer, except that the funds shall be deposited only as and where authorized by the board of directors.

Business and Professions Code § 26226.9

(MAUCRSA, Effective June 27, 2017.)

(a) A member may bring charges against an officer or director by filing them in writing with the secretary of the association, together with a petition that is signed by 5 percent of the members, which requests the removal of the officer or director in question. The removal shall be voted upon at the next regular or special meeting of the association and, by a vote of a majority of the members, the association may remove the officer or director and fill the vacancy. The director or officer, against whom the charges have been brought, shall be informed in writing of the charges previous to the meeting and shall have an opportunity at the meeting to be heard in person or by counsel and to present witnesses. The person bringing the charges against him or her shall have the same opportunity.

(b) If the bylaws provide for election of directors by districts with primary elections in each district, the petition for removal of a director shall be signed by 20 percent of the members that reside in the district from which the director was elected. The board of directors shall call a special meeting of the members who reside in that district to consider the removal of the director. By a vote of the majority of the members of that district at the special meeting, the director in question shall be removed from office.

Article 7. Powers

Business and Professions Code § 26227

(MAUCRSA, Effective June 27, 2017.)

An association may engage in any activity in connection with the growing, harvesting, curing, drying, trimming, packing, grading, storing, or handling of any cannabis product that is produced or delivered to it by its members; or any activity in connection with the purchase, hiring, or use by its members of supplies, machinery, or equipment, or in the financing of any such activities; or in any one or more of the activities that are specified in this section with a valid license.

Business and Professions Code § 26227.1

(MAUCRSA, Effective June 27, 2017.)

An association may borrow without limitation as to the amount of corporate indebtedness or liability and may make advances to members.

Business and Professions Code § 26227.2

(MAUCRSA, Effective June 27, 2017.)

An association may act as the agent or representative of any member or members in any of the activities specified in Section 26226.2 or 26226.3.

Business and Professions Code § 26227.3

(MAUCRSA, Effective June 27, 2017.)

An association may purchase or otherwise acquire, hold, own, and exercise all rights of ownership in, sell, transfer, pledge, or guarantee the payment of dividends or interest on, or the retirement or redemption of, shares of the capital stock or bonds of an association that is engaged in any related activity or in the growing, harvesting, curing, drying, trimming, packing, grading, storing, or handling of a cannabis product that is handled by the association.

Business and Professions Code § 26227.4

(MAUCRSA, Effective June 27, 2017.)

An association may establish reserves and invest the funds of the reserves in bonds or in other property as may be provided in the bylaws.

Business and Professions Code § 26227.5

(MAUCRSA, Effective June 27, 2017.)

An association may buy, hold, and exercise all privileges of ownership over such real or personal property as may be necessary or convenient for the conduct and operation of, or incidental to, the business of the association.

Business and Professions Code § 26227.6

(MAUCRSA, Effective June 27, 2017.)

An association may levy assessments in the manner and in the amount as may be provided in its bylaws.

Business and Professions Code § 26227.7

(MAUCRSA, Effective June 27, 2017.)

An association may do any of the following anywhere:

(a) That which is what is necessary, suitable, or proper for the accomplishment of a purpose, or the attainment of an object, that is enumerated in this article.

(b) That which is conducive to, or expedient for, the interest or benefit of the association.

(c) Contract accordingly.

(d) Exercise and possess all powers, rights, and privileges that are necessary or incidental to the purposes for which the association is organized or to the activities in which it is engaged.

(e) Exercise any other rights, powers, and privileges that are granted by the laws of this state to ordinary corporations, except such as are inconsistent with the express provisions of this chapter.

Business and Professions Code § 26227.75

(MAUCRSA, Effective June 27, 2017.)

An association may use or employ any of its facilities for any purpose, provided the proceeds that arise from such use and employment shall go to reduce the cost of operation for its members. The cannabis products that are handled for, or the services, machinery, equipment, or supplies or facilities that are furnished to, nonmembers shall not, however, exceed in value the cannabis products that are handled for, or the services, merchandise, or facilities that are supplied to, members during the same period.

Business and Professions Code § 26227.8

(MAUCRSA, Effective June 27, 2017.)

(a) An association may organize, form, operate, own, control, have an interest in, own stock of, or be a member of any other association, with or without capital stock, that is engaged in growing, harvesting, curing, drying, trimming, packing, grading, storing, or handling of any cannabis product that is handled by the association, or the byproducts of the cannabis product.

(b) Any two or more associations that are organized pursuant to this section may be merged into one constituent association or consolidated into a new association. The merger or consolidation shall be made in the manner that is prescribed by the general laws of the state that cover domestic corporations.

Business and Professions Code § 26227.9

(Amended by AB 133, Effective September 16, 2017.)

(a) Any association may, upon resolution adopted by its board of directors, enter into all necessary and proper contracts and agreements and make all necessary and proper stipulations and arrangements with another cannabis cooperative or association that is formed in this state for the cannabis cooperative and more economical carrying on of its business or any part of its business.

(b) Any two or more associations may, by agreement between them, unite in employing and using, or may separately employ and use, the same personnel, methods, means, and agencies for carrying on and conducting their respective business.

Article 8. Financial Provisions

Business and Professions Code § 26228

(MAUCRSA, Effective June 27, 2017.)

An association is not subject in any manner to the terms of the Corporate Securities Law (Division 1 (commencing with Section 25000) of Title 4 of the Corporations Code), and any association may issue its membership certificates or stock or other securities as provided in this chapter without the necessity of any qualification under that law.

Business and Professions Code § 26228.1

(MAUCRSA, Effective June 27, 2017.)

If an association issues nonpar value stock, the issuance of the stock shall be governed by the terms of all general laws that cover the issuance of nonpar value stock in domestic corporations.

Business and Professions Code § 26228.2

(MAUCRSA, Effective June 27, 2017.)

If an association with preferred shares of stock purchases the stock or any property, or any interest in any property of any person, it may discharge the obligations that are so incurred, wholly or in part, by exchanging for the acquired interest, shares of its preferred stock to an amount that at par value would equal the fair market value of the stock or interest so purchased, as determined by the board of directors. In that case, the transfer to the association of the stock or interest that is purchased is equivalent to payment in cash for the shares of stock that are issued.

Business and Professions Code § 26228.3

(MAUCRSA, Effective June 27, 2017.)

The board of directors of every association shall cause to be sent to the members of the association not later than 120 days after the close of the fiscal or calendar year an annual report of the operations of the association, unless the report is expressly dispensed with in the bylaws. If required by the bylaws, interim reports of the operations of the association for the three-month, six-month, or nine-month periods of the current fiscal year of the association shall be furnished to the members of the association. Such annual report and any such interim reports shall include a balance sheet as of such closing date. Such financial statement shall be prepared from, and be in accordance with, the books. It shall be prepared in a form that is sanctioned by sound accounting practice for the association or approved by a duly certified public accountant or a public accountant.

Article 9. Members

Business and Professions Code § 26229

(MAUCRSA, Effective June 27, 2017.)

Under the terms and conditions that are prescribed in the bylaws adopted by it, an association may admit as members or issue common stock only to persons engaged in the cultivation of a cannabis product that is to be handled by or through the association.

Business and Professions Code § 26229.1

(MAUCRSA, Effective June 27, 2017.)

If a member of a nonstock association is other than a natural person, the member may be represented by any individual, associate, officer, or manager or member of it, who is duly authorized in writing.

Business and Professions Code § 26229.2

(MAUCRSA, Effective June 27, 2017.)

Any association may become a member or stockholder of any other association.

Business and Professions Code § 26229.3

(MAUCRSA, Effective June 27, 2017.)

If a member of an association that is established without shares of stock has paid his membership fee in full, he or she shall receive a certificate of membership.

Business and Professions Code § 26229.4

(MAUCRSA, Effective June 27, 2017.)

An association shall not issue a certificate for stock to a member until it has been fully paid for. The promissory notes of the members may be accepted by the association as full or partial payment. The association shall hold the stock as security for the payment of the note, but the retention as security does not affect the member's right to vote.

Business and Professions Code § 26229.5

(MAUCRSA, Effective June 27, 2017.)

An association, in its bylaws, may limit the amount of common stock that any member may own.

Business and Professions Code § 26229.6

(MAUCRSA, Effective June 27, 2017.)

The bylaws shall prohibit the transfer of the common stock or membership certificates of the associations to a person that is not qualified to be a shareholder or member as specified in this chapter. These restrictions shall be printed upon every certificate of stock or membership that is subject to them.

Business and Professions Code § 26229.7

(MAUCRSA, Effective June 27, 2017.)

The association may, at any time, as specified in the bylaws, except when the debts of the association exceed 50 percent of its assets, buy in or purchase its common stock at the book value of the common stock, as conclusively determined by the board of directors, and pay for it in cash within one year thereafter.

Business and Professions Code § 26229.8

(MAUCRSA, Effective June 27, 2017.)

A member or stockholder is not liable for the debts of the association to an amount that exceeds the sum that remains unpaid on his membership fee or his subscription to the capital stock, including any unpaid balance on any promissory note that is given in payment of the membership fee or the subscription to the capital stock.

Article 10. Marketing Contracts

Business and Professions Code § 26230

(MAUCRSA, Effective June 27, 2017.)

The association and its members may make and execute marketing contracts that require the members to sell, for any period of time, but not over 15 years, all or a specified part of a cannabis product exclusively to or through the association, or a facility that is created by the association. If the members contract a sale to the association, title to the cannabis product passes absolutely and unreservedly, except for recorded liens, to the association upon delivery or at another specified time that is expressly and definitely agreed in the contract.

Business and Professions Code § 26230.1

(MAUCRSA, Effective June 27, 2017.)

Notwithstanding any provisions of the Civil Code, a contract that is entered into by a member or stockholder of an association that provides for the delivery to the association of a cannabis product that is produced or acquired by the member or stockholder may be specifically enforced by the association to secure the delivery to it of the cannabis product.

Business and Professions Code § 26230.2

(MAUCRSA, Effective June 27, 2017.)

The bylaws or a marketing contract may fix, as liquidated damages, specific sums to be paid by the member or stockholder to the association upon the breach by him or her of any provision of the marketing contract regarding the sale or delivery or withholding of a cannabis product and may provide that the member will pay all costs, premiums for bonds, expenses, and fees, if any action is brought upon the contract by the association. These provisions are valid and enforceable in the courts of this state. The clauses that provide for liquidated damages are enforceable as such and shall not be regarded as penalties.

Business and Professions Code § 26230.3

(MAUCRSA, Effective June 27, 2017.)

If there is a breach or threatened breach of a marketing contract by a member, the association shall be entitled to an injunction to prevent the further breach of the contract and to a decree of specific performance of the contract. Pending the adjudication of the action and upon filing a verified complaint that shows the breach or threatened breach, and upon filing a sufficient bond, the association shall be entitled to a temporary restraining order and preliminary injunction against the member.

Article 11. Reorganization of Corporations Organized Pursuant to Other Laws

Business and Professions Code § 26231

(MAUCRSA, Effective June 27, 2017.)

A corporation that is organized or existing pursuant to any law except Title

23 (commencing with Section 653aa) of Part 4 of Division 1 of the Civil Code may be brought under the provisions of this chapter by amending its articles of incorporation, in the manner that is prescribed by the general corporation laws, to conform to this chapter. If a corporation amends its articles of incorporation to conform to this chapter, it shall be deemed to be organized and existing pursuant to, and entitled to the benefit of, and subject to this chapter for all purposes and as fully as though it had been originally organized pursuant to this chapter.

Business and Professions Code § 26231.1

(MAUCRSA, Effective June 27, 2017.)

Articles of incorporation shall be deemed to conform to this chapter within the meaning of Section 26231 if it clearly appears from the articles of incorporation that the corporation desires to be subject to, and to be organized, exist, and function pursuant to this chapter.

Business and Professions Code § 26231.2

(MAUCRSA, Effective June 27, 2017.)

If the amended articles conform, as provided in Section 26231.1, provisions in the articles of incorporation that appeared in the original articles or some previous amended articles, are ineffective if, and to the extent that, they are inapplicable to, or inconsistent with, this chapter.

II. Civil Code Sections

Civil Code § 1550.5

(Added by AB 1159, Effective January 1, 2018.)

(a) The Legislature finds and declares all of the following:

    (1) The Compassionate Use Act of 1996, an initiative measure enacted by the approval of Proposition 215 at the November 5, 1996, statewide general election, authorized the use of marijuana for medical purposes in this state.

    (2) The Legislature passed the Medical Cannabis Regulation and Safety Act, formerly 3.5 (commencing with Section 19300) of Division 8 of the Business and Professions Code, to regulate and license medical cannabis in the state.

    (3) The Control, Regulate and Tax Adult Use of Marijuana Act (AUMA), an initiative measure enacted by the approval of Proposition 64 at the November 8, 2016, statewide general election, authorized the consumption of nonmedical marijuana by persons over 21 years of age and provided for the licensure and regulation of certain commercial nonmedical marijuana activities in this state.

    (4) The Legislature passed the Medicinal and Adult-Use Cannabis Regulation and Safety Act (Division 10 (commencing with Section 26000) of the Business and Professions Code) to consolidate the licensure and regulation of certain commercial activities with respect to medicinal cannabis and nonmedical marijuana, now known as adult-use cannabis.

(b) Notwithstanding any law, including, but not limited to, Sections 1550, 1667, and 1668 and federal law, commercial activity relating to medicinal cannabis or adult-use cannabis conducted in compliance with California law and any applicable local standards, requirements, and regulations shall be deemed to be all of the following:

    (1) A lawful object of a contract.

(2) Not contrary to, an express provision of law, any policy of express law, or good morals.

(3) Not against public policy.

III. Evidence Code Sections

Evidence Code § 956

(Amended by AB 1159, Effective January 1, 2018.)

(a) There is no privilege under this article if the services of the lawyer were sought or obtained to enable or aid anyone to commit or plan to commit a crime or a fraud.

(b) This exception to the privilege granted by this article shall not apply to legal services rendered in compliance with state and local laws on medicinal cannabis or adult-use cannabis, and confidential communications provided for the purpose of rendering those services are confidential communications between client and lawyer, as defined in Section 952, provided the lawyer also advises the client on conflicts with respect to federal law.

IV. Fish and Game Code Sections

Fish and Game Code § 1602

(MAUCRSA, Effective June 27, 2017.)

(a) An entity shall not substantially divert or obstruct the natural flow of, or substantially change or use any material from the bed, channel, or bank of, any river, stream, or lake, or deposit or dispose of debris, waste, or other material containing crumbled, flaked, or ground pavement where it may pass into any river, stream, or lake, unless all of the following occur:

> (1) The department receives written notification regarding the activity in the manner prescribed by the department. The notification shall include, but is not limited to, all of the following:
>
>> (A) A detailed description of the project's location and a map.
>>
>> (B) The name, if any, of the river, stream, or lake affected.
>>
>> (C) A detailed project description, including, but not limited to, construction plans and drawings, if applicable.
>>
>> (D) A copy of any document prepared pursuant to Division 13 (commencing with Section 21000) of the Public Resources Code.
>>
>> (E) A copy of any other applicable local, state, or federal permit or agreement already issued.
>>
>> (F) Any other information required by the department.
>
> (2) The department determines the notification is complete in accordance with Chapter 4.5 (commencing with Section 65920) of Division 1 of Title 7 of the Government Code, irrespective of whether the activity constitutes a development project for the purposes of that chapter.
>
> (3) The entity pays the applicable fees, pursuant to Section 1609.
>
> (4) One of the following occurs:

(A) (i) The department informs the entity, in writing, that the activity will not substantially adversely affect an existing fish or wildlife resource, and that the entity may commence the activity without an agreement, if the entity conducts the activity as described in the notification, including any measures in the notification that are intended to protect fish and wildlife resources.

(ii) Each region of the department shall log the notifications of activities where no agreement is required. The log shall list the date the notification was received by the department, a brief description of the proposed activity, and the location of the activity. Each item shall remain on the log for one year. Upon written request by any person, a regional office shall send the log to that person monthly for one year. A request made pursuant to this clause may be renewed annually.

(B) The department determines that the activity may substantially adversely affect an existing fish or wildlife resource and issues a final agreement to the entity that includes reasonable measures necessary to protect the resource, and the entity conducts the activity in accordance with the agreement.

(C) A panel of arbitrators issues a final agreement to the entity in accordance with subdivision (b) of Section 1603, and the entity conducts the activity in accordance with the agreement.

(D) The department does not issue a draft agreement to the entity within 60 days from the date notification is complete, and the entity conducts the activity as described in the notification, including any measures in the notification that are intended to protect fish and wildlife resources.

(b) (1) If an activity involves the routine maintenance and operation of water supply, drainage, flood control, or waste treatment and disposal facilities, notice to and agreement with the department shall not be required after the initial notification and agreement, unless the department determines either of the following:

(A) The work described in the agreement has substantially changed.

(B) Conditions affecting fish and wildlife resources have

substantially changed, and those resources are adversely affected by the activity conducted under the agreement.

(2) This subdivision applies only if notice to, and agreement with, the department was attained prior to January 1, 1977, and the department has been provided a copy of the agreement or other proof of the existence of the agreement that satisfies the department, if requested.

(c) Notwithstanding subdivision (a), the department is not required to determine whether the notification is complete or otherwise process the notification until the department has received the applicable fees.

(d) (1) Notwithstanding subdivision (a), an entity shall not be required to obtain an agreement with the department pursuant to this chapter for activities authorized by a license or renewed license for cannabis cultivation issued by the Department of Food and Agriculture for the term of the license or renewed license if all of the following occur:

(A) The entity submits all of the following to the department:

(i) The written notification described in paragraph (1) of subdivision (a).

(ii) A copy of the license or renewed license for cannabis cultivation issued by the Department of Food and Agriculture that includes the requirements specified in subdivisions (d), (e), and (f) of Section 19332.2 of the Business and Professions Code.

(iii) The fee specified in paragraph (3) of subdivision (a).

(B) The department determines in its sole discretion that compliance with the requirements specified in Section 26060.1of the Business and Professions Code that are included in the license will adequately protect existing fish and wildlife resources that may be substantially adversely affected by the cultivation without the need for additional measures that the department would include in a draft streambed alteration agreement in accordance with Section 1603.

(C) The department notifies the entity in writing that the exemption applies to the cultivation authorized by the license or renewed license.

(2) The department shall notify the entity in writing whether the exemption in paragraph (1) applies to the cultivation authorized by the license or renewed license within 60 days from the date that the notification is complete and the fee has been paid.

(3) If an entity receives an exemption pursuant to this subdivision and fails to comply with any of the requirements described in Section 26060.1 of the Business and Professions Code that are included in the license, the failure shall constitute a violation under this section, and the department shall notify the Department of Food and Agriculture of any enforcement action taken.

(e) It is unlawful for any entity to violate this chapter.

Fish and Game Code § 1617

(MAUCRSA, Effective June 27, 2017.)

(a) The department may adopt general agreements for the cultivation of cannabis.

(b) Any general agreement adopted by the department subsequent to adoption of regulations under this section shall be in lieu of an individual agreement described in subparagraph (B) of paragraph (4) of subdivision (a) of Section 1602.

(c) Subparagraph (D) of paragraph (4) of subdivision (a) of Section 1602 and all other time periods to process agreements specified in this chapter do not apply to the issuance of a general agreement adopted by the department pursuant to this section.

(d) Any general agreement issued by the department pursuant to this section is a final agreement and is not subject to Section 1603 or 1604.

(e) The department shall charge a fee for a general agreement adopted by the department under this section in accordance with Section 1609.

(f) If the department adopts or amends a general agreement under this sectio, it shall do so as an emergency regulation. An emergency regulation adopted pursuant to this section, and any amendments to it, shall be adopted by the department in accordance with Chapter 3.5 (commencing with Section 11340) of Part 1 of Division 3 of Title 2 of the Government Code. The adoption of these regulations is an emergency and shall be considered by the

Office of Administrative Law as necessary for the immediate preservation of the public peace, health and safety, and general welfare. Notwithstanding Chapter 3.5 (commencing with Section 11340) of Part 1 of Division 3 of Title 2 of the Government Code, an emergency regulation adopted by the department, or any amendments to it made by the department pursuant to this section, shall stay in effect until revised by the department.

(g) Regulations adopted pursuant to this section, and any amendment thereto, shall not be subject to Division 13 (commencing with Section 21000) of the Public Resources Code.

Fish and Game Code § 2080

(Amended by Statute, Effective January 1, 1995.)

No person shall import into this state, export out of this state, or take, possess, purchase, or sell within this state, any species, or any part or product thereof, that the commission determines to be an endangered species or a threatened species, or attempt any of those acts, except as otherwise provided in this chapter, the Native Plant Protection Act (Chapter 10 (commencing with Section 1900) of this code), or the California Desert Native Plants Act (Division 23 (commencing with Section 80001) of the Food and Agricultural Code).

Fish and Game Code § 3513

(Amended by Statute, Effective 1977.)

It is unlawful to take or possess any migratory nongame bird as designated in the Migratory Bird Treaty Act or any part of such migratory nongame bird except as provided by rules and regulations adopted by the Secretary of the Interior under provisions of the Migratory Treaty Act.

Fish and Game Code § 5650

(Amended by Statute, Effective January 1, 2008.)

(a) Except as provided in subdivision (b), it is unlawful to deposit in, permit to pass into, or place where it can pass into the waters of this state any of the following:

(1) Any petroleum, acid, coal or oil tar, lampblack, aniline, asphalt,

bitumen, or residuary product of petroleum, or carbonaceous material or substance.

(2) Any refuse, liquid or solid, from any refinery, gas house, tannery, distillery, chemical works, mill, or factory of any kind.

(3) Any sawdust, shavings, slabs, or edgings.

(4) Any factory refuse, lime, or slag.

(5) Any cocculus indicus.

(6) Any substance or material deleterious to fish, plant life, mammals, or bird life.

(b) This section does not apply to a discharge or a release that is expressly authorized pursuant to, and in compliance with, the terms and conditions of a waste discharge requirement pursuant to Section 13263 of the Water Code or a waiver issued pursuant to subdivision (a) of Section 13269 of the Water Code issued by the State Water Resources Control Board or a regional water quality control board after a public hearing, or that is expressly authorized pursuant to, and in compliance with, the terms and conditions of a federal permit for which the State Water Resources Control Board or a regional water quality control board has, after a public hearing, issued a water quality certification pursuant to Section 13160 of the Water Code. This section does not confer additional authority on the State Water Resources Control Board, a regional water quality control board, or any other entity.

(c) It shall be an affirmative defense to a violation of this section if the defendant proves, by a preponderance of the evidence, all of the following:

(1) The defendant complied with all applicable state and federal laws and regulations requiring that the discharge or release be reported to a government agency.

(2) The substance or material did not enter the waters of the state or a storm drain that discharges into the waters of the state.

(3) The defendant took reasonable and appropriate measures to effectively mitigate the discharge or release in a timely manner.

(d) The affirmative defense in subdivision (c) does not apply and may not be raised in an action for civil penalties or injunctive relief pursuant to Section 5650.1.

(e) The affirmative defense in subdivision (c) does not apply and may not be raised by any defendant who has on two prior occasions in the preceding five years, in any combination within the same county in which the case is prosecuted, either pleaded nolo contendere, been convicted of a violation of this section, or suffered a judgment for a violation of this section or Section 5650.1. This subdivision shall apply only to cases filed on or after January 1, 1997.

(f) The affirmative defense in subdivision (c) does not apply and may not be raised by the defendant in any case in which a district attorney, city attorney, or Attorney General alleges, and the court finds, that the defendant acted willfully.

Fish and Game Code § 5652

(Amended by Statute, Effective January 1, 2008.)

(a) It is unlawful to deposit, permit to pass into, or place where it can pass into the waters of the state, or to abandon, dispose of, or throw away, within 150 feet of the high water mark of the waters of the state, any cans, bottles, garbage, motor vehicle or parts thereof, rubbish, litter, refuse, waste, debris, or the viscera or carcass of any dead mammal, or the carcass of any dead bird.

(b) The abandonment of any motor vehicle in any manner that violates this section shall constitute a rebuttable presumption affecting the burden of producing evidence that the last registered owner of record, not having complied with Section 5900 of the Vehicle Code, is responsible for that abandonment and is thereby liable for the cost of removal and disposition of the vehicle. This section prohibits the placement of a vehicle body on privately owned property along a streambank by the property owner or tenant for the purpose of preventing erosion of the streambank.

(c) This section does not apply to a refuse disposal site that is authorized by the appropriate local agency having jurisdiction or to the depositing of those materials in a container from which the materials are routinely removed to a legal point of disposal.

(d) This section shall be enforced by all law enforcement officers of this state.

Fish and Game Code § 12025.2

(MCRSA- SB-837, Effective June 27, 2016.)

The director or his or her designee may issue a complaint to any person or entity in accordance with Section 1055 of the Water Code alleging a violation for which liability may be imposed under Section 1052 or 1847 of the Water Code that harms fish and wildlife resources. The complaint is subject to the substantive and procedural requirements set forth in Section 1055 of the Water Code, and the department shall be designated a party to any proceeding before the State Water Resources Control Board regarding a complaint filed pursuant to this section.

Fish and Game Code § 12029

(MCRSA- SB 837, Effective June 27, 2016.)

(a) The Legislature finds and declares all of the following:

> (1) The environmental impacts associated with cannabis cultivation have increased, and unlawful water diversions for cannabis irrigation have a detrimental effect on fish and wildlife and their habitat, which are held in trust by the state for the benefit of the people of the state.

> (2) The remediation of existing cannabis cultivation sites is often complex and the permitting of these sites requires greater department staff time and personnel expenditures. The potential for cannabis cultivation sites to significantly impact the state's fish and wildlife resources requires immediate action on the part of the department's lake and streambed alteration permitting staff.

(b) In order to address unlawful water diversions and other violations of the Fish and Game Code associated with cannabis cultivation, the department shall establish the watershed enforcement program to facilitate the investigation, enforcement, and prosecution of these offenses.

(c) The department, in coordination with the State Water Resources Control Board and the Department of Food and Agriculture, shall establish a permanent multiagency task force to address the environmental impacts of cannabis cultivation. The multiagency task force, to the extent feasible and subject to available resources, shall expand its enforcement efforts on a statewide level to ensure the reduction of adverse impacts of cannabis cultivation on fish and wildlife and their habitats throughout the state.

(d) In order to facilitate the remediation and permitting of cannabis cultivation sites, the department may adopt regulations to enhance the fees on any entity subject to Section 1602 for cannabis cultivation sites that require remediation. The fee schedule established pursuant to this subdivision shall not exceed the fee limits in Section 1609.

V. Food and Agricultural Code Sections

Food and Agricultural Code § 37104

(MAUCRSA, Effective June 27, 2017.)

Notwithstanding Section 26001 of the Business and Professions Code, butter purchased from a licensed milk products plant or retail location that is subsequently infused or mixed with medicinal or adult-use cannabis at the premises or location that is not subject to licensing as a milk product plant is exempt from the provisions of this division.

Food and Agricultural Code § 52452

(MCRSA- SB 837, Effective June 27, 2016.)

(a) Except as otherwise provided in Section 52454, each container of agricultural seed that is for sale or sold within this state for sowing purposes shall bear upon it or have attached to it in a conspicuous place a plainly written or printed label or tag in the English language that includes all of the following information:

(1) The commonly accepted name of the kind, kind and variety, or kind and type of each agricultural seed component in excess of 5 percent of the whole, and the percentage by weight of each. If the aggregate of agricultural seed components, each present in an amount not exceeding 5 percent of the whole, exceeds 10 percent of the whole, each component in excess of 1 percent of the whole shall be named together with the percentage by weight of each. If more than one component is required to be named, the names of all components shall be shown in letters of the same type and size.

(2) The lot number or other lot identification.

(3) The percentage by weight of all weed seeds.

(4) The name and approximate number of each kind of restricted

noxious weed seed per pound.

(5) The percentage by weight of any agricultural seed except that which is required to be named on the label.

(6) The percentage by weight of inert matter. If a percentage by weight is required to be shown by any provision of this section, that percentage shall be exclusive of any substance that is added to the seed as a coating and shown on the label as such.

(7) For each agricultural seed in excess of 5 percent of the whole, stated in accordance with paragraph (1), the percentage of germination exclusive of hard seed, the percentage of hard seed, if present, and the calendar month and year the test was completed to determine the percentages. Following the statement of those percentages, the additional statement "total germination and hard seed" may be stated.

(8) The name and address of the person who labeled the seed or of the person who sells the seed within this state.

(b) Subdivision (a) does not apply in the following instances:

(1) The sale is an occasional sale of seed grain by the producer of the seed grain to his or her neighbor for use by the purchaser within the county of production.

(2) Any cannabis seed, as defined in subdivision (f) of Section 19300.5 of the Business and Professions Code, sold or offered for sale in the state.

(c) All determinations of noxious weed seeds are subject to tolerances and methods of determination prescribed in the regulations that are adopted pursuant to this chapter.

(d) For purposes of this section, "neighbor" means a person who lives in close proximity, not to exceed three miles, to another.

Food and Agricultural Code § 54036

(MAUCRSA, Effective June 27, 2017.)

A person, firm, corporation, or association, that is hereafter organized or doing business in this state, may not use the word "cooperative" as part of its corporate name or other business name or title for producers' cooperative marketing activities, unless it has complied with this chapter or is otherwise authorized by Chapter 22 (commencing with Section 26220) of Division 10 of the Business and Professions Code.

Food and Agricultural Code § 81000

(AUMA, Effective November 9, 2016.)

For purposes of this division, the following terms have the following meanings:

(a) "Board" means the Industrial Hemp Advisory Board.

(b) "Commissioner" means the county agricultural commissioner.

(c) "Established agricultural research institution" means any institution that is either:

> (1) a public or private institution or organization that maintains land or facilities for agricultural research, including colleges, universities, agricultural research centers, and conservation research centers; or

> (2) an institution of higher education (as defined in Section 1001 of the Higher Education Act of 1965 (20 USC. 1001)) that grows, cultivates or manufactures industrial hemp for purposes of research conducted under an agricultural pilot program or other agricultural or academic research.

(d) "Industrial hemp" has the same meaning as the term is defined in Section 11018.5 of the Health and Safety Code.

(e) "Secretary" means the Secretary of Food and Agriculture.

(f) "Seed breeder" means an individual or public or private institution or organization that is registered with the commissioner to develop seed cultivars intended for sale or research.

(g) "Seed cultivar" means a variety of industrial hemp.

(h) "Seed development plan" means a strategy devised by a seed breeder, or applicant seed breeder, detailing his or her plam1ed approach to growing and developing a new seed cultivar for industrial hemp.

Food and Agricultural Code § 81006

(AUMA, Effective November 9, 2016.)

(a)(1) Except when grown by an established agricultural research institution or a registered seed breeder, industrial hemp shall be grown only as a densely planted fiber or oilseed crop, or both, in acreages of not less than one-tenth of an acre at the same time.

(a)(2) Registered seed breeders, for purposes of seed production, shall only grow industrial hemp as a densely planted crop in acreages of not less than one-tenth of an acre at the same time.

(a)(3) Registered seed breeders, for purposes of developing a new California seed cultivar, shall grow industrial hemp as densely as possible in dedicated acreage of not less than one-tenth of an acre and in accordance with the seed development plan. The entire area of the dedicated acreage is not required to be used for the cultivation of the particular seed cultivar.

(b) Ornamental and clandestine cultivation of industrial hemp is prohibited. All plots shall have adequate signage indicating they are industrial hemp.

(c) Pruning and tending of individual industrial hemp plants is prohibited, except when grown by an established agricultural research institution or when the action is necessary to perform the tetrahydrocannabinol (THC) testing described in this section.

(d) Culling of industrial hemp is prohibited, except when grown by an established agricultural research institution, when the action is necessary to perform the THC testing described in this section, or for purposes of seed production and development by a registered seed breeder.

(e) Industrial hemp shall include products imported under the Harmonized Tariff Schedule of the United States (2013) of the United States International Trade Commission, including, but not limited to, hemp seed, per subheading 1207.99.03, hemp oil, per subheading 1515.90.80, oilcake, per subheading 2306.90.01, true hemp, per heading 5302, true hemp yam, per subheading 5308.20.00, and woven fabrics of true hemp fibers, per subheading 5311.00.40.

(f) Except when industrial hemp is grown by an established agricultural research institution, a registrant that grows industrial hemp under this section shall, before the harvest of each crop and as provided below, obtain a laboratory test report indicating the THC levels of a random sampling of the dried flowering tops of the industrial hemp grown.

(1) Sampling shall occur as soon as practicable when the THC content of the leaves surrounding the seeds is at its peak and shall commence as the seeds begin to mature, when the first seeds of approximately 50 percent of the plants are resistant to compression.

(2) The entire fruit-bearing part of the plant including the seeds shall be used as a sample. The sample cut shall be made directly underneath the inflorescence found in the top one-third of the plant.

(3) The sample collected for THC testing shall be accompanied by the following documentation:

(A) The registrant's proof of registration.

(B) Seed certification documentation for the seed cultivar used.

(C) The THC testing report for each certified seed cultivar used.

(4) The laboratory test report shall be issued by a laboratory registered with the federal Drug Enforcement Administration, shall state the percentage content of THC, shall indicate the date and location of samples taken, and shall state the Global Positioning System coordinates and total acreage of the crop. If the laboratory test report indicates a percentage content of THC that is equal to or less than three-tenths of 1 percent, the words "PASSED AS CALIFORNIA INDUSTRIAL HEMP" shall appear at or near the top of the laboratory test report. If the laboratory test report indicates a percentage content of THC that is greater than three-tenths of 1 percent, the words "FAILED AS CALIFORNIA INDUSTRIAL HEMP" shall appear at or near the top of the laboratory test report.

(5) If the laboratory test report indicates a percentage content of THC that is equal to or less than three-tenths of 1 percent, the laboratory shall provide the person who requested the testing not less than 10 original copies signed by an employee authorized by the laboratory and shall retain one or more original copies of the laboratory test report for a minimum of two years from its date of sampling.

(6) If the laboratory test report indicates a percentage content of THC that is greater than three-tenths of 1 percent and does not exceed 1 percent, the registrant that grows industrial hemp shall submit

additional samples for testing of the industrial hemp grown.

(7) A registrant that grows industrial hemp shall destroy the industrial hemp grown upon receipt of a first laboratory test report indicating a percentage content of THC that exceeds 1 percent or a second laboratory test report pursuant to paragraph (6) indicating a percentage content of THC that exceeds three-tenths of 1 percent but is less than 1 percent. If the percentage content of THC exceeds 1 percent, the destruction shall take place within 48 hours after receipt of the laboratory test report. If the percentage content of THC in the second laboratory test report exceeds three-tenths of 1 percent but is less than 1 percent, the destruction shall take place as soon as practicable, but no later than 45 days after receipt of the second test report.

(8) A registrant that intends to grow industrial hemp and who complies with this section shall not be prosecuted for the cultivation or possession of marijuana as a result of a laboratory test report that indicates a percentage content of THC that is greater than three-tenths of 1 percent but does not exceed 1 percent.

(9) Established agricultural research institutions shall be permitted to cultivate or possess industrial hemp with a laboratory test report that indicates a percentage content of THC that is greater than three-tenths of 1 percent if that cultivation or possession contributes to the development of types of industrial hemp that will comply with the three-tenths of 1 percent THC limit established in this division.

(10) Except for an established agricultural research institution, a registrant that grows industrial hemp shall retain an original signed copy of the laboratory test report for two years from its date of sampling, make an original signed copy of the laboratory test report available to the department, the commissioner, or law enforcement officials or their designees upon request, and shall provide an original copy of the laboratory test report to each person purchasing, transporting, or otherwise obtaining from the registrant that grows industrial hemp the fiber, oil, cake, or seed, or any component of the seed, of the plant.

(g) If, in the Attorney General's opinion issued pursuant to Section 8 of the act that added this division, it is determined that the provisions of this section are not sufficient to comply with federal law, the department, in consultation with the board, shall establish procedures for this section that meet the requirements of federal law.

Food and Agricultural Code § 81008

(AUMA, Effective November 9, 2016.)

(a) Not later than January 1, 2019, the Attorney General shall report to the Assembly and Senate Committees on Agriculture and the Assembly and Senate Committees on Public Safety the reported incidents, if any, of the following:

(1) A field of industrial hemp being used to disguise marijuana cultivation.

(2) Claims in a court hearing by persons other than those exempted in subdivision (f) of Section 81006 that marijuana is industrial hemp.

(b) A report submitted pursuant to subdivision (a) shall be submitted in compliance with Section 9795 of the Government Code.

(c) Pursuant to Section 10231.5 of the Government Code, this section is repealed on January 1, 2023, or four years after the date that the report is due, whichever is later.

Food and Agricultural Code § 81010

(MAUCRSA, Effective June 27, 2017.)

This division, and Section 221 shall become operative on January 1, 2017.

VI. Government Code Sections

Government Code § 9147.7

(MCRSA- AB 266, Effective January 1, 2016.)

(a) For the purpose of this section, "eligible agency" means any agency, authority, board, bureau, commission, conservancy, council, department, division, or office of state government, however denominated, excluding an agency that is constitutionally created or an agency related to postsecondary education, for which a date for repeal has been established by statute on or after January 1, 2011.

(b) The Joint Sunset Review Committee is hereby created to identify and eliminate waste, duplication, and inefficiency in government agencies. The purpose of the committee is to conduct a comprehensive analysis over 15 years, and on a periodic basis thereafter, of every eligible agency to determine if the agency is still necessary and cost effective.

(c) Each eligible agency scheduled for repeal shall submit to the committee, on or before December 1 prior to the year it is set to be repealed, a complete agency report covering the entire period since last reviewed, including, but not limited to, the following:

   (1) The purpose and necessity of the agency.

   (2) A description of the agency budget, priorities, and job descriptions of employees of the agency.

   (3) Any programs and projects under the direction of the agency.

   (4) Measures of the success or failures of the agency and justifications for the metrics used to evaluate successes and failures.

   (5) Any recommendations of the agency for changes or reorganization in order to better fulfill its purpose.

(d) The committee shall take public testimony and evaluate the eligible agency prior to the date the agency is scheduled to be repealed. An eligible agency shall be eliminated unless the Legislature enacts a law to extend, consolidate, or reorganize the eligible agency. No eligible agency shall be extended in perpetuity unless specifically exempted from the provisions of this section. The committee may recommend that the Legislature extend the statutory sunset date for no more than one year to allow the committee more time to evaluate the eligible agency.

(e) The committee shall be comprised of 10 members of the Legislature. The Senate Committee on Rules shall appoint five members of the Senate to the committee, not more than three of whom shall be members of the same political party. The Speaker of the Assembly shall appoint five members of the Assembly to the committee, not more than three of whom shall be members of the same political party. Members shall be appointed within 15 days after the commencement of the regular session. Each member of the committee who is appointed by the Senate Committee on Rules or the Speaker of the Assembly shall serve during that committee member's term of office or until that committee member no longer is a Member of the Senate or the Assembly, whichever is applicable. A vacancy on the committee shall be filled in the same manner as the original appointment. Three Assembly Members and three Senators who are members of the committee shall constitute a quorum for the conduct of committee business. Members of the committee shall receive no compensation for their work with the committee.

(f) The committee shall meet not later than 30 days after the first day of the regular session to choose a chairperson and to establish the schedule for eligible agency review provided for in the statutes governing the eligible agencies. The chairperson of the committee shall alternate every two years between a Member of the Senate and a Member of the Assembly, and the vice chairperson of the committee shall be a member of the opposite house as the chairperson.

(g) This section shall not be construed to change the existing jurisdiction of the budget or policy committees of the Legislature.

(h) This section shall not apply to the Bureau of Medical Marijuana Regulation.

Government Code § 11553

(Amended by AB 133, Effective September 16, 2017.)

(a) Effective January 1, 1988, an annual salary of eighty-one thousand six hundred thirty-five dollars ($81,635) shall be paid to each of the following:

(1) Chairperson of the Unemployment Insurance Appeals Board.

(2) Chairperson of the Agricultural Labor Relations Board.

(3) President of the Public Utilities Commission.

(4) Chairperson of the Fair Political Practices Commission.

(5) Chairperson of the Energy Resources Conservation and Development Commission.

(6) Chairperson of the Public Employment Relations Board.

(7) Chairperson of the Workers' Compensation Appeals Board.

(8) Administrative Director of the Division of Industrial Accidents.

(9) Chairperson of the State Water Resources Control Board.

(10) Chairperson of the Cannabis Control Appeals Panel.

(b) The annual compensation provided by this section shall be increased in any fiscal year in which a general salary increase is provided for state employees. The amount of the increase provided by this section shall be comparable to, but shall not exceed, the percentage of the general salary increases provided for state employees during that fiscal year.

(c) Notwithstanding subdivision (b), any salary increase is subject to Section 11565.5.

Government Code § 11553.5

(Amended by AB 133, Effective September 16, 2017.)

(a) Effective January 1, 1988, an annual salary of seventy-nine thousand one hundred twenty-two dollars ($79,122) shall be paid to the following:

(1) Member of the Agricultural Labor Relations Board.

(2) Member of the State Energy Resources Conservation and Development Commission.

(3) Member of the Public Utilities Commission.

(4) Member of the Public Employment Relations Board.

(5) Member of the Unemployment Insurance Appeals Board.

(6) Member of the Workers' Compensation Appeals Board.

(7) Member of the State Water Resources Control Board.

(8) Member of the Cannabis Control Appeals Panel.

(b) The annual compensation provided by this section shall be increased in any fiscal year in which a general salary increase is provided for state employees. The amount of the increase provided by this section shall be comparable to, but shall not exceed, the percentage of the general cost-of-living salary increases provided for state employees during that fiscal year.

(c) Notwithstanding subdivision (b), any salary increase is subject to Section 11565.5.

Government Code § 68152

(Repealed and added by Statute, Effective January 1, 2014.)

The trial court clerk may destroy court records under Section 68153 after notice of destruction, and if there is no request and order for transfer of the records, except the comprehensive historical and sample superior court records preserved for research under the California Rules of Court, when the following times have expired after the date of final disposition of the case in the categories listed:

(a) Civil actions and proceedings, as follows:

(1) Except as otherwise specified: retain 10 years.

(2) Civil unlimited cases, limited cases, and small claims cases, including after trial de novo, if any, except as otherwise specified: retain for 10 years.

(3) Civil judgments for unlimited civil cases: retain permanently.

(4) Civil judgments for limited and small claims cases: retain for 10 years, unless judgment is renewed. If judgment is renewed, retain judgment for length of renewal pursuant to Article 2 (commencing with Section 683.110) of Chapter 3 of Division 1 of Title 9 of Part 2 of the Code of Civil Procedure.

(5) If a party in a civil case appears by a guardian ad litem: retain for 10

years after termination of the court's jurisdiction.

(6) Civil harassment, domestic violence, elder and dependent adult abuse, private postsecondary school violence, and workplace violence cases: retain for the same period of time as the duration of the restraining or other orders and any renewals thereof, then retain the restraining or other orders permanently as a judgment; 60 days after expiration of the temporary restraining or other temporary orders; retain judgments establishing paternity under Section 6323 of the Family Code permanently.

(7) Family law, except as otherwise specified: retain for 30 years.

(8) Adoption: retain permanently.

(9) Parentage: retain permanently.

(10) Change of name, gender, or name and gender: retain permanently.

(11) Probate:

(A) Decedent estates: retain permanently all orders, judgments, and decrees of the court, all inventories and appraisals, and all wills and codicils of the decedent filed in the case, including those not admitted to probate. All other records: retain for five years after final disposition of the estate proceeding.

(B) Wills and codicils transferred or delivered to the court pursuant to Section 732, 734, or 8203 of the Probate Code: retain permanently. For wills and codicils delivered to the clerk of the court under Section 8200 of the Probate Code, retain the original documents as provided in Section 26810.

(C) Substitutes for decedent estate administration:

(i) Affidavit procedures for real property of small value under Chapter 3 (commencing with Section 13100) of Part 1 of Division 8 of the Probate Code: retain permanently.

(ii) Proceedings for determining succession to property under Chapter 4 (commencing with Section 13150) of Part 1 of Division 8 of the Probate Code: retain permanently all inventories and appraisals and court orders. Other records: retain for five years after final disposition of the proceeding.

(iii) Proceedings for determination of property passing or belonging to surviving spouse under Chapter 5 (commencing with Section 13650) of Part 2 of Division 8 of the Probate Code: retain permanently all inventories and appraisals and court orders. Other records: retain for five years after final disposition of the proceeding.

(D) Conservatorships: retain permanently all court orders. Documents of trusts established under substituted judgment pursuant to Section 2580 of the Probate Code: retain as provided in clause (iii) of subparagraph (G). Other records: retain for five years after the later of either (i) the final disposition of the conservatorship proceeding, or (ii) the date of the conservatee's death, if that date is disclosed in the court's file.

(E) Guardianships: retain permanently orders terminating the guardianship, if any, and court orders settling final account and ordering distribution of the estate. Other records: retain for five years after the later of (i) the final disposition of the guardianship proceeding, or (ii) the earlier of the date of the ward's death, if that date is disclosed in the court's file, or the date the ward reaches 23 years of age.

(F) Compromise of minor's or disabled person's claim or action, and disposition of judgment for minors and disabled persons under Section 372 of the Code of Civil Procedure and Chapter 4 (commencing with Section 3600) of Part 8 of Division 4 of the Probate Code:

(i) Retain permanently judgments in favor of minors or disabled persons, orders approving compromises of claims and actions and disposition of the proceeds of judgments, orders directing payment of expenses, costs, and fees, orders directing deposits into blocked accounts and receipts and acknowledgments of those orders, and orders for the withdrawal of funds from blocked accounts.

(ii) Retain other records for the same retention period as for records in the underlying case. If there is no underlying case, retain for five years after the later of either (I) the date the order for payment or delivery of the final balance of the money or property is entered, or (II) the earlier of the date of the minor's death, if that date is disclosed in the court's file, or the date the minor reaches 23 years of age.

(G) Trusts:

(i) Proceedings under Part 5 (commencing with Section 17000) of Division 9 of the Probate Code: retain permanently.

(ii) Trusts created by substituted judgment under Section 2580 of the Probate Code: retain permanently all trust instruments and court orders. Other records: retain as long as the underlying conservatorship file is retained.

(iii) Special needs trusts: retain permanently all trust instruments and court orders. Other records: retain until the later of either (I the retention date of "other records" in the beneficiary's conservatorship or guardianship file under subparagraph (D) or (E), if any, or (II) five years after the date of the beneficiary's death, if that date is disclosed in the court's file.

(H) All other proceedings under the Probate Code: retain as provided for civil cases.

(12) Mental health:

(A) Lanterman Developmental Disabilities Services Act: retain for 10 years.

(B) Lanterman-Petris-Short Act: retain for 20 years.

(C) Riese (capacity) hearings under Sections 5333 and 5334 of the Welfare and Institutions Code: retain for the later of either (i) 20 years after the date of the capacity determination order, or (ii) the court records retention date of the underlying involuntary treatment or commitment proceeding, if any.

(D) Petitions under Chapter 3 (commencing with Section 8100) of Division 8 of the Welfare and Institutions Code for the return of firearms to petitioners who relinquished them to law enforcement while detained in a mental health facility: retain for 10 years.

(13) Eminent domain: retain permanently.

(14) Real property other than unlawful detainer: retain permanently if

the action affects title or an interest in real property.

(15) Unlawful detainer: retain for one year if judgment is only for possession of the premises; retain for 10 years if judgment is for money, or money and possession.

(b) Notwithstanding subdivision (a), any civil or small claims case in the trial court:

(1) Involuntarily dismissed by the court for delay in prosecution or failure to comply with state or local rules: retain for one year.

(2) Voluntarily dismissed by a party without entry of judgment: retain for one year.

(c) Criminal actions and proceedings, as follows:

(1) Capital felony in which the defendant is sentenced to death, and any felony resulting in a sentence of life or life without the possibility of parole: retain permanently, including records of the cases of any codefendants and any related cases, regardless of the disposition. For the purpose of this paragraph, "capital felony" means murder with special circumstances when the prosecution seeks the death penalty. Records of the cases of codefendants and related cases required to be retained under this paragraph shall be limited to those cases that are factually linked or related to the charged offense, that are identified in the courtroom, and that are placed on the record. If a capital felony is disposed of by a sentence less than death, or imprisonment for life or life without the possibility of parole, the judgment shall be retained permanently, and the record shall be retained for 50 years or for 10 years after the official written notification of the death of the defendant. If a capital felony is disposed of by an acquittal, the record shall be retained for 10 years.

(2) Felony, except as otherwise specified, and in any felony or misdemeanor case resulting in a requirement that the defendant register as a sex offender under Section 290 of the Penal Code: retain judgment permanently. For all other documents: retain for 50 years or the maximum term of the sentence, whichever is longer. However, any record other than the judgment may be destroyed 10 years after the death of the defendant. Felony case files that do not include final sentencing or other final disposition because the case was bound over from a former municipal court to the superior court and not already

consolidated with the superior court felony case file: retain for 10 years from the disposition of the superior court case.

(3) Felony reduced to a misdemeanor: retain in accordance with the retention period for the relevant misdemeanor.

(4) Felony, if the charge is dismissed, except as provided in paragraph (6): retain for three years.

(5) Misdemeanor, if the charge is dismissed, except as provided in paragraph (6): retain for one year.

(6) Dismissal under Section 1203.4 or 1203.4a of the Penal Code: retain for the same retention period as for records of the underlying case. If the records in the underlying case have been destroyed, retain for five years after dismissal.

(7) Misdemeanor, except as otherwise specified: retain for five years. For misdemeanors alleging a violation of Section 23109, 23109.5, 23152, or 23153 of the Vehicle Code: retain for 10 years.

(8) Misdemeanor alleging a marijuana violation under subdivision (c), (d), or (e) of Section 11357 of the Health and Safety Code, or subdivision (b) of Section 11360 of the Health and Safety Code: records shall be destroyed, or redacted in accordance with subdivision (c) of Section 11361.5 of the Health and Safety Code, two years from the date of conviction, or from the date of arrest if no conviction, if the case is no longer subject to review on appeal, all applicable fines and fees have been paid, and the defendant has complied with all terms and conditions of the sentence or grant of probation. However, as provided in subdivision (a) of Section 11361.5 of the Health and Safety Code and paragraph (5) of subdivision (e) of this section, records of a misdemeanor alleging a marijuana violation under subdivision (e) of Section 11357 of the Health and Safety Code shall be retained until the offender attains 18 years of age, at which time the records shall be destroyed as provided in subdivision (c) of Section 11361.5 of the Health and Safety Code.

(9) Misdemeanor reduced to an infraction: retain in accordance with the retention period for the relevant infraction.

(10) Infraction, except as otherwise specified: retain for one year. Vehicle Code infraction: retain for three years. Infraction alleging a

marijuana violation under subdivision (b) of Section 11357 of the Health and Safety Code: if records are retained past the one-year minimum retention period, the records shall be destroyed or redacted in accordance with subdivision (c) of Section 11361.5 of the Health and Safety Code two years from the date of conviction, or from the date of arrest if no conviction, if the case is no longer subject to review on appeal, all applicable fines and fees have been paid, and the defendant has complied with all terms and conditions of the sentence or grant of probation.

(11) Criminal protective order: retain until the order expires or is terminated.

(12) Arrest warrant: retain for the same retention period as for records in the underlying case. If there is no underlying case, retain for one year from the date of issue.

(13) Search warrant:

> (A) If there is no underlying case, retain for five years from the date of issue.

> (B) If there is any underlying case, retain for 10 years from the date of issue or, if the retention period for records in the underlying case is less than 10 years or if the underlying case is a capital felony described in paragraph (1) of subdivision (c), retain for the same retention period as for records in the underlying case

(14) Probable cause declarations: retain for the same retention period as for records in the underlying case. If there is no underlying case, retain for one year from the date of declaration.

(15) Proceedings for revocation of postrelease community supervision or postrelease parole supervision: retain for five years after the period of supervision expires or is terminated.

(d) Habeas corpus:

> (1) Habeas corpus in criminal and family law matters: retain for the same retention period as for records in the underlying case, whether granted or denied.

> (2) Habeas corpus in mental health matters: retain all records for the same retention period as for records in the underlying case, whether

granted or denied. If there is no underlying case, retain records for 20 years.

(e) Juveniles:

(1) Dependent pursuant to Section 300 of the Welfare and Institutions Code: upon reaching 28 years of age, or on written request, shall be released to the juvenile five years after jurisdiction over the person has terminated under subdivision (a) of Section 826 of the Welfare and Institutions Code. Sealed records shall be destroyed upon court order five years after the records have been sealed pursuant to subdivision (c) of Section 389 of the Welfare and Institutions Code.

(2) Ward pursuant to Section 601 of the Welfare and Institutions Code: upon reaching 21 years of age, or on written request, shall be released to the juvenile five years after jurisdiction over the person has terminated under subdivision (a) of Section 826 of the Welfare and Institutions Code. Sealed records shall be destroyed upon court order five years after the records have been sealed under subdivision (d) of Section 781 of the Welfare and Institutions Code.

(3) Ward pursuant to Section 602 of the Welfare and Institutions Code: upon reaching 38 years of age under subdivision (a) of Section 826 of the Welfare and Institutions Code. Sealed records shall be destroyed upon court order when the subject of the record reaches 38 years of age under subdivision (d) of Section 781 of the Welfare and Institutions Code.

(4) Traffic and some nontraffic misdemeanors and infractions pursuant to Section 601 of the Welfare and Institutions Code: upon reaching 21 years of age, or five years after jurisdiction over the person has terminated under subdivision (c) of Section 826 of the Welfare and Institutions Code. Records may be microfilmed or photocopied.

(5) Marijuana misdemeanor under subdivision (e) of Section 11357 of the Health and Safety Code in accordance with procedures specified in subdivision (a) of Section 11361.5 of the Health and Safety Code: upon reaching 18 years of age, the records shall be destroyed.

(f) Court records of the appellate division of the superior court: retain for five years.

(g) Other records:

(1) Bench warrant: retain for the same retention period as for records in the underlying case. For a bench warrant issued for a misdemeanor, retain records for the same retention period as for records in the underlying misdemeanor following issuance. If there is no return on the warrant, the court may dismiss on its own motion and immediately destroy the records.

(2) Body attachment: retain for same retention period as for records in the underlying case.

(3) Bond: retain for three years after exoneration and release.

(4) Court reporter notes:

(A) Criminal and juvenile proceedings: retain notes for 10 years, except as otherwise specified. Notes reporting proceedings in capital felony cases (murder with special circumstances when the prosecution seeks the death penalty and the sentence is death), including notes reporting the preliminary hearing, shall be retained permanently, unless the Supreme Court on request of the court clerk authorizes the destruction.

(B) Civil and all other proceedings: retain notes for five years.

(5) Electronic recordings made as the official record of the oral proceedings under the California Rules of Court may be destroyed or deleted as follows:

(A) Any time after final disposition of the case in infraction and misdemeanor proceedings.

(B) After 10 years in all other criminal proceedings.

(C) After five years in all other proceedings.

(6) Electronic recordings not made as the official record of the oral proceedings under the California Rules of Court may be destroyed at any time at the discretion of the court.

(7) Fee waiver applications: retain for the same retention period as for records in the underlying case.

(8) Judgments within the jurisdiction of the superior court other than in a limited civil case, misdemeanor case, or infraction case: retain permanently.

(9) Judgments in misdemeanor cases, infraction cases, and limited civil cases: retain for the same retention period as for records in the underlying case.

(10) Juror proceedings, including sanctions: retain for one year.

(11) Minutes: retain for the same retention period as for records in the underlying case.

(12) Orders not associated with an underlying case, such as orders for the destruction of court records for telephone taps, orders to destroy drugs, and other miscellaneous court orders: retain for one year.

(13) Naturalization index: retain permanently.

(14) Index for cases alleging traffic violations: retain for the same retention period as for records in the underlying case.

(15) Index, except as otherwise specified: retain permanently.

(16) Register of actions or docket: retain for the same retention period as for records in the underlying case, but in no event less than 10 years for civil and small claims cases.

(h) Retention of the court records under this section shall be extended by order of the court on its own motion, or on application of a party or an interested member of the public for good cause shown and on those terms as are just. A fee shall not be charged for making the application.

(i) The record retention periods provided in this section, as amended effective January 1, 2014, apply to all court records in existence prior to that date as well as to records created on or after that date.

VII. Health and Safety Code Sections

Health and Safety Code § 7151.36

(AB 258, Effective January 1, 2016.)

(a) A hospital, physician and surgeon, procurement organization, or other person shall not determine the ultimate recipient of an anatomical gift based solely upon a potential recipient's status as a qualified patient, as defined in Section 11362.7, or based solely upon a positive test for the use of medical marijuana by a potential recipient who is a qualified patient, as defined in Section 11362.7, except to the extent that the qualified patient's use of medical marijuana has been found by a physician and surgeon, following a case-by-case evaluation of the potential recipient, to be medically significant to the provision of the anatomical gift.

(b) Subdivision (a) shall apply to each part of the organ transplant process. The organ transplant process includes, but is not limited to, all of the following:

(1) The referral from a primary care provider to a specialist.

(2) The referral from a specialist to a transplant center.

(3) The evaluation of the patient for the transplant by the transplant center.

(4) The consideration of the patient for placement on the official waiting list.

(c) The court shall accord priority on its calendar and handle expeditiously any action brought to seek any remedy authorized by law for purposes of enforcing compliance with this section.

(d) This section shall not be deemed to require referrals or recommendations for, or the performance of, medically inappropriate organ transplants.

Health and Safety Code § 11006.5

(MAUCRSA, Effective June 27, 2017.)

"Concentrated cannabis" means the separated resin, whether crude or purified, obtained from cannabis.

Health and Safety Code § 11007

(Added by Statute, Effective September 26, 1987.)

"Controlled substance," unless otherwise specified, means a drug, substance, or immediate precursor which is listed in any schedule in Section 11054, 11055, 11056, 11057, or 11058.

Health and Safety Code § 11014.5

(MAUCRSA, Effective June 27, 2017.)

(a) "Drug paraphernalia" means all equipment, products and materials of any kind which are designed for use or marketed for use, in planting, propagating, cultivating, growing, harvesting, manufacturing, compounding, converting, producing, processing, preparing, testing, analyzing, packaging, repackaging, storing, containing, concealing, injecting, ingesting, inhaling, or otherwise introducing into the human body a controlled substance in violation of this division. It includes, but is not limited to:

(1) Kits designed for use or marketed for use in planting, propagating, cultivating, growing, or harvesting of any species of plant which is a controlled substance or from which a controlled substance can be derived.

(2) Kits designed for use or marketed for use in manufacturing, compounding, converting, producing, processing, or preparing controlled substances.

(3) Isomerization devices designed for use or marketed for use in increasing the potency of any species of plant which is a controlled substance.

(4) Testing equipment designed for use or marketed for use in identifying, or in analyzing the strength, effectiveness, or purity of controlled substances.

(5) Scales and balances designed for use or marketed for use in weighing or measuring controlled substances.

(6) Containers and other objects designed for use or marketed for use in storing or concealing controlled substances.

(7) Hypodermic syringes, needles, and other objects designed for use or marketed for use in parenterally injecting controlled substances into the human body.

(8) Objects designed for use or marketed for use in ingesting, inhaling, or otherwise introducing marijuana, cocaine, hashish, or hashish oil into the human body, such as:

(A) Carburetion tubes and devices.

(B) Smoking and carburetion masks.

(C) Roach clips, meaning objects used to hold burning material, such as a cannabis cigarette, that has become too small or too short to be held in the hand.

(D) Miniature cocaine spoons, and cocaine vials.

(E) Chamber pipes.

(F) Carburetor pipes.

(G) Electric pipes.

(H) Air-driven pipes.

(I) Chillums.

(J) Bongs.

(K) Ice pipes or chillers.

(b) For the purposes of this section, the phrase "marketed for use" means advertising, distributing, offering for sale, displaying for sale, or selling in a manner which promotes the use of equipment, products, or materials with controlled substances.

(c) In determining whether an object is drug paraphernalia, a court or other authority may consider, in addition to all other logically relevant factors, the following:

(1) Statements by an owner or by anyone in control of the object concerning its use.

(2) Instructions, oral or written, provided with the object concerning its use for ingesting, inhaling, or otherwise introducing a controlled substance into the human body.

(3) Descriptive materials accompanying the object which explain or depict its use.

(4) National and local advertising concerning its use.

(5) The manner in which the object is displayed for sale.

(6) Whether the owner, or anyone in control of the object, is a legitimate supplier of like or related items to the community, such as a licensed distributor or dealer of tobacco products.

(7) Expert testimony concerning its use.

(d) If any provision of this section or the application thereof to any person or circumstance is held invalid, it is the intent of the Legislature that the invalidity shall not affect other provisions or applications of the section which can be given effect without the invalid provision or application and to this end the provisions of this section are severable.

Health and Safety Code § 11018

(MAUCRSA, Effective June 27, 2017.)

"Cannabis" means all parts of the plant Cannabis sativa L., whether growing or not; the seeds thereof; the resin extracted from any part of the plant; and every compound, manufacture, salt, derivative, mixture, or preparation of the plant, its seeds or resin. It does not include either of the following:

(a) Industrial hemp, as defined in Section 11018.5; or

(b) The weight of any other ingredient combined with cannabis to prepare topical or oral administrations, food, drink, or other product.

Health and Safety Code § 11018.1

(MAUCRSA, Effective June 27, 2017.)

"Cannabis products" means cannabis that has undergone a process whereby the plant material has been transformed into a concentrate, including, but not limited to, concentrated cannabis, or an edible or topical product containing cannabis or concentrated cannabis and other ingredients.

Health and Safety Code § 11018.2

(MAUCRSA, Effective June 27, 2017.)

"Cannabis accessories" means any equipment, products or materials of any kind which are used, intended for use, or designed for use in planting, propagating, cultivating, growing, harvesting, manufacturing, compounding, converting, producing, processing, preparing, testing, analyzing, packaging, repackaging, storing, smoking, vaporizing, or containing cannabis, or for ingesting, inhaling, or otherwise introducing cannabis or cannabis products into the human body.

Health and Safety Code § 11018.5

(MAUCRSA, Effective June 27, 2017.)

Industrial Hemp

(a) "Industrial hemp" means a fiber or oilseed crop, or both, that is limited to types of the plant Cannabis sativa L., having no more than three-tenths of 1 percent tetrahydrocannabinol (THC) contained in the dried flowering tops, whether growing or not; the seeds of the plant;, the resin extracted from any part of the plant; and every compound, manufacture, salt, derivative, mixture, or preparation of the plant, its seeds or resin produced therefrom.

(b) Industrial hemp shall not be subject to the provisions of this division or of Division 10 (commencing with Section 26000) of the Business and Professions Code, but instead shall be regulated by the Department of Food and Agriculture in accordance with the provisions of Division 24 (commencing with Section 81000) of the Food and Agricultural Code, inclusive.

Health and Safety Code § 11032

(MAUCRSA, Effective June 27, 2017.)

If reference is made to the term "narcotics" in any law not in this division, unless otherwise expressly provided, it means those controlled substances classified in Schedules I and II, as defined in this division. If reference is made to "restricted dangerous drugs" not in this division, unless otherwise expressly provided, it means those controlled substances classified in Schedules III and IV. If reference is made to the term "marijuana" in any law not in this division, unless otherwise expressly provided, it means cannabis as defined in this division.

Health and Safety Code § 11054

(MAUCRSA, Effective June 27, 2017.)

(a) The controlled substances listed in this section are included in Schedule I.

(b) Opiates. Unless specifically excepted or unless listed in another schedule, any of the following opiates, including their isomers, esters, ethers, salts, and salts of isomers, esters, and ethers whenever the existence of those isomers, esters, ethers, and salts is possible within the specific chemical designation:

(1) Acetylmethadol.

(2) Allylprodine.

(3) Alphacetylmethadol (except levoalphacetylmethadol, also known as levo-alpha- acetylmethadol, levomethadyl acetate, or LAAM).

(4) Alphameprodine.

(5) Alphamethadol.

(6) Benzethidine.

(7) Betacetylmethadol.

(8) Betameprodine.

(9) Betamethadol.

(10) Betaprodine.

(11) Clonitazene.

(12) Dextromoramide.

(13) Diampromide.

(14) Diethylthiambutene.

(15) Difenoxin.

(16) Dimenoxadol.

(17) Dimepheptanol.

(18) Dimethylthiambutene.

(19) Dioxaphetyl butyrate.

(20) Dipipanone.

(21) Ethylmethylthiambutene.

(22) Etonitazene.

(23) Etoxeridine.

(24) Furethidine.

(25) Hydroxypethidine.

(26) Ketobemidone.

(27) Levomoramide.

(28) Levophenacylmorphan.

(29) Morpheridine.

(30) Noracymethadol.

(31) Norlevorphanol.

(32) Normethadone.

(33) Norpipanone.

(34) Phenadoxone.

(35) Phenampromide.

(36) Phenomorphan.

(37) Phenoperidine.

(38) Piritramide.

(39) Proheptazine.

(40) Properidine.

(41) Propiram.

(42) Racemoramide.

(43) Tilidine.

(44) Trimeperidine.

(45) Any substance which contains any quantity of acetylfentanyl (N-[1-phenethyl-4-piperidinyl] acetanilide) or a derivative thereof.

(46) Any substance which contains any quantity of the thiophene analog of acetylfentanyl (N-[1-[2-(2-thienyl)ethyl]-4-piperidinyl] acetanilide) or a derivative thereof.

(47) 1-Methyl-4-Phenyl-4-Propionoxypiperidine (MPPP).

(48) 1-(2-Phenethyl)-4-Phenyl-4-Acetyloxypiperidine (PEPAP).

(c) Opium derivatives. Unless specifically excepted or unless listed in another schedule, any of the following opium derivatives, its salts, isomers, and salts of isomers whenever the existence of those salts, isomers, and salts of isomers is possible within the specific chemical designation:

(1) Acetorphine.

(2) Acetyldihydrocodeine.

(3) Benzylmorphine.

(4) Codeine methylbromide.

(5) Codeine-N-Oxide.

(6) Cyprenorphine.

(7) Desomorphine.

(8) Dihydromorphine.

(9) Drotebanol.

(10) Etorphine (except hydrochloride salt).

(11) Heroin.

(12) Hydromorphinol.

(13) Methyldesorphine.

(14) Methyldihydromorphine.

(15) Morphine methylbromide.

(16) Morphine methylsulfonate.

(17) Morphine-N-Oxide.

(18) Myrophine.

(19) Nicocodeine.

(20) Nicomorphine.

(21) Normorphine.

(22) Pholcodine.

(23) Thebacon.

(d) Hallucinogenic substances. Unless specifically excepted or unless listed in another schedule, any material, compound, mixture, or preparation, which contains any quantity of the following hallucinogenic substances, or which contains any of its salts, isomers, and salts of isomers whenever the existence of those salts, isomers, and salts of isomers is possible within the specific chemical designation (for purposes of this subdivision only, the term "isomer" includes the optical, position, and geometric isomers):

(1) 4-bromo-2,5-dimethoxy-amphetamine—Some trade or other names: 4-bromo-2,5-dimethoxy-alphamethylphenethylamine; 4-bromo-2,5-DMA.

(2) 2,5-dimethoxyamphetamine—Some trade or other names: 2,5-dimethoxy-alpha-methylphenethylamine; 2,5-DMA.

(3) 4-methoxyamphetamine—Some trade or other names: 4-methoxy-alpha-methylphenethylamine, paramethoxyamphetamine, PMA.

(4) 5-methoxy-3,4-methylenedioxy-amphetamine.

(5) 4-methyl-2,5-dimethoxy-amphetamine—Some trade or other names: 4-methyl-2,5-dimethoxy-alphamethylphenethylamine; "DOM"; and "STP."

(6) 3,4-methylenedioxy amphetamine.

(7) 3,4,5-trimethoxy amphetamine.

(8) Bufotenine—Some trade or other names: 3-(beta-dimethylaminoethyl)-5-hydroxyindole; 3-(2-dimethylaminoethyl)-5 indolol; N,N-dimethylserolonin, 5-hydroxy-N,N-dimethyltryptamine; mappine.

(9) Diethyltryptamine—Some trade or other names: N,N-Diethyltryptamine; DET.

(10) Dimethyltryptamine—Some trade or other names: DMT.

(11) Ibogaine—Some trade or other names: 7-Ethyl-6,6beta, 7,8,9,10,12,13-octahydro-2-methoxy-6,9-methano-5H-pyrido [1',2':1,2] azepino [5,4-b] indole; Tabernantheiboga.

(12) Lysergic acid diethylamide.

(13) Cannabis.

(14) Mescaline.

(15) Peyote—Meaning all parts of the plant presently classified botanically as Lophophora williamsii Lemaire, whether growing or not, the seeds thereof, any extract from any part of the plant, and every compound, manufacture, salts, derivative, mixture, or preparation of the plant, its seeds or extracts (interprets 21 U.S.C. Sec. 812(c), Schedule 1(c)(12)).

(16) N-ethyl-3-piperidyl benzilate.

(17) N-methyl-3-piperidyl benzilate.

(18) Psilocybin.

(19) Psilocyn.

(20) Tetrahydrocannabinols. Synthetic equivalents of the substances contained in the plant, or in the resinous extractives of Cannabis, sp. and/or synthetic substances, derivatives, and their isomers with similar chemical structure and pharmacological activity such as the following: delta 1 cis or trans tetrahydrocannabinol, and their optical isomers; delta 6 cis or trans tetrahydrocannabinol, and their optical isomers; delta 3,4 cis or trans tetrahydrocannabinol, and its optical isomers.

Because nomenclature of these substances is not internationally standardized, compounds of these structures, regardless of numerical designation of atomic positions covered.

(21) Ethylamine analog of phencyclidine—Some trade or other names: N-ethyl-1-phenylcyclohexylamine, (1-phenylcyclohexyl) ethylamine, N-(1-phenylcyclohexyl) ethylamine, cyclohexamine, PCE.

(22) Pyrrolidine analog of phencyclidine—Some trade or other names: 1-(1-phenylcyclohexyl)-pyrrolidine, PCP, PHP.

(23) Thiophene analog of phencyclidine—Some trade or other names: 1-[1-(2 thienyl)-cyclohexyl]-piperidine, 2-thienyl analog of phencyclidine, TPCP, TCP.

(e) Depressants. Unless specifically excepted or unless listed in another schedule, any material, compound, mixture, or preparation which contains any quantity of the following substances having a depressant effect on the central nervous system, including its salts, isomers, and salts of isomers whenever the existence of those salts, isomers, and salts of isomers is possible within the specific chemical designation:

(1) Mecloqualone.

(2) Methaqualone.

(3) Gamma hydroxybutyric acid (also known by other names such as GHB; gamma hydroxy butyrate; 4-hydroxybutyrate; 4-hydroxybutanoic acid; sodium oxybate; sodium oxybutyrate), including its immediate precursors, isomers, esters, ethers, salts, and salts of isomers, esters, and ethers, including, but not limited to, gammabutyrolactone, for which an application has not been approved under Section 505 of the Federal Food, Drug, and Cosmetic Act (21 U.S.C. Sec. 355).

(f) Unless specifically excepted or unless listed in another schedule, any material, compound, mixture, or preparation which contains any quantity of the following substances having a stimulant effect on the central nervous system, including its isomers:

> (1) Cocaine base.

> (2) Fenethylline, including its salts.

> (3) N-Ethylamphetamine, including its salts.

Health and Safety Code § 11357

(Amended by AB 133, Effective September 16, 2017.)

(a) Except as authorized by law, possession of not more than 28.5 grams of cannabis, or not more than eight grams of concentrated cannabis, or both, shall be punished or adjudicated as follows:

> (1) Persons under 18 years of age are guilty of an infraction and shall be required to:

>> (A) Upon a finding that a first offense has been committed, complete four hours of drug education or counseling and up to 10 hours of community service over a period not to exceed 60 days.

>> (B) Upon a finding that a second offense or subsequent offense has been committed, complete six hours of drug education or counseling and up to 20 hours of community service over a period not to exceed 90 days.

> (2) Persons at least 18 years of age but less than 21 years of age are guilty of an infraction and punishable by a fine of not more than one hundred dollars ($100).

(b) Except as authorized by law, possession of more than 28.5 grams of cannabis, or more than eight grams of concentrated cannabis, shall be punished as follows:

> (1) Persons under 18 years of age who possess more than 28.5 grams of cannabis or more than eight grams of concentrated cannabis, or both, are guilty of an infraction and shall be required to:

>> (A) Upon a finding that a first offense has been committed,

complete eight hours of drug education or counseling and up to 40 hours of community service over a period not to exceed 90 days.

(B) Upon a finding that a second or subsequent offense has been committed, complete 10 hours of drug education or counseling and up to 60 hours of community service over a period not to exceed 120 days.

(2) Persons 18 years of age or older who possess more than 28.5 grams of cannabis, or more than eight grams of concentrated cannabis, or both, shall be punished by imprisonment in a county jail for a period of not more than six months or by a fine of not more than five hundred dollars ($500), or by both that fine and imprisonment.

(c) Except as authorized by law, a person 18 years of age or older who possesses not more than 28.5 grams of cannabis, or not more than eight grams of concentrated cannabis, upon the grounds of, or within, any school providing instruction in kindergarten or any of grades 1 to 12, inclusive, during hours the school is open for classes or school-related programs is guilty of a misdemeanor and shall be punished as follows:

(1) A fine of not more than two hundred fifty dollars ($250), upon a finding that a first offense has been committed.

(2) A fine of not more than five hundred dollars ($500), or by imprisonment in a county jail for a period of not more than 10 days, or both, upon a finding that a second or subsequent offense has been committed.

(d) Except as authorized by law, a person under 18 years of age who possesses not more than 28.5 grams of cannabis, or not more than eight grams of concentrated cannabis, upon the grounds of, or within, any school providing instruction in kindergarten or any of grades 1 to 12, inclusive, during hours the school is open for classes or school-related programs is guilty of an infraction and shall be punished in the same manner provided in paragraph (1) of subdivision (b).

Health and Safety Code § 11357.5

(Amended by Statute, Effective September 25, 2016.)

(a) Every person who sells, dispenses, distributes, furnishes, administers, or gives, or offers to sell, dispense, distribute, furnish, administer, or give, or possesses for sale any synthetic cannabinoid compound, or any synthetic cannabinoid derivative, to any person, is guilty of a misdemeanor, punishable by imprisonment in a county jail not to exceed six months, or by a fine not to exceed one thousand dollars ($1,000), or by both that fine and imprisonment.

(b) Every person who uses or possesses any synthetic cannabinoid compound, or any synthetic cannabinoid derivative, is guilty of a public offense, punishable as follows:

(1) A first offense is an infraction punishable by a fine not exceeding two hundred fifty dollars ($250).

(2) A second offense is an infraction punishable by a fine not exceeding two hundred fifty dollars ($250) or a misdemeanor punishable by imprisonment in a county jail not exceeding six months, a fine not exceeding five hundred dollars ($500), or by both that fine and imprisonment.

(3) A third or subsequent offense is a misdemeanor punishable by imprisonment in a county jail not exceeding six months, or by a fine not exceeding one thousand dollars ($1,000), or by both that fine and imprisonment.

(c) As used in this section, the term "synthetic cannabinoid compound" refers to any of the following substances or an analog of any of the following substances:

(1) Adamantoylindoles or adamantoylindazoles, which includes adamantyl carboxamide indoles and adamantyl carboxamide indazoles, or any compound structurally derived from 3-(1-adamantoyl)indole, 3-(1-adamantoyl)indazole, 3-(2-adamantoyl)indole, N-(1-adamantyl)-1H-indole-3-carboxamide, or N-(1-adamantyl)-1H-indazole-3-carboxamide by substitution at the nitrogen atom of the indole or indazole ring with alkyl, haloalkyl, alkenyl, cyanoalkyl, hydroxyalkyl, cycloalkylmethyl, cycloalkylethyl, 1-(N-methyl-2-piperidinyl)methyl, 2-(4-morpholinyl)ethyl, or 1-(N-methyl-2-pyrrolidinyl)methyl, 1-(N-methyl-3-morpholinyl)methyl, or (tetrahydropyran-4-yl)methyl group, whether or not further substituted in the indole or indazole ring to any extent and whether or not substituted in the adamantyl ring to any extent, including, but not limited to, 2NE1, 5F-AKB-48, AB-001, AKB-48, AM-1248, JWH-018 adamantyl carboxamide, STS-135.

(2) Benzoylindoles, which includes any compound structurally derived from a 3-(benzoyl)indole structure with substitution at the nitrogen atom of the indole ring with alkyl, haloalkyl, cyanoalkyl, hydroxyalkyl, alkenyl, cycloalkylmethyl, cycloalkylethyl, 1-(N-methyl-2-piperidinyl) methyl, 2-(4-morpholinyl)ethyl, or 1-(N-methyl-2-pyrrolidinyl)methyl, 1-(N-methyl-3-morpholinyl)methyl, or (tetrahydropyran-4-yl)methyl group, whether or not further substituted in the indole ring to any extent and whether or not substituted in the phenyl ring to any extent, including, but not limited to, AM-630, AM-661, AM-679, AM-694, AM-1241, AM-2233, RCS-4, WIN 48,098 (Pravadoline).

(3) Cyclohexylphenols, which includes any compound structurally derived from 2-(3-hydroxycyclohexyl)phenol by substitution at the 5-position of the phenolic ring by alkyl, haloalkyl, cyanoalkyl, hydroxyalkyl, alkenyl, cycloalkylmethyl, cycloalkylethyl, 1-(N-methyl-2-piperidinyl)methyl, 2-(4-morpholinyl)ethyl, or 1-(N-methyl-2-pyrrolidinyl)methyl, 1-(N-methyl-3-morpholinyl)methyl, or tetrahydropyran-4-yl)methyl group, whether or not further substituted in the cyclohexyl ring to any extent, including, but not limited to, CP 47,497, CP 55,490, CP 55,940, CP 56,667, cannabicyclohexanol.

(4) Cyclopropanoylindoles, which includes any compound structurally derived from 3-(cyclopropylmethanoyl)indole, 3-(cyclopropylmethanone)indole, 3-(cyclobutylmethanone)indole or 3-(cyclopentylmethanone)indole by substitution at the nitrogen atom of the indole ring, whether or not further substituted in the indole ring to any extent, whether or not substituted on the cyclopropyl, cyclobutyl, or cyclopentyl rings to any extent.

(5) Naphthoylindoles, which includes any compound structurally derived from 3-(1-naphthoyl)indole or 1H-indol-3-yl-(1-naphthyl) methane by substitution at the nitrogen atom of the indole ring by alkyl, haloalkyl, cyanoalkyl, hydroxyalkyl, alkenyl, cycloalkylmethyl, cycloalkylethyl, 1-(N-methyl-2-piperidinyl)methyl, 2-(4-morpholinyl) ethyl group, 1-(N-methyl-2-pyrrolidinyl)methyl, 1-(N-methyl-3-morpholinyl)methyl, or (tetrahydropyran-4-yl)methyl group, whether or not further substituted in the naphthyl ring to any extent, including, but not limited to, AM-678, AM-1220, AM-1221, AM-1235, AM-2201, AM-2232, EAM-2201, JWH-004, JWH-007, JWH-009, JWH-011, JWH-015, JWH-016, JWH-018, JWH-019, JWH-020, JWH-022,

JWH-046, JWH-047, JWH-048, JWH-049, JWH-050, JWH-070, JWH-071, JWH-072, JWH-073, JWH-076, JWH-079, JWH-080, JWH-081, JWH-082, JWH-094, JWH-096, JWH-098, JWH-116, JWH-120, JWH-122, JWH-148, JWH-149, JWH-164, JWH-166, JWH-180, JWH-181, JWH-182, JWH-189, JWH-193, JWH-198, JWH-200, JWH-210, JWH-211, JWH-212, JWH-213, JWH-234, JWH-235, JWH-236, JWH-239, JWH-240, JWH-241, JWH-242, JWH-258, JWH-262, JWH-386, JWH-387, JWH-394, JWH-395, JWH-397, JWH-398, JWH-399, JWH-400, JWH-412, JWH-413, JWH-414, JWH-415, JWH-424, MAM-2201, WIN 55,212.

(6) Naphthoylnaphthalenes, which includes any compound structurally derived from naphthalene-1-yl-(naphthalene-1-yl) methanone with substitutions on either of the naphthalene rings to any extent, including, but not limited to, CB-13.

(7) Naphthoylpyrroles, which includes any compound structurally derived from 3-(1-naphthoyl)pyrrole by substitution at the nitrogen atom of the pyrrole ring by alkyl, haloalkyl, cyanoalkyl, hydroxyalkyl, alkenyl, cycloalkylmethyl, cycloalkylethyl, 1-(N-methyl-2-piperidinyl) methyl, 2-(4-morpholinyl)ethyl, or 1-N-methyl-2-pyrrolidinyl)methyl, 1-(N-methyl-3-morpholinyl)methyl, or (tetrahydropyran-4-yl)methyl group, whether or not further substituted in the pyrrole ring to any extent and whether or not substituted in the naphthyl ring to any extent, including, but not limited to, JWH-030, JWH-031, JWH-145, JWH-146, JWH-147, JWH-150, JWH-156, JWH-243, JWH-244, JWH-245, JWH-246, JWH-292, JWH-293, JWH-307, JWH-308, JWH-309, JWH-346, JWH-348, JWH-363, JWH-364, JWH-365, JWH-367, JWH-368, JWH-369, JWH-370, JWH-371, JWH-373, JWH-392.

(8) Naphthylmethylindenes, which includes any compound containing a naphthylideneindene structure or which is structurally derived from 1-(1-naphthylmethyl)indene with substitution at the 3-position of the indene ring by alkyl, haloalkyl, cyanoalkyl, hydroxyalkyl, alkenyl, cycloalkylmethyl, cycloalkylethyl, 1-(N-methyl-2-piperidinyl) methyl, 2-(4-morpholinyl)ethyl, or 1-(N-methyl-2-pyrrolidinyl)methyl, 1-(N-methyl-3-morpholinyl)methyl, or (tetrahydropyran-4-yl)methyl group, whether or not further substituted in the indene ring to any extent and whether or not substituted in the naphthyl ring to any extent, including, but not limited to, JWH-171, JWH-176, JWH-220.

(9) Naphthylmethylindoles, which includes any compound structurally

derived from an H-indol-3-yl-(1-naphthyl) methane by substitution at the nitrogen atom of the indole ring by alkyl, haloalkyl, cyanoalkyl, hydroxyalkyl, alkenyl, cycloalkylmethyl, cycloalkylethyl, 1-(N-methyl-2-piperidinyl)methyl, 2-(4-morpholinyl)ethyl, or 1-(N-methyl-2-pyrrolidinyl)methyl, 1-(N-methyl-3-morpholinyl)methyl, or (tetrahydropyran-4-yl)methyl group, whether or not further substituted in the indole ring to any extent and whether or not substituted in the naphthyl ring to any extent, including, but not limited to, JWH-175, JWH-184, JWH-185, JWH-192, JWH-194, JWH-195, JWH-196, JWH-197, JWH-199.

(10) Phenylacetylindoles, which includes any compound structurally derived from 3-phenylacetylindole by substitution at the nitrogen atom of the indole ring with alkyl, haloalkyl, cyanoalkyl, hydroxyalkyl, alkenyl, cycloalkylmethyl, cycloalkylethyl, 1-(N-methyl-2-piperidinyl) methyl, 2-(4-morpholinyl)ethyl, or 1-N-methyl-2-pyrrolidinyl)methyl, 1-(N-methyl-3-morpholinyl)methyl, or (tetrahydropyran-4-yl)methyl group, whether or not further substituted in the indole ring to any extent and whether or not substituted in the phenyl ring to any extent, including, but not limited to, cannabipiperidiethanone, JWH-167, JWH-201, JWH-202, JWH-203, JWH-204, JWH-205, JWH-206, JWH-207, JWH-208, JWH-209, JWH-237, JWH-248, JWH-249, JWH-250, JWH-251, JWH-253, JWH-302, JWH-303, JWH-304, JWH-305, JWH-306, JWH-311, JWH-312, JWH-313, JWH-314, JWH-315, JWH-316, RCS-8.

(11) Quinolinylindolecarboxylates, which includes any compound structurally derived from quinolin-8-yl-1H-indole-3-carboxylate by substitution at the nitrogen atom of the indole ring with alkyl, haloalkyl, benzyl, halobenzyl, alkenyl, haloalkenyl, alkoxy, cyanoalkyl, hydroxyalkyl, cycloalkylmethyl, cycloalkylethyl, (N-methylpiperidin-2-yl)alkyl, (4-tetrahydropyran)alkyl, or 2-(4-morpholinyl)alkyl, whether or not further substituted in the indole ring to any extent, whether or not substituted in the quinoline ring to any extent, including, but not limited to, BB-22, 5-Fluoro-PB-22, PB-22.

(12) Tetramethylcyclopropanoylindoles, which includes any compound structurally derived from 3-tetramethylcyclopropanoylindole, 3-(1-tetramethylcyclopropyl)indole, 3-(2,2,3,3-tetramethylcyclopropyl)indole or 3-(2,2,3,3-tetramethylcyclopropylcarbonyl)indole with substitution at the nitrogen atom of the indole ring by an alkyl, haloalkyl,

cyanoalkyl, hydroxyalkyl, alkenyl, cycloalkylmethyl, cycloalkylethyl, 1-(N-methyl-2-piperidinyl)methyl, 2-(4-morpholinyl)ethyl, 1-(N-methyl-2-pyrrolidinyl)methyl, 1-(N-methyl-3-morpholinyl)methyl, or (tetrahydropyran-4-yl)methyl group whether or not further substituted in the indole ring to any extent and whether or not substituted in the tetramethylcyclopropanoyl ring to any extent, including, but not limited to, 5-bromo-UR-144, 5-chloro-UR-144, 5-fluoro-UR-144, A-796,260, A-834,735, AB-034, UR-144, XLR11.

(13) Tetramethylcyclopropane-thiazole carboxamides, which includes any compound structurally derived from 2,2,3,3-tetramethyl-N-(thiazol-2-ylidene)cyclopropanecarboxamide by substitution at the nitrogen atom of the thiazole ring by alkyl, haloalkyl, benzyl, halobenzyl, alkenyl, haloalkenyl, alkoxy, cyanoalkyl, hydroxyalkyl, cycloalkylmethyl, cycloalkylethyl, (N-methylpiperidin-2-yl)alkyl, (4-tetrahydropyran)alkyl, or 2-(4-morpholinyl)alkyl, whether or not further substituted in the thiazole ring to any extent, whether or not substituted in the tetramethylcyclopropyl ring to any extent, including, but not limited to, A-836,339.

(14) Unclassified synthetic cannabinoids, which includes all of the following:

(A) AM-087, (6aR,10aR)-3-(2-methyl-6-bromohex-2-yl)-6,6,9-t rimethyl-6a,7,10,10a-tetrahydrobenzo[c]chromen-1-ol.

(B) AM-356, methanandamide, including (5Z,8Z,11Z,14Z)-[(1R)-2-hydroxy-1-methylethyl]icosa-5,8,11,14-tetraenamide and arachidonyl-1'-hydroxy-2'-propylamide.

(C) AM-411, (6aR,10aR)-3-(1-adamantyl)-6,6,9-trimethyl-6 a,7,10,10a-tetrahydrobenzo[c]chromen-1-ol.

(D) AM-855, (4aR,12bR)-8-hexyl-2,5,5-trimethyl-1,4,4a,8,9,10,11,12b-octahydronaphtho[3,2-c]isochromen-12-ol.

(E) AM-905, (6aR,9R,10aR)-3-[(E)-hept-1-enyl]-9-(hydroxymethyl)-6,6-dimethyl-6a,7,8,9,10,10a-hexahydrobenzo[c]chromen-1-ol.

(F) AM-906, (6aR,9R,10aR)-3-[(Z)-hept-1-enyl]-9-(hydroxymethyl)-6,6-dimethyl-6a,7,8,9,10,10a-hexahydrobenzo[c]chromen-1-ol.

(G) AM-2389, (6aR,9R,10aR)-3-(1-hexyl-cyclobut-1-yl)-6 a,7,8,9,10,10a-hexahydro-6,6-dimethyl-6H-dibenzo[b,d]pyran-1 ,9 diol.

(H) BAY 38-7271, (-)-(R)-3-(2-Hydroxymethylindanyl-4-o xy) phenyl-4,4,4-trifluorobutyl-1-sulfonate.

(I) CP 50,556-1, Levonantradol, including 9-hydroxy-6-methyl-3 -[5-phenylpentan-2-yl]oxy-5,6,6a,7,8,9,10,10a-octahydrophenant hridin-1-yl]acetate; [(6S,6aR,9R, 10aR)-9-hydroxy-6-methyl-3-[(2R)-5-phenylpentan-2-yl] oxy-5,6,6a,7,8,9,10,10a-octahydrophenanthridin-1-yl] acetate; and [9-hydroxy-6-methyl-3-[5-phenylpentan-2-yl]oxy-5,6,6a,7,8,9,10,10a-octahydrophenanthridin-1-yl]acetate.

(J) HU-210, including (6aR,10aR)-9-(hydroxymethyl)-6,6-d imethyl-3-(2-methyloctan-2-yl)-6a,7,10,10a-tetrahydrobenzo[c] chromen-1-ol; [(6aR,10aR)-9-(hydroxymethyl)-6,6-dimethyl-3-(2-methyl octan-2-yl)-6a,7,10,10a-tetrahydrobenzo[c]chromen-1-o l and 1,1-Dimethylheptyl-11-hydroxytetrahydrocannabinol.

(K) HU-211, Dexanabinol, including (6aS, 10aS)-9-(hydroxy methyl)-6,6-dimethyl-3-(2-methyloctan-2-yl)-6a,7,10,10a-tetrahydrobenzo[c]chromen-1-ol and (6aS, 10aS)-9-(hydroxy methyl)-6,6-dimethyl- 3-(2-methyloctan-2-yl)-6a,7,10,10a-tetrahydrobenzo[c]chromen-1-ol.

(L) HU-243, 3-dimethylheptyl-11-hydroxyhexahydrocannabinol.

(M) HU-308, [(91R,2R,5R)-2-[2,6-dimethoxy-4-(2-methyloctan-2 - yl)phenyl]-7,7-dimethyl-4-bicyclo[3.1.1]hept-3-enyl]methanol.

(N) HU-331, 3-hydroxy-2-[(1R,6R)-3-methyl-6-(1-m ethylethenyl)-2-cyclohexen-1-yl]-5-pentyl-2,5-cyclohexadiene-1 ,4-dione.

(O) HU-336, (6aR,10aR)-6,6,9-trimethyl-3-pentyl-6a,7,10,10a-tetrahydro-1H-benzo[c]chromene-1,4(6H)-dione.

(P) JTE-907, N-(benzol[1,3]dioxol-5-ylmethyl)-7-methoxy-2-o xo-8-pentyloxy-1,2-dihydroquinoline-3-carboxamide.

(Q) JWH-051, ((6aR,10aR)-6,6-dimethyl-3-(2-methyloctan-2-y l)-6a,7,10,10a-tetrahydrobenzo[c]chromen-9-yl)methanol.

(R) JWH-057 (6aR,10aR)-3-(1,1-dimethylheptyl)-6a,7,10,10a-t etrahydro-6,6,9-trimethyl-6H-Dibenzo[b,d]pyran.

(S) JWH-133 (6aR,10aR)-3-(1,1-Dimethylbutyl)-6a,7,10,10a-t etrahydro -6,6,9-trimethyl-6H-dibenzo[b,d]pyran.

(T) JWH-359, (6aR,10aR)- 1-methoxy- 6,6,9-trimethyl- 3-[(2R)-1 ,1,2-trimethylbutyl]- 6a,7,10,10a-tetrahydrobenzo[c]chromene.

(U) URB-597 [3-(3-carbamoylphenyl)phenyl]-N-cyclohexylcarb amate.

(V) URB-602 [1,1'-Biphenyl]-3-yl-carbamic acid, cyclohexyl ester; OR cyclohexyl [1,1'-biphenyl]-3-ylcarbamate.

(W) URB-754 6-methyl-2-[(4-methylphenyl)amino]-4H-3,1-b enzoxazin-4-one.

(X) URB-937 3'-carbamoyl-6-hydroxy-[1,1'-biphenyl]-3-yl cyclohexylcarbamate.

(Y) WIN 55,212-2, including (R)-(+)-[2,3-dihydro-5-methyl-3 -(4-morpholinylmethyl)pyrrolo[1,2,3-de]-1,4-benzoxazin-6- yl]-1 -napthalenylmethanone and [2,3-Dihydro-5-methyl-3-(4- morpholinylmethyl)pyrrolo[(1,2,3-de)-1,4-benzoxazin-6-yl]-1- napthalenylmethanone.

(d) The substances or analogs of substances identified in subdivision (c) may be lawfully obtained and used for bona fide research, instruction, or analysis if that possession and use does not violate federal law.

(e) As used in this section, "synthetic cannabinoid compound" does not include either of the following:

(1) Any substance for which there is an approved new drug application, as defined in Section 505 of the federal Food, Drug, and Cosmetic Act (21 U.S.C. Sec. 355) or which is generally recognized as safe and effective for use pursuant to Section 501, 502, and 503 of the federal Food, Drug, and Cosmetic Act and Title 21 of the Code of Federal Regulations.

(2) With respect to a particular person, any substance for which an exemption is in effect for investigational use for that person pursuant to Section 505 of the federal Food, Drug, and Cosmetic Act (21 U.S.C.

Sec. 355), to the extent that the conduct with respect to that substance is pursuant to the exemption.

Health and Safety Code § 11358

(MAUCRSA, Effective June 27, 2017.)

Every person who plants, cultivates, harvests, dries, or processes cannabis plants, or any part thereof, except as otherwise provided by law, shall be punished as follows:

(a) Every person under the age of 18 who plants, cultivates, harvests, dries, or processes any cannabis plants shall be punished in the same manner provided in paragraph (1) of subdivision (b) of section 11357.

(b) Every person at least 18 years of age but less than 21 years of age who plants, cultivates, harvests, dries, or processes not more than six living cannabis plants shall be guilty of an infraction and a fine of not more than one hundred dollars ($100).

(c) Every person 18 years of age or over who plants, cultivates, harvests, dries, or processes more than six living cannabis plants shall be punished by imprisonment in a county jail for a period of not more than six months or by a fine of not more than five hundred dollars ($500), or by both such fine and imprisonment.

(d) Notwithstanding subdivision (c), a person 18 years of age or over who plants, cultivates, harvests, dries, or processes more than six living cannabis plants, or any part thereof, except as otherwise provided by law, may be punished by imprisonment pursuant to subdivision (h) of Section 1170 of the Penal Code if any of the following conditions exist:

(1) the person has one or more prior convictions for an offense specified in clause (iv) of subparagraph (C) of paragraph (2) of subdivision (e) of Section 667 of the Penal Code or for an offense requiring registration pursuant to subdivision (c) of Section 290 of the Penal Code.

(2) the person has two or more prior convictions under subdivision (c).

(3) the offense resulted in any of the following:

(A) Violation of Section 1052 of the Water Code relating to illegal diversion of water.

(B) Violation of Section 13260, 13264, 13272, or 13387 of the Water Code relating to discharge of water.

(C) Violation of Section 5650 or Section 5652 of the Fish and Game Code relating to waters of the state.

(D) Violation of Section 1602 of the Fish and Game Code relating to rivers, streams and lakes.

(E) Violation of Section 374.8 of the Penal Code relating to hazardous substances or Sections 25189.5, 25189.6, or 25189.7 of the Health and Safety Code relating to hazardous waste.

(F) Violation of Section 2080 of the Fish and Game Code relating to endangered and threatened species or Section 3513 of the Fish and Game Code relating to the Migratory Bird Treaty Act, or Section 2000 of the Fish and Game Code relating to the unlawful taking of fish and wildlife.

(G) Intentionally or with gross negligence causing substantial environmental harm to public lands or other public resources.

Health and Safety Code § 11359

(MAUCRSA, Effective June 27, 2017.)

Every person who possesses for sale any cannabis, except as otherwise provided by law, shall be punished as follows:

(a) Every person under the age of 18 who possesses cannabis for sale shall be punished in the same manner provided in paragraph (1) of subdivision (b) of Section 11357.

(b) Every person 18 years of age or over who possesses cannabis for sale shall be punished by imprisonment in a county jail for a period of not more than six months or by a fine of not more than five hundred dollars ($500), or by both such fine and imprisonment.

(c) Notwithstanding subdivision (b), a person 18 years of age or over who possesses cannabis for sale may be punished by imprisonment pursuant to subdivision (h) of Section 1170 of the Penal Code if:

(1) the person has one or more prior convictions for an offense specified in clause (iv) of subparagraph (C) of paragraph (2) of subdivision (e) of

Section 667 of the Penal Code or for an offense requiring registration pursuant to subdivision (c) of Section 290 of the Penal Code;

(2) the person has two or more prior convictions under subdivision (b); or

(3) the offense occurred in connection with the knowing sale or attempted sale of cannabis to a person under the age of 18 years.

(d) Notwithstanding subdivision (b), a person 21 years of age or over who possesses cannabis for sale may be punished by imprisonment pursuant to subdivision (h) of Section 1170 of the Penal Code if the offense involves knowingly hiring, employing, or using a person 20 years of age or younger in unlawfully cultivating, transporting, carrying, selling, offering to sell, giving away, preparing for sale, or peddling any cannabis.

Health and Safety Code § 11360

(MAUCRSA, Effective June 27, 2017.)

(a) Except as otherwise provided by this section or as authorized by law, every person who transports, imports into this state, sells, furnishes, administers, or gives away, or offers to transport, import into this state, sell, furnish, administer, or give away, or attempts to import into this state or transport any cannabis shall be punished as follows:

(1) Persons under the age of 18 years shall be punished in the same manner as provided in paragraph (1) of subdivision (b) of section 11357.

(2) Persons 18 years of age or over shall be punished by imprisonment in a county jail for a period of not more than six months or by a fine of not more than five hundred dollars ($500), or by both such fine and imprisonment.

(3) Notwithstanding paragraph (2), a person 18 years of age or over may be punished by imprisonment pursuant to subdivision (h) of Section 1170 of the Penal Code for a period two, three, or four years if:

(A) The person has one or more prior convictions for an offense specified in clause (iv) of subparagraph (C) of paragraph (2) of subdivision (e) of Section 667 of the Penal Code or for an offense requiring registration pursuant to subdivision (c) of Section 290 of the Penal Code;

(B) The person has two or more prior convictions under paragraph (2);

(C) The offense involved the knowing sale, attempted sale, or the knowing offer to sell, furnish, administer or give away cannabis to a person under the age of 18 years; or

(D) The offense involved the import, offer to import; or attempted import into this state, or the transport for sale, offer to transport for sale, or attempted transport for sale out of this state, of more than 28.5 grams of cannabis or more than four grams of concentrated cannabis.

(b) Except as authorized by law, every person who gives away, offers to give away, transports, offers to transport, or attempts to transport not more than 28.5 grams of cannabis, other than concentrated cannabis, is guilty of an infraction and shall be punished by a fine of not more than one hundred dollars ($100). In any case in which a person is arrested for a violation of this subdivision and does not demand to be taken before a magistrate, such person shall be released by the arresting officer upon presentation of satisfactory evidence of identity and giving his or her written promise to appear in court, as provided in Section 853.6 of the Penal Code, and shall not be subjected to booking.

(c) For purposes of this section, "transport" means to transport for sale.

(d) This section does not preclude or limit prosecution for any aiding and abetting or conspiracy offenses.

Health & Safety Code § 11361

(MAUCRSA, Effective June 27, 2017.)

(a) A person 18 years of age or over who hires, employs, or uses a minor in unlawfully transporting, carrying, selling, giving away, preparing for sale, or peddling any cannabis, who unlawfully sells, or offers to sell, any cannabis to a minor, or who furnishes, administers, or gives, or offers to furnish, administer, or give any cannabis to a minor under 14 years of age, or who induces a minor to use cannabis in violation of law shall be punished by imprisonment in the state prison for a period of three, five, or seven years.

(b) A person 18 years of age or over who furnishes, administers, or gives, or offers to furnish, administer, or give, any cannabis to a minor 14 years of age or older in violation of law shall be punished by imprisonment in the state prison for a period of three, four, or five years.

Health and Safety Code § 11361.1

(MAUCRSA, Effective June 27, 2017.)

(a) The drug education and counseling requirements under sections 11357, 11358, 11359, and 11360 shall be:

> (1) Mandatory, unless the court finds that such drug education or counseling is unnecessary for the person, or that a drug education or counseling program is unavailable;

> (2) Free to participants, and shall consist of at least four hours of group discussion or instruction based on science and evidence-based principles and practices specific to the use and abuse of cannabis and other controlled substances.

(b) For good cause, the court may grant an extension of time not to exceed 30 days for a person to complete the drug education and counseling required under sections 11357, 11358, 11359, and 11360.

Health and Safety Code § 11361.5

(MAUCRSA, Effective June 27, 2017.)

(a) Records of any court of this state, any public or private agency that provides services upon referral under Section 1000.2 of the Penal Code, or of any state agency pertaining to the arrest or conviction of any person for a violation of Section 11357 or subdivision (b) of Section 11360, or pertaining to the arrest or conviction of any person under the age of 18 for a violation of any provision of this article except Section 11357.5, shall not be kept beyond two years from the date of the conviction, or from the date of the arrest if there was no conviction, except with respect to a violation of subdivision (d) of Section 11357, or any other violation by a person under the age of 18 occurring upon the grounds of, or within, any school providing instruction in kindergarten or any of grades 1 to 12, inclusive, during hours the school is open for classes or school-related programs, the records shall be retained until the offender attains the age of 18 years at which time the records shall be destroyed as provided in this section. Any court or agency having custody of the records, including the statewide criminal databases, shall provide for the timely destruction of the records in accordance with subdivision (c), and those records shall also be purged from the statewide criminal databases. As used in this subdivision, "records pertaining to the arrest or conviction" shall include records of arrests resulting in the criminal proceeding and records relating to other offenses charged in the accusatory pleading, whether the defendant was acquitted or charges were dismissed. The two-year period beyond which records shall not be kept pursuant to this subdivision shall not apply to any person who is, at the time at which this subdivision would otherwise require record destruction, incarcerated for an offense subject to this subdivision. For such persons, the two-year period shall commence from the date the person is released from custody. The requirements of this subdivision do not apply to records of any conviction occurring prior to January 1, 1976, or records of any arrest not followed by a conviction occurring prior to that date, or records of any arrest for an offense specified in subdivision (c) of Section 1192.7, or subdivision (c) of Section 667.5 of the Penal Code.

(b) This subdivision applies only to records of convictions and arrests not followed by conviction occurring prior to January 1, 1976, for any of the following offenses:

(1) Any violation of Section 11357 or a statutory predecessor thereof.

(2) Unlawful possession of a device, contrivance, instrument, or paraphernalia used for unlawfully smoking cannabis, in violation of Section 11364, as it existed prior to January 1, 1976, or a statutory predecessor thereof.

(3) Unlawful visitation or presence in a room or place in which cannabis is being unlawfully smoked or used, in violation of Section 11365, as it existed prior to January 1, 1976, or a statutory predecessor thereof.

(4) Unlawfully using or being under the influence of cannabis, in violation of Section 11550, as it existed prior to January 1, 1976, or a statutory predecessor thereof.

Any person subject to an arrest or conviction for those offenses may apply to the Department of Justice for destruction of records pertaining to the arrest or conviction if two or more years have elapsed since the date of the conviction, or since the date of the arrest if not followed by a conviction. The application shall be submitted upon a form supplied by the Department of Justice and shall be accompanied by a fee, which shall be established by the department in an amount which will defray the cost of administering this subdivision and costs incurred by the state under subdivision (c), but which shall not exceed thirty-seven dollars and fifty cents ($37.50). The application form may be made available at every local police or sheriff's department and from the Department of Justice and may require that information which the department determines is necessary for purposes of identification.

The department may request, but not require, the applicant to include a self-administered fingerprint upon the application. If the department is unable to sufficiently identify the applicant for purposes of this subdivision without the fingerprint or without additional fingerprints, it shall so notify the applicant and shall request the applicant to submit any fingerprints which may be required to effect identification, including a complete set if necessary, or, alternatively, to abandon the application and request a refund of all or a portion of the fee submitted with the application, as provided in this section. If the applicant fails or refuses to submit fingerprints in accordance with the department's request within a reasonable time which shall be established by the department, or if the applicant requests a refund of the fee, the department shall promptly mail a refund to the applicant at the address specified in the application or at any other address which may be specified by the applicant. However, if the department has notified the applicant that election to abandon the application will result in forfeiture of a specified amount which is a portion of the fee, the department may retain a portion of the fee which the department determines will defray the actual costs of processing the application, provided the amount of the portion retained shall not exceed ten dollars ($10).

Upon receipt of a sufficient application, the Department of Justice shall destroy records of the department, if any, pertaining to the arrest or conviction in the manner prescribed by subdivision (c) and shall notify the Federal Bureau of Investigation, the law enforcement agency which arrested the applicant, and, if the applicant was convicted, the probation department which investigated the applicant and the Department of Motor Vehicles, of the application.

(c) Destruction of records of arrest or conviction pursuant to subdivision (a) or (b) shall be accomplished by permanent obliteration of all entries or notations upon the records pertaining to the arrest or conviction, and the record shall be prepared again so that it appears that the arrest or conviction never occurred. However, where (1) the only entries upon the record pertain to the arrest or conviction and (2) the record can be destroyed without necessarily effecting the destruction of other records, then the document constituting the record shall be physically destroyed.

(d) Notwithstanding subdivision (a) or (b), written transcriptions of oral testimony in court proceedings and published judicial appellate reports are not subject to this section. Additionally, no records shall be destroyed pursuant to subdivision (a) if the defendant or a codefendant has filed a civil action against the peace officers or law enforcement jurisdiction which made the arrest or instituted the prosecution and if the agency which is the custodian of those records has received a certified copy of the complaint in the civil action, until the civil action has finally been resolved. Immediately following the final resolution of the civil action, records subject to subdivision (a) shall be destroyed pursuant to subdivision (c) if more than two years have elapsed from the date of the conviction or arrest without conviction.

Health and Safety Code § 11361.7

(Added by Statute, Effective 1976.)

(a) Any record subject to destruction or permanent obliteration pursuant to Section 11361.5, or more than two years of age, or a record of a conviction for an offense specified in subdivision (a) or (b) of Section 11361.5 which became final more than two years previously, shall not be considered to be accurate, relevant, timely, or complete for any purposes by any agency or person. The provisions of this subdivision shall be applicable for purposes of the Privacy Act of 1974 (5 U.S.C. Section 552a) to the fullest extent permissible by law, whenever any information or record subject to destruction or permanent obliteration under Section 11361.5 was obtained by any state agency, local public agency, or any public or private agency that provides services upon referral under Section 1000.2 of the Penal Code, and is thereafter shared with or disseminated to any agency of the federal government.

(b) No public agency shall alter, amend, assess, condition, deny, limit, postpone, qualify, revoke, surcharge, or suspend any certificate, franchise, incident, interest, license, opportunity, permit, privilege, right, or title of any person because of an arrest or conviction for an offense specified in subdivision (a) or (b) of Section 11361.5, or because of the facts or events leading to such an arrest or conviction, on or after the date the records of such arrest or conviction are required to be destroyed by subdivision (a) of Section 11361.5, or two years from the date of such conviction or arrest without conviction with respect to arrests and convictions occurring prior to January 1, 1976. As used in this subdivision, "public agency" includes, but is not limited to, any state, county, city and county, city, public or constitutional corporation or entity, district, local or regional political subdivision, or any department, division, bureau, office, board, commission or other agency thereof.

(c) Any person arrested or convicted for an offense specified in subdivision (a) or (b) of Section 11361.5 may, two years from the date of such a conviction, or from the date of the arrest if there was no conviction, indicate in response to any question concerning his prior criminal record that he was not arrested or convicted for such offense.

(d) The provisions of this section shall be applicable without regard to whether destruction or obliteration of records has actually been implemented pursuant to Section 11361.5.

Health and Safety Code § 11361.8

(AUMA, Effective November 9, 2016.)

(a) A person currently serving a sentence for a conviction, whether by trial or by open or negotiated plea, who would not have been guilty of an offense or who would have been guilty of a lesser offense under the Control, Regulate and Tax Adult Use of Marijuana Act had that Act been in effect at the time of the offense may petition for a recall or dismissal of sentence before the trial court that entered the judgment of conviction in his or her case to request resentencing or dismissal in accordance with Sections 11357, 11358, 11359, 11360, 11362.1, 11362.2, 11362.3, and 11362. 4 as those sections have been amended or added by this Act.

(b) Upon receiving a petition under subdivision (a), the court shall presume the petitioner satisfies the criteria in subdivision (a) unless the party opposing the petition proves by clear and convincing evidence that the petitioner does not satisfy the criteria. If the petitioner satisfies the criteria in subdivision (a), the court shall grant the petition to recall the sentence or dismiss the sentence because it is legally invalid unless the court determines that granting the petition would pose an unreasonable risk of danger to public safety.

(1) In exercising its discretion, the court may consider, but shall not be

limited to evidence provided for in subdivision (b) of Section 1170.18 of the Penal Code.

(2) As used in this section, "unreasonable risk of danger to public safety" has the same meaning as provided in subdivision (c) of Section 1170.18 of the Penal Code.

(c) A person who is serving a sentence and resentenced pursuant to subdivision (b) shall be given credit for any time already served and shall be subject to supervision for one year following completion of his or her time in custody or shall be subject to whatever supervision time he or she would have otherwise been subject to after release, whichever is shorter, unless the court, in its discretion, as part of its resentencing order, releases the person from supervision. Such person is subject to parole supervision under Penal Code Section 3000.08 or post-release community supervision under subdivision (a) of Section 3451 of the Penal Code by the designated agency and the jurisdiction of the court in the county in which the offender is released or resides, or in which an alleged violation of supervision has occurred, for the purpose of hearing petitions to revoke supervision and impose a term of custody.

(d) Under no circumstances may resentencing under this section result in the imposition of a term longer than the original sentence, or the reinstatement of charges dismissed pursuant to a negotiated plea agreement.

(e) A person who has completed his or her sentence for a conviction under Sections 11357, 11358, 11359, and 11360, whether by trial or open or negotiated plea, who would not have been guilty of an offense or who would have been guilty of a lesser offense under the Control, Regulate and Tax Adult Use of Marijuana Act had that Act been in effect at the time of the offense, may file an application before the trial court that entered the judgment of conviction in his or her case to have the conviction dismissed and sealed because the prior conviction is now legally invalid or redesignated as a misdemeanor or infraction in accordance with Sections 11357, 11358, 11359, 11360, 11362.1, 11362.2, 11362.3, and 11362.4 as those sections have been amended or added by this Act.

(f) The court shall presume the petitioner satisfies the criteria in subdivision (e) unless the party opposing the application proves by clear and convincing evidence that the petitioner does not satisfy the criteria in subdivision (e). Once the applicant satisfies the criteria in subdivision (e), the court shall redesignate the conviction as a misdemeanor or infraction or dismiss and seal the conviction as legally invalid as now established under the Control, Regulate and Tax Adult Use of Marijuana Act.

(g) Unless requested by the applicant, no hearing is necessary to grant or deny an application filed under subdivision (e).

(h) Any felony conviction that is recalled and resentenced under subdivision (b) or designated as a misdemeanor or infraction under subdivision (f) shall be considered a misdemeanor or infraction for all purposes. Any misdemeanor conviction that is recalled and resentenced under subdivision (b) or designated as an infraction under subdivision (f) shall be considered an infraction for all purposes.

(i) If the court that originally sentenced the petitioner is not available, the presiding judge shall designate another judge to rule on the petition or application.

(j) Nothing in this section is intended to diminish or abrogate any rights or remedies otherwise available to the petitioner or applicant.

(k) Nothing in this and related sections is intended to diminish or abrogate the finality of judgments in any case not falling within the purview of the Control, Regulate and Tax Adult Use of Marijuana Act.

(l) A resentencing hearing ordered under this act shall constitute a "post-conviction release proceeding" under paragraph (7) of subdivision (b) of Section 28 of Article I of the California Constitution (Marsy's Law).

(m) The provisions of this section shall apply equally to juvenile delinquency adjudications and dispositions under Section 602 of the Welfare and Institutions Code if the juvenile would not have been guilty of an offense or would have been guilty of a lesser offense under the Control, Regulate and Tax Adult Use of Marijuana Act.

(n) The Judicial Council shall promulgate and make available all necessary forms to enable the filing of the petitions and applications provided in this section.

Health and Safety Code § 11362

(Amended by Statute, Effective April 4, 2011, and Operative October 1, 2011.)

As used in this article "felony offense," and offense "punishable as a felony" refer to an offense prior to July 1, 2011, for which the law prescribes imprisonment in the state prison, or for an offense on or after July 1, 2011, imprisonment in either the state prison or pursuant to subdivision (h) of Section 1170 of the Penal Code, as either an alternative or the sole penalty, regardless of the sentence the particular defendant received.

Health and Safety Code § 11362.1

(MAUCRSA, Effective June 27, 2017.)

(a) Subject to Sections 11362.2, 11362.3, 11362.4, and 11362.45, but notwithstanding any other provision of law, it shall be lawful under state and local law, and shall not be a violation of state or local law, for persons 21 years of age or older to:

> (1) Possess, process, transport, purchase, obtain, or give away to persons 21 years of age or older without any compensation whatsoever, not more than 28.5 grams of cannabis not in the form of concentrated cannabis;

> (2) Possess, process, transport, purchase, obtain, or give away to persons 21 years of age or older without any compensation whatsoever, not more than eight grams of cannabis in the form of concentrated cannabis, including as contained in cannabis products;

> (3) Possess, plant, cultivate, harvest, dry, or process not more than six living cannabis plants and possess the cannabis produced by the plants;

> (4) Smoke or ingest cannabis or cannabis products; and

> (5) Possess, transport, purchase, obtain, use, manufacture, or give away cannabis accessories to persons 21 years of age or older without any compensation whatsoever.

(b) Paragraph (5) of subdivision (a) is intended to meet the requirements of subdivision (f) of Section 863 a/Title 21 of the United States Code (21 US.C. § 863(f)) by authorizing, under state law, any person in compliance with this section to manufacture, possess, or distribute cannabis accessories.

(c) Cannabis and cannabis products involved in any way with conduct deemed lawful by this section are not contraband nor subject to seizure, and no conduct deemed lawful by this section shall constitute the basis for detention, search, or arrest.

Health and Safety Code § 11362.2

(MAUCRSA, Effective June 27, 2017.)

(a) Personal cultivation of cannabis under paragraph (3) of subdivision (a) of Section 11362.1 is subject to the following restrictions:

> (1) A person shall plant, cultivate, harvest, dry, or process plants in accordance with local ordinances, if any, adopted in accordance with subdivision (b).

> (2) The living plants and any cannabis produced by the plants in excess of 28.5 grams are kept within the person's private residence, or upon the grounds of that private residence (e.g., in an outdoor garden area), are in a locked space, and are not visible by normal unaided vision from a public place.

> (3) Not more than six living plants may be planted, cultivated, harvested, dried, or processed within a single private residence, or upon the grounds of that private residence, at one time.

(b)(1) A city, county, or city and county may enact and enforce reasonable regulations to regulate the actions and conduct in paragraph (3) of subdivision (a) of Section 11362.1.

(2) Notwithstanding paragraph (1), a city, county, or city and county shall not completely prohibit persons engaging in the actions and conduct under paragraph (3) of subdivision (a) of Section 11362.1 inside a private residence, or inside an accessory structure to a private residence located upon the grounds of a private residence that is fully enclosed and secure.

(3) Notwithstanding paragraph (3) of subdivision (a) of Section 11362.1, a city, county, or city and county may completely prohibit persons from engaging in actions and conduct under paragraph (3) of subdivision (a) of Section 11362.1 outdoors upon the grounds of a private residence.

(4) Paragraph (3) shall become inoperable upon a determination by the California Attorney General that adult use of cannabis is lawful in the State of California under federal law, and an act taken by a city, county, or city and county under paragraph (3) is unenforceable upon the date of that

determination by the Attorney General.

(5) For purposes of this section, "private residence" means a house, an apartment unit, a mobile home, or other similar dwelling.

Health and Safety Code § 11362.3

(MAUCRSA, Effective June 27, 2017.)

(a) Section 11362.1 does not permit any person to:

(1) Smoke or ingest cannabis or cannabis products in a public place, except in accordance with Section 26200 of the Business and Professions Code.

(2) Smoke cannabis or cannabis products in a location where smoking tobacco is prohibited.

(3) Smoke cannabis or cannabis products within 1,000 feet of a school, day care center, or youth center while children are present at the school, day care center, or youth center, except in or upon the grounds of a private residence or in accordance with Section 26200 of the Business and Professions Code and only if such smoking is not detectable by others on the grounds of the school, day care center, or youth center while children are present.

(4) Possess an open container or open package of cannabis or cannabis products while driving, operating, or riding in the passenger seat or compartment of a motor vehicle, boat, vessel, aircraft, or other vehicle used for transportation.

(5) Possess, smoke or ingest cannabis or cannabis products in or upon the grounds of a school, day care center, or youth center while children are present.

(6) Manufacture concentrated cannabis using a volatile solvent, unless done in accordance with a license under Division 10 (commencing with section 26000) of the Business and Professions Code.

(7) Smoke or ingest cannabis or cannabis products while driving, operating a motor vehicle, boat, vessel, aircraft, or other vehicle used for transportation.

(8) Smoke or ingest cannabis or cannabis products while riding in the

passenger seat or compartment of a motor vehicle, boat, vessel, aircraft, or other vehicle used for transportation except as permitted on a motor vehicle, boat, vessel, aircraft, or other vehicle used for transportation that is operated in accordance with Section 26200 of the Business and Professions Code and while no persons under the age of 21 years are present.

(b) For purposes of this section, the following definitions apply:

(1) "Day care center" has the same meaning as in Section 1596.76.

(2) "Smoke" means to inhale, exhale, burn, or carry any lighted or heated device or pipe, or any other lighted or heated cannabis or cannabis product intended for inhalation, whether natural or synthetic, in any manner or in any form. "Smoke" includes the use of an electronic smoking device that creates an aerosol or vapor, in any manner or in any form, or the use of any oral smoking device for the purpose of circumventing the prohibition of smoking in a place.

(3) "Volatile solvent" means a solvent that is or produces a flammable gas or vapor that, when present in the air in sufficient quantities, will create explosive or ignitable mixtures.

(4) "Youth center" has the same meaning as in Section 11353.1.

(c) Nothing in this section shall be construed or interpreted to amend, repeal, affect, restrict, or preempt laws pertaining to the Compassionate Use Act of 1996.

Health and Safety Code § 11362.4

(MAUCRSA, Effective June 27, 2017.)

(a) A person who engages in the conduct described in paragraph (1) of subdivision (a) of Section 11362.3 is guilty of an infraction punishable by no more than a one-hundred-dollar ($100) fine; provided, however, that persons under the age of 18 shall instead be required to complete four hours of a drug education program or counseling, and up to 10 hours of community service, over a period not to exceed 60 days once the drug education program or counseling and community service opportunity are made available to the person.

(b) A person who engages in the conduct described in paragraphs (2), (3), or

(4) of subdivision (a) of Section 11362.3 is guilty of an infraction punishable by no more than a two-hundred-fifty-dollar ($250) fine, unless such activity is otherwise permitted by state and local law; provided, however, that persons under the age of 18 shall instead be required to complete four hours of drug education or counseling, and up to 20 hours of community service, over a period not to exceed 90 days once the drug education program or counseling and community service opportunity are made available to the person.

(c) A person who engages in the conduct described in paragraph (5) of subdivision (a) of Section 11362.3 shall be subject to the same punishment as provided under subdivision (c) or (d) of Section 11357.

(d) A person who engages in the conduct described in paragraph (6) of subdivision (a) of Section 11362.3 shall be subject to punishment under Section 11379.6.

(e) A person who violates the restrictions in subdivision (a) of Section 11362.2 is guilty of an infraction punishable by no more than a two-hundred-fifty-dollar ($250) fine.

(f) Notwithstanding subdivision (e), a person under the age of 18 who violates the restrictions in subdivision (a) of Section 11362.2 shall be punished under subdivision (a) of Section 11358.

(g) (1) The drug education program or counseling hours required by this section shall be mandatory unless the court makes a finding that such a program or counseling is unnecessary for the person or that a drug education program or counseling is unavailable.

(2) The drug education program required by this section for persons under the age of 18 shall be free to participants and provide at least four hours of group discussion or instruction based on science and evidence-based principles and practices specific to the use and abuse of cannabis and other controlled substances.

(h) Upon a finding of good cause, the court may extend the time for a person to complete the drug education or counseling, and community service required under this section.

Health and Safety Code § 11362.45

(MAUCRSA, Effective June 27, 2017.)

Section 11362.1 does not amend, repeal, affect, restrict, or preempt:

(a) Laws making it unlawful to drive or operate a vehicle, boat, vessel, or aircraft, while smoking, ingesting, or impaired by, cannabis or cannabis products, including, but not limited to, subdivision (e) of Section 23152 of the Vehicle Code, or the penalties prescribed for violating those laws.

(b) Laws prohibiting the sale, administering, furnishing, or giving away of cannabis, cannabis products, or cannabis accessories, or the offering to sell, administer, furnish, or give away cannabis, cannabis products, or cannabis accessories to a person younger than 21 years of age.

(c) Laws prohibiting a person younger than 21 years of age from engaging in any of the actions or conduct otherwise permitted under Section 11362.1.

(d) Laws pertaining to smoking or ingesting cannabis or cannabis products on the grounds of, or within, any facility or institution under the jurisdiction of the Department of Corrections and Rehabilitation or the Division of Juvenile Justice, or on the grounds of, or within, any other facility or institution referenced in Section 4573 of the Penal Code.

(e) Laws providing that it would constitute negligence or professional malpractice to undertake any task while impaired from smoking or ingesting cannabis or cannabis products.

(f) The rights and obligations of public and private employers to maintain a drug and alcohol free workplace or require an employer to permit or accommodate the use, consumption, possession, transfer, display, transportation, sale, or growth of cannabis in the workplace, or affect the ability of employers to have policies prohibiting the use of cannabis by employees and prospective employees, or prevent employers from complying with state or federal law.

(g) The ability of a state or local government agency to prohibit or restrict any of the actions or conduct otherwise permitted under Section 11362.1 within a building owned, leased, or occupied by the state or local government agency.

(h) The ability of an individual or private entity to prohibit or restrict any of the actions or conduct otherwise permitted under Section 11362.1 on the individual's or entity's privately owned property.

(i) Laws pertaining to the Compassionate Use Act of 1996.

Health And Safety Code § 11362.5

(Proposition 215, Effective November 5, 1996.)

SEC. 1.

(a) This section shall be known and may be cited as the Compassionate Use Act of 1996.

(b)(1) The people of the State of California hereby find and declare that the purposes of the Compassionate Use Act of 1996 are as follows:

(A) To ensure that seriously ill Californians have the right to obtain and use marijuana for medical purposes where that medical use is deemed appropriate and has been recommended by a physician who has determined that the person's health would benefit from the use of marijuana in the treatment of cancer, anorexia, AIDS, chronic pain, spasticity, glaucoma, arthritis, migraine, or any other illness for which marijuana provides relief.

(B) To ensure that patients and their primary caregivers who obtain and use marijuana for medical purposes upon the recommendation of a physician are not subject to criminal prosecution or sanction.

(C) To encourage the federal and state governments to implement a plan to provide for the safe and affordable distribution of marijuana to all patients in medical need of marijuana.

(b)(2) Nothing in this section shall be construed to supersede legislation prohibiting persons from engaging in conduct that endangers others, nor to condone the diversion of marijuana for nonmedical purposes.

(c) Notwithstanding any other provision of law, no physician in this state shall be punished, or denied any right or privilege, for having recommended marijuana to a patient for medical purposes.

(d) Section 11357, relating to the possession of marijuana, and Section 11358, relating to the cultivation of marijuana, shall not apply to a patient, or to a patient's primary caregiver, who possesses or cultivates marijuana for the personal medical purposes of the patient upon the written or oral recommendation or approval of a physician.

(e) For the purposes of this section, "primary caregiver" means the individual designated by the person exempted under this section who has consistently assumed responsibility for the housing, health, or safety of that person.

SEC. 2.

If any provision of this measure or the application thereof to any person or circumstance is held invalid, that invalidity shall not affect other provisions or applications of the measure that can be given effect without the invalid provision or application, and to this end the provisions of this measure are severable.

Heath and Safety Code § 11362.7

(MAUCRSA, Effective June 27, 2017.)

For purposes of this article, the following definitions shall apply:

(a) "Attending physician" means an individual who possesses a license in good standing to practice medicine or osteopathy issued by the Medical Board of California or the Osteopathic Medical Board of California and who has taken responsibility for an aspect of the medical care, treatment, diagnosis, counseling, or referral of a patient and who has conducted a medical examination of that patient before recording in the patient's medical record the physician's assessment of whether the patient has a serious medical condition and whether the medical use of cannabis is appropriate.

(b) "Department" means the State Department of Public Health.

(c) "Person with an identification card" means an individual who is a qualified patient who has applied for and received a valid identification card pursuant to this article.

(d) "Primary caregiver" means the individual, designated by a qualified patient, who has consistently assumed responsibility for the housing, health, or safety of that patient, and may include any of the following:

(1) In a case in which a qualified patient or person with an identification card receives medical care or supportive services, or both, from a clinic licensed pursuant to Chapter 1 (commencing with Section 1200) of Division 2, a health care facility licensed pursuant to Chapter 2 (commencing with Section 1250) of Division 2, a residential care facility for persons with chronic life-threatening illness licensed pursuant to Chapter 3.01 (commencing with Section 1568.01) of Division 2, a residential care facility for the elderly licensed pursuant to Chapter 3.2

(commencing with Section 1569) of Division 2, a hospice, or a home health agency licensed pursuant to Chapter 8 (commencing with Section 1725) of Division 2, the owner or operator, or no more than three employees who are designated by the owner or operator, of the clinic, facility, hospice, or home health agency, if designated as a primary caregiver by that qualified patient or person with an identification card.

(2) An individual who has been designated as a primary caregiver by more than one qualified patient or person with an identification card, if every qualified patient or person with an identification card who has designated that individual as a primary caregiver resides in the same city or county as the primary caregiver.

(3) An individual who has been designated as a primary caregiver by a qualified patient or person with an identification card who resides in a city or county other than that of the primary caregiver, if the individual has not been designated as a primary caregiver by any other qualified patient or person with an identification card.

(e) A primary caregiver shall be at least 18 years of age, unless the primary caregiver is the parent of a minor child who is a qualified patient or a person with an identification card or the primary caregiver is a person otherwise entitled to make medical decisions under state law pursuant to Section 6922, 7002, 7050, or 7120 of the Family Code.

(f) "Qualified patient" means a person who is entitled to the protections of Section 11362.5, but who does not have an identification card issued pursuant to this article.

(g) "Identification card" means a document issued by the department that identifies a person authorized to engage in the medical use of cannabis and the person's designated primary caregiver, if any.

(h) "Serious medical condition" means all of the following medical conditions:

(1) Acquired immune deficiency syndrome (AIDS).

(2) Anorexia.

(3) Arthritis.

(4) Cachexia.

(5) Cancer.

(6) Chronic pain.

(7) Glaucoma.

(8) Migraine.

(9) Persistent muscle spasms, including, but not limited to, spasms associated with multiple sclerosis.

(10) Seizures, including, but not limited to, seizures associated with epilepsy.

(11) Severe nausea.

(12) Any other chronic or persistent medical symptom that either:

> (A) Substantially limits the ability of the person to conduct one or more major life activities as defined in the federal Americans with Disabilities Act of 1990 (Public Law 101-336).

> (B) If not alleviated, may cause serious harm to the patient's safety or physical or mental health.

(i) "Written documentation" means accurate reproductions of those portions of a patient's medical records that have been created by the attending physician, that contain the information required by paragraph (2) of subdivision (a) of Section 11362.715, and that the patient may submit as part of an application for an identification card.

Health and Safety Code § 11362.71

(MAUCRSA, Effective June 27, 2017.)

(a) (1) The department shall establish and maintain a voluntary program for the issuance of identification cards to qualified patients who satisfy the requirements of this article and voluntarily apply to the identification card program.

(2) The department shall establish and maintain a 24-hour, toll-free telephone number that will enable state and local law enforcement officers to have immediate access to information necessary to verify the validity of an identification card issued by the department, until a cost-effective Internet

Web-based system can be developed for this purpose.

(b) Every county health department, or the county's designee, shall do all of the following:

(1) Provide applications upon request to individuals seeking to join the identification card program.

(2) Receive and process completed applications in accordance with Section 11362.72.

(3) Maintain records of identification card programs.

(4) Utilize protocols developed by the department pursuant to paragraph (1) of subdivision (d).

(5) Issue identification cards developed by the department to approved applicants and designated primary caregivers.

(c) The county board of supervisors may designate another health-related governmental or nongovernmental entity or organization to perform the functions described in subdivision (b), except for an entity or organization that cultivates or distributes cannabis.

(d) The department shall develop all of the following:

(1) Protocols that shall be used by a county health department or the county's designee to implement the responsibilities described in subdivision (b), including, but not limited to, protocols to confirm the accuracy of information contained in an application and to protect the confidentiality of program records.

(2) Application forms that shall be issued to requesting applicants.

(3) An identification card that identifies a person authorized to engage in the medical use of cannabis and an identification card that identifies the person's designated primary caregiver, if any. The two identification cards developed pursuant to this paragraph shall be easily distinguishable from each other.

(e) No person or designated primary caregiver in possession of a valid identification card shall be subject to arrest for possession, transportation, delivery, or cultivation of medicinal cannabis in an amount established pursuant to this article, unless there is probable cause to believe that the information contained in the card is false or falsified, the card has been obtained by means of fraud, or the person is otherwise in violation of the provisions of this article.

(f) It shall not be necessary for a person to obtain an identification card in order to claim the protections of Section 11362.5.

Health and Safety Code § 11362.712

(AUMA, Effective November 9, 2016.)

(a) Commencing on January 1, 2018, a qualified patient must possess a physician's recommendation that complies with Article 25 (commencing with Section 2525) of Chapter 5 of Division 2 of the Business and Professions Code. Failure to comply with this requirement shall not, however, affect any of the protections provided to patients or their primary caregivers by Section 11362.5.

(b) A county health department or the county's designee shall develop protocols to ensure that, commencing upon January 1, 2018, all identification cards issued pursuant to Section 11362.71 are supported by a physician's recommendation that complies with Article 25 (commencing with Section 2525) of Chapter 5 of Division 2 of the Business and Professions Code.

Health and Safety Code § 11362.713

(AUMA, Effective November 9, 2016.)

(a) Information identifying the names, addresses, or social security numbers of patients, their medical conditions, or the names of their primary caregivers, received and contained in the records of the Department of Public Health and by any county public health department are hereby deemed "medical information" within the meaning of the Confidentiality of Medical Information Act (Civil Code§ 56, et seq.) and shall not be disclosed by the Department or by any county public health department except in accordance with the restrictions on disclosure of individually identifiable information under the Confidentiality of Medical Information Act.

(b) Within 24 hours of receiving any request to disclose the name, address, or social security number of a patient, their medical condition, or the name of their primary caregiver, the Department of Public Health or any county public health agency shall contact the patient and inform the patient of the request and if the request was made in writing, a copy of the request.

(c) Notwithstanding Section 56.10 of the Civil Code, neither the Department of Public Health, nor any county public health agency, shall disclose, nor shall they be ordered by agency or court to disclose, the names, addresses, or social security numbers of patients, their medical conditions, or the names of their primary caregivers, sooner than the 10th day after which the patient whose records are sought to be disclosed has been contacted.

(d) No identification card application system or database used or maintained by the Department of Public Health or by any county department of public health or the county's designee as provided in Section 11362.71 shall contain any personal information of any qualified patient, including but not limited to, the patient's name, address, social security number, medical conditions, or the names of their primary caregivers. Such an application system or database may only contain a unique user identification number, and when that number is entered, the only information that may be provided is whether the card is valid or invalid.

Health and Safety Code § 11362.715

(MAUCRSA, Effective June 27, 2017.)

(a) A person who seeks an identification card shall pay the fee, as provided in Section 11362.755, and provide all of the following to the county health department or the county's designee on a form developed and provided by the department:

> (1) The name of the person and proof of his or her residency within the county.

> (2) Written documentation by the attending physician in the person's medical records stating that the person has been diagnosed with a serious medical condition and that the medicinal use of cannabis is appropriate.

> (3) The name, office address, office telephone number, and California medical license number of the person's attending physician.

> (4) The name and the duties of the primary caregiver.

> (5) A government-issued photo identification card of the person and of the designated primary caregiver, if any. If the applicant is a person under 18 years of age, a certified copy of a birth certificate shall be deemed sufficient proof of identity.

(b) If the person applying for an identification card lacks the capacity to make medical decisions, the application may be made by the person's legal representative, including, but not limited to, any of the following:

(1) A conservator with authority to make medical decisions.

(2) An attorney-in-fact under a durable power of attorney for health care or surrogate decisionmaker authorized under another advanced health care directive.

(3) Any other individual authorized by statutory or decisional law to make medical decisions for the person.

(c) The legal representative described in subdivision (b) may also designate in the application an individual, including himself or herself, to serve as a primary caregiver for the person, provided that the individual meets the definition of a primary caregiver.

(d) The person or legal representative submitting the written information and documentation described in subdivision (a) shall retain a copy thereof.

Health and Safety Code § 11362.72

(SB 420, Effective January 1, 2004.)

(a) Within 30 days of receipt of an application for an identification card, a county health department or the county's designee shall do all of the following:

(1) For purposes of processing the application, verify that the information contained in the application is accurate. If the person is less than 18 years of age, the county health department or its designee shall also contact the parent with legal authority to make medical decisions, legal guardian, or other person or entity with legal authority to make medical decisions, to verify the information.

(2) Verify with the Medical Board of California or the Osteopathic Medical Board of California that the attending physician has a license in good standing to practice medicine or osteopathy in the state.

(3) Contact the attending physician by facsimile, telephone, or mail to confirm that the medical records submitted by the patient are a true and correct copy of those contained in the physician's office records. When

contacted by a county health department or the county's designee, the attending physician shall confirm or deny that the contents of the medical records are accurate.

(4) Take a photograph or otherwise obtain an electronically transmissible image of the applicant and of the designated primary caregiver, if any.

(5) Approve or deny the application. If an applicant who meets the requirements of Section 11362.715 can establish that an identification card is needed on an emergency basis, the county or its designee shall issue a temporary identification card that shall be valid for 30 days from the date of issuance. The county, or its designee, may extend the temporary identification card for no more than 30 days at a time, so long as the applicant continues to meet the requirements of this paragraph.

(b) If the county health department or the county's designee approves the application, it shall, within 24 hours, or by the end of the next working day of approving the application, electronically transmit the following information to the department:

(1) A unique user identification number of the applicant.

(2) The date of expiration of the identification card.

(3) The name and telephone number of the county health department or the county's designee that has approved the application.

(c) The county health department or the county's designee shall issue an identification card to the applicant and to his or her designated primary caregiver, if any, within five working days of approving the application.

(d) In any case involving an incomplete application, the applicant shall assume responsibility for rectifying the deficiency. The county shall have 14 days from the receipt of information from the applicant pursuant to this subdivision to approve or deny the application.

Health and Safety Code § 11362.735

(SB 420, Effective January 1, 2004.)

(a) An identification card issued by the county health department shall be serially numbered and shall contain all of the following:

(1) A unique user identification number of the cardholder.

(2) The date of expiration of the identification card.

(3) The name and telephone number of the county health department or the county's designee that has approved the application.

(4) A 24-hour, toll-free telephone number, to be maintained by the department, that will enable state and local law enforcement officers to have immediate access to information necessary to verify the validity of the card.

(5) Photo identification of the cardholder.

(b) A separate identification card shall be issued to the person's designated primary caregiver, if any, and shall include a photo identification of the caregiver.

Health and Safety Code § 11362.74

(SB 420, Effective January 1, 2004.)

(a) The county health department or the county's designee may deny an application only for any of the following reasons:

(1) The applicant did not provide the information required by Section 11362.715, and upon notice of the deficiency pursuant to subdivision (d) of Section 11362.72, did not provide the information within 30 days.

(2) The county health department or the county's designee determines that the information provided was false.

(3) The applicant does not meet the criteria set forth in this article.

(b) Any person whose application has been denied pursuant to subdivision (a) may not reapply for six months from the date of denial unless otherwise authorized by the county health department or the county's designee or by a court of competent jurisdiction.

(c) Any person whose application has been denied pursuant to subdivision (a) may appeal that decision to the department. The county health department or the county's designee shall make available a telephone number or address to which the denied applicant can direct an appeal.

Health and Safety Code § 11362.745

(SB 420, Effective January 1, 2004.)

(a) An identification card shall be valid for a period of one year.

(b) Upon annual renewal of an identification card, the county health department or its designee shall verify all new information and may verify any other information that has not changed.

(c) The county health department or the county's designee shall transmit its determination of approval or denial of a renewal to the department.

Health and Safety Code § 11362.755

(AUMA, Effective November 9, 2016.)

(a) Each county health department or the county's designee may charge a fee for all costs incurred by the county or the county's designee for administering the program pursuant to this article.

(b) In no event shall the amount of the fee charged by a county health department exceed $100 per application or renewal.

(c) Upon satisfactory proof of participation and eligibility in the Medi-Cal program, a Medi-Cal beneficiary shall receive a 50 percent reduction in the fees established pursuant to this section.

(d) Upon satisfactory proof that a qualified patient, or the legal guardian of a qualified patient under the age of 18, is a medically indigent adult who is eligible for and participates in the County Medical Services Program, the fee established pursuant to this section shall be waived.

(e) In the event the fees charged and collected by a county health department are not sufficient to pay for the administrative costs incurred in discharging the county health department's duties with respect to the mandatory identification card system, the Legislature, upon request by the county health department, shall reimburse the county health department for those reasonable administrative costs in excess of the fees charged and collected by the county health department.

Health and Safety Code § 11362.76

(SB 420, Effective January 1, 2004.)

(a) A person who possesses an identification card shall:

(1) Within seven days, notify the county health department or the county's designee of any change in the person's attending physician or designated primary caregiver, if any.

(2) Annually submit to the county health department or the county's designee the following:

(A) Updated written documentation of the person's serious medical condition.

(B) The name and duties of the person's designated primary caregiver, if any, for the forthcoming year.

(b) If a person who possesses an identification card fails to comply with this section, the card shall be deemed expired. If an identification card expires, the identification card of any designated primary caregiver of the person shall also expire.

(c) If the designated primary caregiver has been changed, the previous primary caregiver shall return his or her identification card to the department or to the county health department or the county's designee.

(d) If the owner or operator or an employee of the owner or operator of a provider has been designated as a primary caregiver pursuant to paragraph (1) of subdivision (d) of Section 11362.7, of the qualified patient or person with an identification card, the owner or operator shall notify the county health department or the county's designee, pursuant to Section 11362.715, if a change in the designated primary caregiver has occurred.

Health and Safety Code § 11362.765

(MAUCRSA, Effective June 27, 2017.)

(a) Subject to the requirements of this article, the individuals specified in subdivision (b) shall not be subject, on that sole basis, to criminal liability under Section 11357, 11358, 11359, 11360, 11366, 11366.5, or 11570. This section does not authorize the individual to smoke or otherwise consume cannabis unless otherwise authorized by this article, nor shall anything in this section authorize any individual or group to cultivate or distribute cannabis for profit.

(b) Subdivision (a) shall apply to all of the following:

(1) A qualified patient or a person with an identification card who transports or processes cannabis for his or her own personal medical use.

(2) A designated primary caregiver who transports, processes, administers, delivers, or gives away cannabis for medical purposes, in amounts not exceeding those established in subdivision (a) of Section 11362.77, only to the qualified patient of the primary caregiver, or to the person with an identification card who has designated the individual as a primary caregiver.

(3) An individual who provides assistance to a qualified patient or a person with an identification card, or his or her designated primary caregiver, in administering medicinal cannabis to the qualified patient or person or acquiring the skills necessary to cultivate or administer cannabis for medical purposes to the qualified patient or person.

(c) A primary caregiver who receives compensation for actual expenses, including reasonable compensation incurred for services provided to an eligible qualified patient or person with an identification card to enable that person to use cannabis under this article, or for payment for out-of-pocket expenses incurred in providing those services, or both, shall not, on the sole basis of that fact, be subject to prosecution or punishment under Section 11359 or 11360.

(Health and Safety Code § 11362.768

(MAUCRSA, Effective June 27, 2017.)

(a) This section shall apply to individuals specified in subdivision (b) of Section 11362.765.

(b) No medicinal cannabis cooperative, collective, dispensary, operator, establishment, or provider who possesses, cultivates, or distributes medicinal cannabis pursuant to this article shall be located within a 600-foot radius of a school.

(c) The distance specified in this section shall be the horizontal distance measured in a straight line from the property line of the school to the closest property line of the lot on which the medicinal cannabis cooperative, collective, dispensary, operator, establishment, or provider is to be located without regard to intervening structures.

(d) This section shall not apply to a medicinal cannabis cooperative, collective, dispensary, operator, establishment, or provider that is also a licensed residential medical or elder care facility.

(e) This section shall apply only to a medicinal cannabis cooperative, collective, dispensary, operator, establishment, or provider that is authorized by law to possess, cultivate, or distribute medicinal cannabis and that has a storefront or mobile retail outlet which ordinarily requires a local business license.

(f) Nothing in this section shall prohibit a city, county, or city and county from adopting ordinances or policies that further restrict the location or establishment of a medicinal cannabis cooperative, collective, dispensary, operator, establishment, or provider.

(g) This section does not preempt local ordinances, adopted prior to January 1, 2011, that regulate the location or establishment of a medicinal cannabis cooperative, collective, dispensary, operator, establishment, or provider.

(h) For the purposes of this section, "school" means any public or private school providing instruction in kindergarten or any of grades 1 to 12, inclusive, but does not include any private school in which education is primarily conducted in private homes.

Health and Safety Code § 11362.769

(MCRSA- SB 837, Effective June 27, 2016.)

Indoor and outdoor medical cannabis cultivation shall be conducted in accordance with state and local laws. State agencies, including, but not limited to, the Department of Food and Agriculture, the State Board of Forestry and Fire Protection, the Department of Fish and Wildlife, the State Water Resources Control Board, the California regional water quality control boards, and traditional state law enforcement agencies shall address environmental impacts of medical cannabis cultivation and shall coordinate, when appropriate, with cities and counties and their law enforcement agencies in enforcement efforts.

Health and Safety Code § 11362.77

(MAUCRSA, Effective June 27, 2017.)

(a) A qualified patient or primary caregiver may possess no more than eight ounces of dried cannabis per qualified patient. In addition, a qualified patient or primary caregiver may also maintain no more than six mature or 12 immature cannabis plants per qualified patient.

(b) If a qualified patient or primary caregiver has a physician's recommendation that this quantity does not meet the qualified patient's medical needs, the qualified patient or primary caregiver may possess an amount of cannabis consistent with the patient's needs.

(c) Counties and cities may retain or enact medicinal cannabis guidelines allowing qualified patients or primary caregivers to exceed the state limits set forth in subdivision (a).

(d) Only the dried mature processed flowers of female cannabis plant or the plant conversion shall be considered when determining allowable quantities of cannabis under this section.

(e) A qualified patient or a person holding a valid identification card, or the designated primary caregiver of that qualified patient or person, may possess amounts of cannabis consistent with this article.

Health and Safety Code § 11362.775

(MAUCRSA, Effective June 27, 2017.)

(a) Subject to subdivision (d), qualified patients, persons with valid identification cards, and the designated primary caregivers of qualified patients and persons with identification cards, who associate within the State of California in order collectively or cooperatively to cultivate cannabis for medicinal purposes, shall not solely on the basis of that fact be subject to state criminal sanctions under Section 11357, 11358, 11359, 11360, 11366, 11366.5, or 11570.

(b) A collective or cooperative that operates pursuant to this section and manufactures medicinal cannabis products shall not, solely on the basis of that fact, be subject to state criminal sanctions under Section 11379.6 if the collective or cooperative abides by all of the following requirements:

(1) The collective or cooperative does either or both of the following:

(A) Utilizes only manufacturing processes that are either solventless or that employ only nonflammable, nontoxic solvents that are generally recognized as safe pursuant to the federal Food, Drug, and Cosmetic Act (21 U.S.C. Sec. 301 et seq.).

(B) Utilizes only manufacturing processes that use solvents exclusively within a closed-loop system that meets all of the following requirements:

(i) The system uses only solvents that are generally recognized as safe pursuant to the federal Food, Drug, and Cosmetic Act (21 U.S.C. Sec. 301 et seq.).

(ii) The system is designed to recapture and contain solvents during the manufacturing process, and otherwise prevent the off-gassing of solvents into the ambient atmosphere to mitigate the risks of ignition and explosion during the manufacturing process.

(iii) A licensed engineer certifies that the system was commercially manufactured, safe for its intended use, and built to codes of recognized and generally accepted good engineering practices, including, but not limited to, the American Society of Mechanical Engineers (ASME), the American National Standards Institute (ANSI), Underwriters Laboratories (UL), the American Society for Testing and Materials (ASTM), or OSHA Nationally Recognized Testing Laboratories (NRTLs).

(iv) The system has a certification document that contains the signature and stamp of a professional engineer and the serial number of the extraction unit being certified.

(2) The collective or cooperative receives and maintains approval from the local fire official for the closed-loop system, other equipment, the extraction operation, and the facility.

(3) The collective or cooperative meets required fire, safety, and building code requirements in one or more of the following:

(A) The California Fire Code.

(B) The National Fire Protection Association (NFPA) standards.

(C) International Building Code (IBC).

(D) The International Fire Code (IFC).

(E) Other applicable standards, including complying with all applicable fire, safety, and building codes in processing, handling, and storage of solvents or gasses.

(4) The collective or cooperative is in possession of a valid seller's permit issued by the State Board of Equalization.

(5) The collective or cooperative is in possession of a valid local license, permit, or other authorization specific to the manufacturing of medicinal cannabis products, and in compliance with any additional conditions imposed by the city or county issuing the local license, permit, or other authorization.

(c) For purposes of this section, "manufacturing" means compounding, converting, producing, deriving, processing, or preparing, either directly or indirectly by chemical extraction or independently by means of chemical synthesis, medicinal cannabis products.

(d) This section shall remain in effect only until one year after the Bureau of Cannabis Control posts a notice on its Internet Web site that the licensing authorities have commenced issuing licenses pursuant to the Medicinal and Adult-Use Cannabis Regulation and Safety Act (Division 10 (commencing with Section 26000) of the Business and Professions Code).

(e) This section is repealed one year after the date upon which the notice is posted pursuant to subdivision (d).

Health and Safety Code § 11362.78

(MAUCRSA, Effective June 27, 2017.)

A state or local law enforcement agency or officer shall not refuse to accept an identification card issued pursuant to this article unless the state or local law enforcement agency or officer has probable cause to believe that the information contained in the card is false or fraudulent, or the card is being used fraudulently.

Health and Safety Code § 11362.785

(MAUCRSA, Effective June 27, 2017.)

(a) Nothing in this article shall require any accommodation of medicinal use of cannabis on the property or premises of a place of employment or during the hours of employment or on the property or premises of a jail, correctional facility, or other type of penal institution in which prisoners reside or persons under arrest are detained.

(b) Notwithstanding subdivision (a), a person shall not be prohibited or prevented from obtaining and submitting the written information and documentation necessary to apply for an identification card on the basis that the person is incarcerated in a jail, correctional facility, or other penal institution in which prisoners reside or persons under arrest are detained.

(c) This article does not prohibit a jail, correctional facility, or other penal institution in which prisoners reside or persons under arrest are detained, from permitting a prisoner or a person under arrest who has an identification card, to use cannabis for medicinal purposes under circumstances that will not endanger the health or safety of other prisoners or the security of the facility.

(d) This article does not require a governmental, private, or any other health insurance provider or health care service plan to be liable for a claim for reimbursement for the medicinal use of cannabis.

Health and Safety Code § 11362.79

(MAUCRSA, Effective June 27, 2017.)

This article does not authorize a qualified patient or person with an identification card to engage in the smoking of medicinal cannabis under any of the following circumstances:

(a) In a place where smoking is prohibited by law.

(b) In or within 1,000 feet of the grounds of a school, recreation center, or youth center, unless the medicinal use occurs within a residence.

(c) On a schoolbus.

(d) While in a motor vehicle that is being operated.

(e) While operating a boat.

Health and Safety Code § 11362.795

(MAUCRSA, Effective June 27, 2017.)

(a) (1) Any criminal defendant who is eligible to use cannabis pursuant to Section 11362.5 may request that the court confirm that he or she is allowed to use medicinal cannabis while he or she is on probation or released on bail.

(2) The court's decision and the reasons for the decision shall be stated on the record and an entry stating those reasons shall be made in the minutes of the court.

(3) During the period of probation or release on bail, if a physician recommends that the probationer or defendant use medicinal cannabis, the probationer or defendant may request a modification of the conditions of probation or bail to authorize the use of medicinal cannabis.

(4) The court's consideration of the modification request authorized by this subdivision shall comply with the requirements of this section.

(b) (1) Any person who is to be released on parole from a jail, state prison, school, road camp, or other state or local institution of confinement and who is eligible to use medicinal cannabis pursuant to Section 11362.5 may request that he or she be allowed to use medicinal cannabis during the period he or she is released on parole. A parolee's written conditions of parole shall reflect whether or not a request for a modification of the conditions of his or her parole to use medicinal cannabis was made, and whether the request was granted or denied.

(2) During the period of the parole, where a physician recommends that the parolee use medicinal cannabis, the parolee may request a modification of the conditions of the parole to authorize the use of medicinal cannabis.

(3) Any parolee whose request to use medicinal cannabis while on parole was denied may pursue an administrative appeal of the decision. Any decision on the appeal shall be in writing and shall reflect the reasons for the decision.

(4) The administrative consideration of the modification request authorized by this subdivision shall comply with the requirements of this section.

Health and Safety Code § 11362.8

(MAUCRSA, Effective June 27, 2017.)

A professional licensing board shall not impose a civil penalty or take other disciplinary action against a licensee based solely on the fact that the licensee has performed acts that are necessary or appropriate to carry out the licensee's role as a designated primary caregiver to a person who is a qualified patient or who possesses a lawful identification card issued pursuant to Section 11362.72. However, this section shall not apply to acts performed by a physician relating to the discussion or recommendation of the medical use of cannabis to a patient. These discussions or recommendations, or both, shall be governed by Section 11362.5.

Health and Safey Code § 11362.81

(MAUCRSA, Effective June 27, 2017.)

(a) A person specified in subdivision (b) shall be subject to the following penalties:

(1) For the first offense, imprisonment in the county jail for no more than six months or a fine not to exceed one thousand dollars ($1,000), or both.

(2) For a second or subsequent offense, imprisonment in the county jail for no more than one year, or a fine not to exceed one thousand dollars ($1,000), or both.

(b) Subdivision (a) applies to any of the following:

(1) A person who fraudulently represents a medical condition or fraudulently provides any material misinformation to a physician, county health department or the county's designee, or state or local law enforcement agency or officer, for the purpose of falsely obtaining an identification card.

(2) A person who steals or fraudulently uses any person's identification card in order to acquire, possess, cultivate, transport, use, produce, or distribute cannabis.

(3) A person who counterfeits, tampers with, or fraudulently produces an identification card.

(4) A person who breaches the confidentiality requirements of this article to information provided to, or contained in the records of, the department or of a county health department or the county's designee

pertaining to an identification card program.

(c) In addition to the penalties prescribed in subdivision (a), a person described in subdivision (b) may be precluded from attempting to obtain, or obtaining or using, an identification card for a period of up to six months at the discretion of the court.

(d) In addition to the requirements of this article, the Attorney General shall develop and adopt appropriate guidelines to ensure the security and nondiversion of cannabis grown for medicinal use by patients qualified under the Compassionate Use Act of 1996.

Health and Safety Code § 11362.82

(SB 420, Effective January 1, 2004.)

If any section, subdivision, sentence, clause, phrase, or portion of this article is for any reason held invalid or unconstitutional by any court of competent jurisdiction, that portion shall be deemed a separate, distinct, and independent provision, and that holding shall not affect the validity of the remaining portion thereof.

Health and Safety Code § 11362.83

(MAUCRSA, Effective June 27, 2017.)

Nothing in this article shall prevent a city or other local governing body from adopting and enforcing any of the following:

(a) Adopting local ordinances that regulate the location, operation, or establishment of a medicinal cannabis cooperative or collective.

(b) The civil and criminal enforcement of local ordinances described in subdivision (a).

(c) Enacting other laws consistent with this article.

Health and Safety Code § 11362.84

(AUMA, Effective November 9, 2016.)

The status and conduct of a qualified patient who acts in accordance with the Compassionate Use Act shall not, by itself, be used to restrict or abridge custodial or parental rights to minor children in any action or proceeding under the jurisdiction of family or juvenile court.

Health and Safety Code § 11362.85

(MAUCRSA, Effective June 27, 2017.)

Upon a determination by the California Attorney General that the federal schedule of controlled substances has been amended to reclassify or declassify cannabis, the Legislature may amend or repeal the provisions of this code, as necessary, to conform state law to such changes in federal law.

Health and Safety Code § 11362.9

(MAUCRSA, Effective June 27, 2017.)

(a) (1) It is the intent of the Legislature that the state commission objective scientific research by the premier research institute of the world, the University of California, regarding the efficacy and safety of administering cannabis as part of medical treatment. If the Regents of the University of California, by appropriate resolution, accept this responsibility, the University of California shall create a program, to be known as the California Cannabis Research Program. Whenever "California Marijuana Research Program" appears in any statute, regulation, or contract, or in any other code, it shall be construed to refer to the California Cannabis Research Program.

(2) The program shall develop and conduct studies intended to ascertain the general medical safety and efficacy of cannabis and, if found valuable, shall develop medical guidelines for the appropriate administration and use of cannabis. The studies may include studies to ascertain the effect of cannabis on motor skills.

(b) The program may immediately solicit proposals for research projects to be included in the cannabis studies. Program requirements to be used when evaluating responses to its solicitation for proposals, shall include, but not be limited to, all of the following:

(1) Proposals shall demonstrate the use of key personnel, including clinicians or scientists and support personnel, who are prepared to develop a program of research regarding cannabis' general medical efficacy and safety.

(2) Proposals shall contain procedures for outreach to patients with various medical conditions who may be suitable participants in research on cannabis.

(3) Proposals shall contain provisions for a patient registry.

(4) Proposals shall contain provisions for an information system that is designed to record information about possible study participants, investigators, and clinicians, and deposit and analyze data that accrues as part of clinical trials.

(5) Proposals shall contain protocols suitable for research on cannabis, addressing patients diagnosed with acquired immunodeficiency syndrome (AIDS) or human immunodeficiency virus (HIV), cancer, glaucoma, or seizures or muscle spasms associated with a chronic, debilitating condition. The proposal may also include research on other serious illnesses, provided that resources are available and medical information justifies the research.

(6) Proposals shall demonstrate the use of a specimen laboratory capable of housing plasma, urine, and other specimens necessary to study the concentration of cannabinoids in various tissues, as well as housing specimens for studies of toxic effects of cannabis.

(7) Proposals shall demonstrate the use of a laboratory capable of analyzing cannabis, provided to the program under this section, for purity and cannabinoid content and the capacity to detect contaminants.

(c) In order to ensure objectivity in evaluating proposals, the program shall use a peer review process that is modeled on the process used by the National Institutes of Health, and that guards against funding research that is biased in favor of or against particular outcomes. Peer reviewers shall be selected for their expertise in the scientific substance and methods of the proposed research, and their lack of bias or conflict of interest regarding the applicants or the topic of an approach taken in the proposed research. Peer reviewers shall judge research proposals on several criteria, foremost among which shall be both of the following:

(1) The scientific merit of the research plan, including whether the research design and experimental procedures are potentially biased for or against a particular outcome.

(2) Researchers' expertise in the scientific substance and methods of the proposed research, and their lack of bias or conflict of interest regarding the topic of, and the approach taken in, the proposed research.

(d) If the program is administered by the Regents of the University of California, any grant research proposals approved by the program shall also require review and approval by the research advisory panel.

(e) It is the intent of the Legislature that the program be established as follows:

(1) The program shall be located at one or more University of California campuses that have a core of faculty experienced in organizing multidisciplinary scientific endeavors and, in particular, strong experience in clinical trials involving psychopharmacologic agents. The campuses at which research under the auspices of the program is to take place shall accommodate the administrative offices, including the director of the program, as well as a data management unit, and facilities for storage of specimens.

(2) When awarding grants under this section, the program shall utilize principles and parameters of the other well-tested statewide research programs administered by the University of California, modeled after programs administered by the National Institutes of Health, including peer review evaluation of the scientific merit of applications.

(3) The scientific and clinical operations of the program shall occur, partly at University of California campuses, and partly at other postsecondary institutions, that have clinicians or scientists with expertise to conduct the required studies. Criteria for selection of research locations shall include the elements listed in subdivision (b) and, additionally, shall give particular weight to the organizational plan, leadership qualities of the program director, and plans to involve investigators and patient populations from multiple sites.

(4) The funds received by the program shall be allocated to various research studies in accordance with a scientific plan developed by the Scientific Advisory Council. As the first wave of studies is completed, it is anticipated that the program will receive requests for funding of additional studies. These requests shall be reviewed by the Scientific Advisory Council.

(5) The size, scope, and number of studies funded shall be

commensurate with the amount of appropriated and available program funding.

(f) All personnel involved in implementing approved proposals shall be authorized as required by Section 11604.

(g) Studies conducted pursuant to this section shall include the greatest amount of new scientific research possible on the medical uses of, and medical hazards associated with, cannabis. The program shall consult with the Research Advisory Panel analogous agencies in other states, and appropriate federal agencies in an attempt to avoid duplicative research and the wasting of research dollars.

(h) The program shall make every effort to recruit qualified patients and qualified physicians from throughout the state.

(i) The cannabis studies shall employ state-of-the-art research methodologies.

(j) The program shall ensure that all cannabis used in the studies is of the appropriate medical quality and shall be obtained from the National Institute on Drug Abuse or any other federal agency designated to supply cannabis for authorized research. If these federal agencies fail to provide a supply of adequate quality and quantity within six months of the effective date of this section, the Attorney General shall provide an adequate supply pursuant to Section 11478.

(k) The program may review, approve, or incorporate studies and research by independent groups presenting scientifically valid protocols for medical research, regardless of whether the areas of study are being researched by the committee.

(l) (1) To enhance understanding of the efficacy and adverse effects of cannabis as a pharmacological agent, the program shall conduct focused controlled clinical trials on the usefulness of cannabis in patients diagnosed with AIDS or HIV, cancer, glaucoma, or seizures or muscle spasms associated with a chronic, debilitating condition. The program may add research on other serious illnesses, provided that resources are available and medical information justifies the research. The studies shall focus on comparisons of both the efficacy and safety of methods of administering the drug to patients, including inhalational, tinctural, and oral, evaluate possible uses of cannabis as a primary or adjunctive treatment, and develop further information on optimal dosage, timing, mode of administration, and variations in the effects of different cannabinoids and varieties of cannabis.

(2) The program shall examine the safety of cannabis in patients with various medical disorders, including cannabis's interaction with other drugs, relative safety of inhalation versus oral forms, and the effects on mental function in medically ill persons.

(3) The program shall be limited to providing for objective scientific research to ascertain the efficacy and safety of cannabis as part of medical treatment, and should not be construed as encouraging or sanctioning the social or recreational use of cannabis.

(m) (1) Subject to paragraph (2), the program shall, prior to any approving proposals, seek to obtain research protocol guidelines from the National Institutes of Health and shall, if the National Institutes of Health issues research protocol guidelines, comply with those guidelines.

(2) If, after a reasonable period of time of not less than six months and not more than a year has elapsed from the date the program seeks to obtain guidelines pursuant to paragraph (1), no guidelines have been approved, the program may proceed using the research protocol guidelines it develops.

(n) In order to maximize the scope and size of the cannabis studies, the program may do any of the following:

(1) Solicit, apply for, and accept funds from foundations, private individuals, and all other funding sources that can be used to expand the scope or timeframe of the cannabis studies that are authorized under this section. The program shall not expend more than 5 percent of its General Fund allocation in efforts to obtain money from outside sources.

(2) Include within the scope of the cannabis studies other cannabis research projects that are independently funded and that meet the requirements set forth in subdivisions (a) to (c), inclusive. In no case shall the program accept any funds that are offered with any conditions other than that the funds be used to study the efficacy and safety of cannabis as part of medical treatment. Any donor shall be advised that funds given for purposes of this section will be used to study both the possible benefits and detriments of cannabis and that he or she will have no control over the use of these funds.

(o) (1) Within six months of the effective date of this section, the program shall report to the Legislature, the Governor, and the Attorney General on the progress of the cannabis studies.

(2) Thereafter, the program shall issue a report to the Legislature every six months detailing the progress of the studies. The interim reports required under this paragraph shall include, but not be limited to, data on all of the following:

(A) The names and number of diseases or conditions under study.

(B) The number of patients enrolled in each study by disease.

(C) Any scientifically valid preliminary findings.

(p) If the Regents of the University of California implement this section, the President of the University of California shall appoint a multidisciplinary Scientific Advisory Council, not to exceed 15 members, to provide policy guidance in the creation and implementation of the program. Members shall be chosen on the basis of scientific expertise. Members of the council shall serve on a voluntary basis, with reimbursement for expenses incurred in the course of their participation. The members shall be reimbursed for travel and other necessary expenses incurred in their performance of the duties of the council.

(q) No more than 10 percent of the total funds appropriated may be used for all aspects of the administration of this section.

(r) This section shall be implemented only to the extent that funding for its purposes is appropriated by the Legislature in the annual Budget Act.

Health & Safety Code § 11364.5

(MAUCRSA, Effective June 27, 2017.)

(a) Except as authorized by law, no person shall maintain or operate any place of business in which drug paraphernalia is kept, displayed or offered in any manner, sold, furnished, transferred or given away unless such drug paraphernalia is completely and wholly kept, displayed or offered within a separate room or enclosure to which persons under the age of 18 years not accompanied by a parent or legal guardian are excluded. Each entrance to such a room or enclosure shall be signposted in reasonably visible and legible words to the effect that drug paraphernalia is kept, displayed or offered in such room or enclosure and that minors, unless accompanied by a parent or legal guardian, are excluded.

(b) Except as authorized by law, no owner, manager, proprietor or other person in charge of any room or enclosure, within any place of business, in which drug paraphernalia is kept, displayed or offered in any manner, sold, furnished, transferred or given away shall permit or allow any person under the age of 18 years to enter, be in, remain in or visit such room or enclosure unless that minor person is accompanied by one of his or her parents or by his or her legal guardian.

(c) Unless authorized by law, no person under the age of 18 years shall enter, be in, remain in, or visit any room or enclosure in any place of business in which drug paraphernalia is kept, displayed or offered in any manner, sold, furnished, transferred, or given away unless accompanied by one of his or her parents or by his or her legal guardian.

(d) As used in this section, "drug paraphernalia" means all equipment, products, and materials of any kind which are intended for use or designed for use, in planting, propagating, cultivating, growing, harvesting, manufacturing, compounding, converting, producing, processing, preparing, testing, analyzing, packaging, repackaging, storing, containing, concealing, injecting, ingesting, inhaling, or otherwise introducing into the human body a controlled substance. "Drug paraphernalia" includes, but is not limited to, all of the following:

(1) Kits intended for use or designed for use in planting, propagating, cultivating, growing, or harvesting of any species of plant which is a controlled substance or from which a controlled substance can be derived.

(2) Kits intended for use or designed for use in manufacturing, compounding, converting, producing, processing, or preparing controlled substances.

(3) Isomerization devices intended for use or designed for use in increasing the potency of any species of plant which is a controlled substance.

(4) Testing equipment intended for use or designed for use in identifying, or in analyzing the strength, effectiveness, or purity of controlled substances.

(5) Scales and balances intended for use or designed for use in weighing or measuring controlled substances.

(6) Diluents and adulterants, such as quinine hydrochloride, mannitol,

mannite, dextrose, and lactose, intended for use or designed for use in cutting controlled substances.

(7) Separation gins and sifters intended for use or designed for use in removing twigs and seeds from, or in otherwise cleaning or refining, cannabis.

(8) Blenders, bowls, containers, spoons, and mixing devices intended for use or designed for use in compounding controlled substances.

(9) Capsules, balloons, envelopes, and other containers intended for use or designed for use in packaging small quantities of controlled substances.

(10) Containers and other objects intended for use or designed for use in storing or concealing controlled substances.

(11) Hypodermic syringes, needles, and other objects intended for use or designed for use in parenterally injecting controlled substances into the human body.

(12) Objects intended for use or designed for use in ingesting, inhaling, or otherwise introducing cannabis, cocaine, hashish, or hashish oil into the human body, such as the following:

> (A) Metal, wooden, acrylic, glass, stone, plastic, or ceramic pipes with or without screens, permanent screens, hashish heads, or punctured metal bowls.

> (B) Water pipes.

> (C) Carburetion tubes and devices.

> (D) Smoking and carburetion masks.

> (E) Roach clips, meaning objects used to hold burning material, such as a cannabis cigarette that has become too small or too short to be held in the hand.

> (F) Miniature cocaine spoons, and cocaine vials.

> (G) Chamber pipes.

> (H) Carburetor pipes.

> (I) Electric pipes.

(J) Air-driven pipes.

(K) Chillums.

(L) Bongs.

(M) Ice pipes or chillers.

(e) In determining whether an object is drug paraphernalia, a court or other authority may consider, in addition to all other logically relevant factors, the following:

(1) Statements by an owner or by anyone in control of the object concerning its use.

(2) Prior convictions, if any, of an owner, or of anyone in control of the object, under any state or federal law relating to any controlled substance.

(3) Direct or circumstantial evidence of the intent of an owner, or of anyone in control of the object, to deliver it to persons whom he or she knows, or should reasonably know, intend to use the object to facilitate a violation of this section. The innocence of an owner, or of anyone in control of the object, as to a direct violation of this section shall not prevent a finding that the object is intended for use, or designed for use, as drug paraphernalia.

(4) Instructions, oral or written, provided with the object concerning its use.

(5) Descriptive materials, accompanying the object which explain or depict its use.

(6) National and local advertising concerning its use.

(7) The manner in which the object is displayed for sale.

(8) Whether the owner, or anyone in control of the object, is a legitimate supplier of like or related items to the community, such as a licensed distributor or dealer of tobacco products.

(9) The existence and scope of legitimate uses for the object in the community.

(10) Expert testimony concerning its use.

(f) This section shall not apply to any of the following:

(1) Any pharmacist or other authorized person who sells or furnishes drug paraphernalia described in paragraph (11) of subdivision (d) upon the prescription of a physician, dentist, podiatrist, or veterinarian.

(2) Any physician, dentist, podiatrist, or veterinarian who furnishes or prescribes drug paraphernalia described in paragraph (11) of subdivision (d) to his or her patients.

(3) Any manufacturer, wholesaler, or retailer licensed by the California State Board of Pharmacy to sell or transfer drug paraphernalia described in paragraph (11) of subdivision (d).

(g) Notwithstanding any other provision of law, including Section 11374, violation of this section shall not constitute a criminal offense, but operation of a business in violation of the provisions of this section shall be grounds for revocation or nonrenewal of any license, permit, or other entitlement previously issued by a city, county, or city and county for the privilege of engaging in such business and shall be grounds for denial of any future license, permit, or other entitlement authorizing the conduct of such business or any other business, if the business includes the sale of drug paraphernalia.

Health & Safety Code § 11366

(Amended by Statute, Effective 1991.)

Every person who opens or maintains any place for the purpose of unlawfully selling, giving away, or using any controlled substance which is

(1) specified in subdivision (b), (c), or (e), or paragraph (1) of subdivision (f) of Section 11054, specified in paragraph (13), (14), (15), or (20) of subdivision (d) of Section 11054, or specified in subdivision (b), (c), paragraph (1) or (2) of subdivision (d), or paragraph (3) of subdivision (e) of Section 11055, or

(2) which is a narcotic drug classified in Schedule III, IV, or V, shall be punished by imprisonment in the county jail for a period of not more than one year or the state prison.

Health & Safety Code § 11366.5

(Amended by Statute, Effective April 4, 2011, and Operative October 1, 2011.)

(a) Any person who has under his or her management or control any building, room, space, or enclosure, either as an owner, lessee, agent, employee, or mortgagee, who knowingly rents, leases, or makes available for use, with or without compensation, the building, room, space, or enclosure for the purpose of unlawfully manufacturing, storing, or distributing any controlled substance for sale or distribution shall be punished by imprisonment in the county jail for not more than one year, or pursuant to subdivision (h) of Section 1170 of the Penal Code.

(b) Any person who has under his or her management or control any building, room, space, or enclosure, either as an owner, lessee, agent, employee, or mortgagee, who knowingly allows the building, room, space, or enclosure to be fortified to suppress law enforcement entry in order to further the sale of any amount of cocaine base as specified in paragraph (1) of subdivision (f) of Section 11054, cocaine as specified in paragraph (6) of subdivision (b) of Section 11055, heroin, phencyclidine, amphetamine, methamphetamine, or lysergic acid diethylamide and who obtains excessive profits from the use of the building, room, space, or enclosure shall be punished by imprisonment pursuant to subdivision (h) of Section 1170 of the Penal Code for two, three, or four years.

(c) Any person who violates subdivision (a) after previously being convicted of a violation of subdivision (a) shall be punished by imprisonment pursuant to subdivision (h) of Section 1170 of the Penal Code for two, three, or four years.

(d) For the purposes of this section, excessive profits means the receipt of consideration of a value substantially higher than fair market value.

Health & Safety Code § 11379.6

(Amended by Statute, Effective January 1, 2016.)

(a) Except as otherwise provided by law, every person who manufactures, compounds, converts, produces, derives, processes, or prepares, either directly or indirectly by chemical extraction or independently by means of chemical synthesis, any controlled substance specified in Section 11054, 11055, 11056,

11057, or 11058 shall be punished by imprisonment pursuant to subdivision (h) of Section 1170 of the Penal Code for three, five, or seven years and by a fine not exceeding fifty thousand dollars ($50,000).

(b) Except when an enhancement pursuant to Section 11379.7 is pled and proved, the fact that a person under 16 years of age resided in a structure in which a violation of this section involving methamphetamine occurred shall be considered a factor in aggravation by the sentencing court.

(c) Except when an enhancement pursuant to Section 11379.7 is pled and proved, the fact that a violation of this section involving methamphetamine occurred within 200 feet of an occupied residence or any structure where another person was present at the time the offense was committed may be considered a factor in aggravation by the sentencing court.

(d) The fact that a violation of this section involving the use of a volatile solvent to chemically extract concentrated cannabis occurred within 300 feet of an occupied residence or any structure where another person was present at the time the offense was committed may be considered a factor in aggravation by the sentencing court.

(e) Except as otherwise provided by law, every person who offers to perform an act which is punishable under subdivision (a) shall be punished by imprisonment pursuant to subdivision (h) of Section 1170 of the Penal Code for three, four, or five years.

(f) All fines collected pursuant to subdivision (a) shall be transferred to the State Treasury for deposit in the Clandestine Drug Lab Clean-up Account, as established by Section 5 of Chapter 1295 of the Statutes of 1987. The transmission to the State Treasury shall be carried out in the same manner as fines collected for the state by the county.

Health and Safety Code § 11470

(MAUCRSA, Effective June 27, 2017.)

The following are subject to forfeiture:

(a) All controlled substances which have been manufactured, distributed, dispensed, or acquired in violation of this division.

(b) All raw materials, products, and equipment of any kind which are used, or intended for use, in manufacturing, compounding, processing, delivering, importing, or exporting any controlled substance in violation of this division.

(c) All property except real property or a boat, airplane, or any vehicle which is used, or intended for use, as a container for property described in subdivision (a) or (b).

(d) All books, records, and research products and materials, including formulas, microfilm, tapes, and data which are used, or intended for use, in violation of this division.

(e) The interest of any registered owner of a boat, airplane, or any vehicle other than an implement of husbandry, as defined in Section 36000 of the Vehicle Code, which has been used as an instrument to facilitate the manufacture of, or possession for sale or sale of 14.25 grams or more of heroin, or a substance containing 14.25 grams or more of heroin, or 14.25 grams or more of a substance containing heroin, or 28.5 grams or more of Schedule I controlled substances except cannabis, peyote, or psilocybin; 10 pounds dry weight or more of cannabis, peyote, or psilocybin; or 28.5 grams or more of cocaine, as specified in paragraph (6) of subdivision (b) of Section 11055, cocaine base as specified in paragraph (1) of subdivision (f) of Section 11054, or methamphetamine; or a substance containing 28.5 grams or more of cocaine, as specified in paragraph (6) of subdivision (b) of Section 11055, cocaine base as specified in paragraph (1) of subdivision (f) of Section 11054, or methamphetamine; or 57 grams or more of a substance containing cocaine, as specified in paragraph (6) of subdivision (b) of Section 11055, cocaine base as specified in paragraph (1) of subdivision (f) of Section 11054, or methamphetamine; or 28.5 grams or more of Schedule II controlled substances. An interest in a vehicle which may be lawfully driven on the highway with a class C, class M1, or class M2 license, as prescribed in Section 12804.9 of the Vehicle Code, shall not be forfeited under this subdivision if there is a community property interest in the vehicle by a person other than the defendant and the vehicle is the sole class C, class M1, or class M2 vehicle available to the defendant's immediate family.

(f) All moneys, negotiable instruments, securities, or other things of value furnished or intended to be furnished by any person in exchange for a controlled substance, all proceeds traceable to such an exchange, and all moneys, negotiable instruments, or securities used or intended to be used to facilitate any violation of Section 11351, 11351.5, 11352, 11355, 11359, 11360, 11378, 11378.5, 11379, 11379.5, 11379.6, 11380, 11382, or 11383 of this code, or Section 182 of the Penal Code, or a felony violation of Section 11366.8 of this code, insofar as the offense involves manufacture, sale, possession for sale, offer for sale, or offer to manufacture, or conspiracy to commit at least one of those offenses, if the exchange, violation, or other conduct which is the basis for the forfeiture occurred within five years of the seizure of the property, or the filing of a petition under this chapter, or the issuance of an order of forfeiture of the property, whichever comes first.

(g) The real property of any property owner who is convicted of violating Section 11366, 11366.5, or 11366.6 with respect to that property. However, property which is used as a family residence or for other lawful purposes, or which is owned by two or more persons, one of whom had no knowledge of its unlawful use, shall not be subject to forfeiture.

(h) (1) Subject to the requirements of Section 11488.5 and except as further limited by this subdivision to protect innocent parties who claim a property interest acquired from a defendant, all right, title, and interest in any personal property described in this section shall vest in the state upon commission of the act giving rise to forfeiture under this chapter, if the state or local governmental entity proves a violation of Section 11351, 11351.5, 11352, 11355, 11359, 11360, 11378, 11378.5, 11379, 11379.5, 11379.6, 11380, 11382, or 11383 of this code, or Section 182 of the Penal Code, or a felony violation of Section 11366.8 of this code, insofar as the offense involves the manufacture, sale, possession for sale, offer for sale, offer to manufacture, or conspiracy to commit at least one of those offenses, in accordance with the burden of proof set forth in paragraph (1) of subdivision (i) of Section 11488.4 or, in the case of cash or negotiable instruments in excess of twenty-five thousand dollars ($25,000), paragraph (4) of subdivision (i) of Section 11488.4.

(2) The operation of the special vesting rule established by this subdivision shall be limited to circumstances where its application will not defeat the claim of any person, including a bona fide purchaser or encumbrancer who, pursuant to Section 11488.5, 11488.6, or 11489, claims an interest in the property seized, notwithstanding that the interest in the property being claimed was acquired from a defendant whose property interest would otherwise have been subject to divestment pursuant to this subdivision.

Health & Safety Code § 11478

(MAUCRSA, Effective June 27, 2017.)

Cannabis may be provided by the Attorney General to the heads of research projects which have been registered by the Attorney General, and which have been approved by the research advisory panel pursuant to Section 11480.

The head of the approved research project shall personally receipt for such quantities of cannabis and shall make a record of their disposition. The receipt and record shall be retained by the Attorney General. The head of the approved research project shall also, at intervals and in the manner required by the research advisory panel, report the progress or conclusions of the research project.

Health & Safety Code § 11479

(MAUCRSA, Effective June 27, 2017.)

Notwithstanding Sections 11473 and 11473.5, at any time after seizure by a law enforcement agency of a suspected controlled substance, except in the case of growing or harvested cannabis, that amount in excess of 10 pounds in gross weight may be destroyed without a court order by the chief of the law enforcement agency or a designated subordinate. In the case of growing or harvested cannabis, that amount in excess of two pounds, or the amount of cannabis a medicinal cannabis patient or designated caregiver is authorized to possess by ordinance in the city or county where the cannabis was seized, whichever is greater, may be destroyed without a court order by the chief of the law enforcement agency or a designated subordinate. Destruction shall not take place pursuant to this section until all of the following requirements are satisfied:

(a) At least five random and representative samples have been taken, for evidentiary purposes, from the total amount of suspected controlled substances to be destroyed. These samples shall be in addition to the 10 pounds required above. When the suspected controlled substance consists of growing or harvested cannabis plants, at least one 2-pound sample or a sample in the amount of medicinal cannabis a medicinal cannabis patient or designated caregiver is authorized to possess by ordinance in the city or county where the cannabis was seized, whichever is greater, shall be retained. This sample may include stalks, branches, or leaves. In addition, five representative samples of leaves or buds shall be retained for evidentiary purposes from the total amount of suspected controlled substances to be destroyed.

(b) Photographs and videos have been taken that reasonably and accurately demonstrate the total amount of the suspected controlled substance to be destroyed.

(c) The gross weight of the suspected controlled substance has been determined, either by actually weighing the suspected controlled substance or by estimating that weight after dimensional measurement of the total suspected controlled substance.

(d) The chief of the law enforcement agency has determined that it is not reasonably possible to preserve the suspected controlled substance in place, or to remove the suspected controlled substance to another location. In making this determination, the difficulty of transporting and storing the suspected controlled substance to another site and the storage facilities may be taken into consideration.

Subsequent to any destruction of a suspected controlled substance pursuant to this section, an affidavit shall be filed within 30 days in the court that has jurisdiction over any pending criminal proceedings pertaining to that suspected controlled substance, reciting the applicable information required by subdivisions (a), (b), (c), and (d) together with information establishing the location of the suspected controlled substance, and specifying the date and time of the destruction. In the event that there are no criminal proceedings pending that pertain to that suspected controlled substance, the affidavit may be filed in any court within the county that would have jurisdiction over a person against whom those criminal charges might be filed.

Health & Safety Code § 11479.2

(MAUCRSA, Effective June 27, 2017.)

Notwithstanding the provisions of Sections 11473, 11473.5, 11474, 11479, and 11479.1, at any time after seizure by a law enforcement agency of a suspected controlled substance, except cannabis, any amount, as determined by the court, in excess of 57 grams may, by court order, be destroyed by the chief of a law enforcement agency or a designated subordinate. Destruction shall not take place pursuant to this section until all of the following requirements are satisfied:

(a) At least five random and representative samples have been taken, for evidentiary purposes, from the total amount of suspected controlled substances to be destroyed. Those samples shall be in addition to the 57 grams required above and each sample shall weigh not less than one gram at the time the sample is collected.

(b) Photographs have been taken which reasonably demonstrate the total amount of the suspected controlled substance to be destroyed.

(c) The gross weight of the suspected controlled substance has been determined, either by actually weighing the suspected controlled substance or by estimating such weight after dimensional measurement of the total suspected controlled substance.

(d) In cases involving controlled substances suspected of containing cocaine or methamphetamine, an analysis has determined the qualitative and quantitative nature of the suspected controlled substance.

(e) The law enforcement agency with custody of the controlled substance sought to be destroyed has filed a written motion for the order of destruction in the court which has jurisdiction over any pending criminal proceeding in which a defendant is charged by accusatory pleading with a crime specifically involving the suspected controlled substance sought to be destroyed. The motion shall, by affidavit of the chief of the law enforcement agency or designated subordinate, recite the applicable information required by subdivisions (a), (b), (c), and (d), together with information establishing the location of the suspected controlled substance and the title of any pending criminal proceeding as defined in this subdivision. The motion shall bear proof of service upon all parties to any pending criminal proceeding. No motion shall be made when a defendant is without counsel until the defendant has entered his or her plea to the charges.

(f) The order for destruction shall issue pursuant to this section upon the motion and affidavit in support of the order, unless within 20 days after application for the order, a defendant has requested, in writing, a hearing on the motion. Within 10 days after the filing of that request, or a longer period of time upon good cause shown by either party, the court shall conduct a hearing on the motion in which each party to the motion for destruction shall be permitted to call and examine witnesses. The hearing shall be recorded. Upon conclusion of the hearing, if the court finds that the defendant would not be prejudiced by the destruction, it shall grant the motion and make an order for destruction. In making the order, the court shall ensure that the representative samples to be retained are of sufficient quantities to allow for qualitative analyses by both the prosecution and the defense. Any order for destruction pursuant to this section shall include the applicable information required by subdivisions (a), (b), (c), (d), and (e) and the name of the agency responsible for the destruction. Unless waived, the order shall provide for a 10-day delay prior to destruction in order to allow expert analysis of the controlled substance by the defense.

Subsequent to any destruction of a suspected controlled substance pursuant to this section, an affidavit shall be filed within 30 days in the court which ordered destruction stating the location of the retained, suspected controlled substance and specifying the date and time of destruction.

This section does not apply to seizures involving hazardous chemicals or controlled substances in mixture or combination with hazardous chemicals.

Health and Safety Code § 11480

(MAUCRSA, Effective June 27, 2017.)

(a) The Legislature finds that there is a need to encourage further research into the nature and effects of cannabis and hallucinogenic drugs and to coordinate research efforts on such subjects.

(b) There is a Research Advisory Panel that consists of a representative of the State Department of Health Services, a representative of the California State Board of Pharmacy, the State Public Health Officer, a representative of the Attorney General, a representative of the University of California who shall be a pharmacologist, a physician, or a person holding a doctorate degree in the health sciences, a representative of a private university in this state who shall be a pharmacologist, a physician, or a person holding a doctorate degree in the health sciences, a representative of a statewide professional medical society in this state who shall be engaged in the private practice of medicine and shall be experienced in treating controlled substance dependency, a representative appointed by and serving at the pleasure of the Governor who shall have experience in drug abuse, cancer, or controlled substance research and who is either a registered nurse, licensed pursuant to Chapter 6 (commencing with Section 2700) of Division 2 of the Business and Professions Code, or other health professional. The Governor shall annually designate the private university and the professional medical society represented on the panel. Members of the panel shall be appointed by the heads of the entities to be represented, and they shall serve at the pleasure of the appointing power.

(c) The Research Advisory Panel shall appoint two special members to the Research Advisory Panel, who shall serve at the pleasure of the Research Advisory Panel only during the period Article 6 (commencing with Section 11260) of Chapter 5 remains effective. The additional members shall be physicians and surgeons, and who are board certified in oncology, ophthalmology, or psychiatry.

(d) The panel shall annually select a chairperson from among its members.

(e) The panel may hold hearings on, and in other ways study, research projects concerning cannabis or hallucinogenic drugs in this state. Members of the panel shall serve without compensation, but shall be reimbursed for any actual and necessary expenses incurred in connection with the performance of their duties.

(f) The panel may approve research projects, which have been registered by the Attorney General, into the nature and effects of cannabis or hallucinogenic drugs, and shall inform the Attorney General of the head of the approved research projects that are entitled to receive quantities of cannabis pursuant to Section 11478.

(g) The panel may withdraw approval of a research project at any time, and when approval is withdrawn shall notify the head of the research project to return any quantities of cannabis to the Attorney General.

(h) The panel shall report annually to the Legislature and the Governor those research projects approved by the panel, the nature of each research project, and, where available, the conclusions of the research project.

Health and Safety Code § 11485

(MAUCRSA, Effective June 27, 2017.)

Any peace officer of this state who, incident to a search under a search warrant issued for a violation of Section 11358 with respect to which no prosecution of a defendant results, seizes personal property suspected of being used in the planting, cultivation, harvesting, drying, processing, or transporting of cannabis, shall, if the seized personal property is not being held for evidence or destroyed as contraband, and if the owner of the property is unknown or has not claimed the property, provide notice regarding the seizure and manner of reclamation of the property to any owner or tenant of real property on which the property was seized. In addition, this notice shall be posted at the location of seizure and shall be published at least once in a newspaper of general circulation in the county in which the property was seized. If, after 90 days following the first publication of the notice, no owner appears and proves his or her ownership, the seized personal property shall be deemed to be abandoned and may be disposed of by sale to the public at public auction as set forth in Article 1 (commencing with Section 2080) of Chapter 4 of Title 6 of Part 4 of Division 3 of the

Civil Code, or may be disposed of by transfer to a government agency or community service organization. Any profit from the sale or transfer of the property shall be expended for investigative services with respect to crimes involving cannabis.

Health and Safety Code § 11532

(MAUCRSA, Effective June 27, 2017.)

(a) It is unlawful for any person to loiter in any public place in a manner and under circumstances manifesting the purpose and with the intent to commit an offense specified in Chapter 6 (commencing with Section 11350) and Chapter 6.5 (commencing with Section 11400).

(b) Among circumstances that may be considered in determining whether a person has the requisite intent to engage in drug-related activity are that the person:

(1) Acts as a "look-out."

(2) Transfers small objects or packages for currency in a furtive fashion.

(3) Tries to conceal himself or herself or any object that reasonably could be involved in an unlawful drug-related activity.

(4) Uses signals or language indicative of summoning purchasers of illegal drugs.

(5) Repeatedly beckons to, stops, attempts to stop, or engages in conversations with passersby, whether on foot or in a motor vehicle, indicative of summoning purchasers of illegal drugs.

(6) Repeatedly passes to or receives from passersby, whether on foot or in a motor vehicle, money or small objects.

(7) Is under the influence of a controlled substance or possesses narcotic or drug paraphernalia. For the purposes of this paragraph, "narcotic or drug paraphernalia" means any device, contrivance, instrument, or apparatus designed or marketed for the use of smoking, injecting, ingesting, or consuming cannabis, hashish, PCP, or any controlled substance, including, but not limited to, roach clips, cigarette papers, and rollers designed or marketed for use in smoking a controlled substance.

(8) Has been convicted in any court within this state, within five years prior to the arrest under this chapter, of any violation involving the use, possession, or sale of any of the substances referred to in Chapter 6 (commencing with Section 11350) or Chapter 6.5 (commencing with Section 11400), or has been convicted of any violation of those provisions or substantially similar laws of any political subdivision of this state or of any other state.

(9) Is currently subject to any order prohibiting his or her presence in any high drug activity geographic area.

(10) Has engaged, within six months prior to the date of arrest under this section, in any behavior described in this subdivision, with the exception of paragraph (8), or in any other behavior indicative of illegal drug-related activity.

(c) The list of circumstances set forth in subdivision (b) is not exclusive. The circumstances set forth in subdivision (b) should be considered particularly salient if they occur in an area that is known for unlawful drug use and trafficking, or if they occur on or in premises that have been reported to law enforcement as a place suspected of unlawful drug activity. Any other relevant circumstances may be considered in determining whether a person has the requisite intent. Moreover, no one circumstance or combination of circumstances is in itself determinative of intent. Intent must be determined based on an evaluation of the particular circumstances of each case.

Health and Safety Code § 11553

(MAUCRSA, Effective June 27, 2017.)

The fact that a person is or has been, or is suspected of being, a user of cannabis is not alone sufficient grounds upon which to invoke Section 11551 or 11552.

This section shall not be construed to limit the discretion of a judge to invoke Section 11551 or 11552 if the court has reason to believe a person is or has been a user of narcotics or drugs other than cannabis.

Health & Safety Code § 11570

(Amended by Statute, Effective 1986.)

Every building or place used for the purpose of unlawfully selling, serving, storing, keeping, manufacturing, or giving away any controlled substance, precursor, or analog specified in this division, and every building or place wherein or upon which those acts take place, is a nuisance which shall be enjoined, abated, and prevented, and for which damages may be recovered, whether it is a public or private nuisance.

Health & Safety Code § 11590

(Amended by statute, Effective January 1, 1996.)

(a) Except as provided in subdivisions (c) and (d), any person who is convicted in the State of California of any offense defined in Section 11350, 11351, 11351.5, 11352, 11353, 11353.5, 11353.7, 11354, 11355, 11357, 11358, 11359, 11360, 11361, 11363, 11366, 11366.5, 11366.6, 11368, 11370.1, 11378, 11378.5, 11379, 11379.5, 11379.6, 11380, 11380.5, 11383, or 11550, or subdivision (a) of Section 11377, or any person who is discharged or paroled from a penal institution where he or she was confined because of the commission of any such offense, or any person who is convicted in any other state of any offense which, if committed or attempted in this state, would have been punishable as one or more of the above-mentioned offenses, shall within 30 days of his or her coming into any county or city, or city and county in which he or she resides or is temporarily domiciled for that length of time, register with the chief of police of the city in which he or she resides or the sheriff of the county if he or she resides in an unincorporated area.

For persons convicted of an offense defined in Section 11377, 11378, 11379, or 11380, this subdivision shall apply only to offenses involving controlled substances specified in paragraph (12) of subdivision (d) of Section 11054 and paragraph (2) of subdivision (d) of Section 11055, and to analogs of these substances, as defined in Section 11401. For persons convicted of an offense defined in Section 11379 or 11379.5, this subdivision shall not apply if the conviction was for transporting, offering to transport, or attempting to transport a controlled substance.

(b) Any person who is convicted in any federal court of any offense which, if committed or attempted in this state would have been punishable as one or more of the offenses enumerated in subdivision (a) shall, within 30 days of his or her coming into any county or city, or city and county, in which he or she resides or is temporarily domiciled for that length of time, register with the chief of police of the city in which he or she resides or the sheriff of the county if he or she resides in an unincorporated area.

(c) This section does not apply to a conviction of a misdemeanor under Section 11357, 11360, or 11377.

(d) The registration requirements imposed by this section for the conviction of offenses defined in Section 11353.7, 11366.5, 11366.6, 11370.1, 11377, 11378, 11378.5, 11379, 11379.5, 11379.6, 11380, 11380.5, or 11383, shall apply to any person who commits any of those offenses on and after January 1, 1990.

Health & Safety Code § 25189.5

(Amended by Statute, Effective April 4, 2011, and Operative October 1, 2011. Subd. (e) Amended on Nov. 4, 1986, by Prop. 65.)

(a) The disposal of any hazardous waste, or the causing thereof, is prohibited when the disposal is at a facility which does not have a permit from the department issued pursuant to this chapter, or at any point which is not authorized according to this chapter.

(b) Any person who is convicted of knowingly disposing or causing the disposal of any hazardous waste, or who reasonably should have known that he or she was disposing or causing the disposal of any hazardous waste, at a facility which does not have a permit from the department issued pursuant to this chapter, or at any point which is not authorized according to this chapter shall, upon conviction, be punished by imprisonment in a county jail for not more than one year or by imprisonment pursuant to subdivision (h) of Section 1170 of the Penal Code.

(c) Any person who knowingly transports or causes the transportation of hazardous waste, or who reasonably should have known that he or she was causing the transportation of any hazardous waste, to a facility which does not have a permit from the department issued pursuant to this chapter, or at any point which is not authorized according to this chapter, shall, upon conviction, be punished by imprisonment in a county jail for not more than one year or by imprisonment pursuant to subdivision (h) of Section 1170 of the Penal Code.

(d) Any person who knowingly treats or stores any hazardous waste at a facility which does not have a permit from the department issued pursuant to this chapter, or at any point which is not authorized according to this chapter, shall, upon conviction, be punished by imprisonment in a county jail for not more than one year or by imprisonment pursuant to subdivision (h) of Section 1170 of the Penal Code.

(e) The court also shall impose upon a person convicted of violating subdivision (b), (c), or (d), a fine of not less than five thousand dollars ($5,000) nor more than one hundred thousand dollars ($100,000) for each day of violation, except as further provided in this subdivision. If the act which violated subdivision (b), (c), or (d) caused great bodily injury, or caused a substantial probability that death could result, the person convicted of violating subdivision (b), (c), or (d) may be punished by imprisonment pursuant to subdivision (h) of Section 1170 of the Penal Code for one, two, or three years, in addition and consecutive to the term specified in subdivision (b), (c), or (d), and may be fined up to two hundred fifty thousand dollars ($250,000) for each day of violation.

(f) For purposes of this section, except as otherwise provided in this subdivision, "each day of violation" means each day on which a violation continues. In any case where a person has disposed or caused the disposal of any hazardous waste in violation of this section, each day that the waste remains disposed of in violation of this section and the person has knowledge thereof is a separate additional violation, unless the person has filed a report of the disposal with the department and is complying with any order concerning the disposal issued by the department, a hearing officer, or court of competent jurisdiction.

Health & Safety Code § 25189.6

(Amended by Statute, Effective April 4, 2011, and Operative October 1, 2011.)

(a) Any person who knowingly, or with reckless disregard for the risk, treats, handles, transports, disposes, or stores any hazardous waste in a manner which causes any unreasonable risk of fire, explosion, serious injury, or death is guilty of a public offense and shall, upon conviction, be punished by a fine of not less than five thousand dollars ($5,000) nor more than two hundred fifty thousand dollars ($250,000) for each day of violation, or by imprisonment in a county jail for not more than one year, or by imprisonment pursuant to subdivision (h) of Section 1170 of the Penal Code, or by both that fine and imprisonment.

(b) Any person who knowingly, at the time the person takes the actions specified in subdivision (a), places another person in imminent danger of death or serious bodily injury, is guilty of a public offense and shall, upon conviction, be punished by a fine of not less than five thousand dollars ($5,000) nor more than two hundred fifty thousand dollars ($250,000) for each day of violation, and by imprisonment pursuant to subdivision (h) of Section 1170 of the Penal Code for three, six, or nine years.

Health & Safety Code § 25189.7

(Amended by Statute, Effective April 4, 2011, and Operative October 1, 2011.)

(a) The burning or incineration of any hazardous waste, or the causing thereof, is prohibited when the burning or incineration is at a facility which does not have a permit from the department issued pursuant to this chapter, or at any point which is not authorized according to this chapter.

(b) Any person who is convicted of knowingly burning or incinerating, or causing the burning or incineration of, any hazardous waste, or who reasonably should have known that he or she was burning or incinerating, or causing the burning or incineration of, any hazardous waste, at a facility which does not have a permit from the department issued pursuant to this chapter, or at any point which is not authorized according to this chapter, shall, upon conviction, be punished by imprisonment in a county jail for not more than one year or by imprisonment pursuant to subdivision (h) of Section 1170 of the Penal Code.

(c) The court also shall impose upon a person convicted of violating subdivision (b) a fine of not less than five thousand dollars ($5,000) nor more than one hundred thousand dollars ($100,000) for each day of violation, except as otherwise provided in this subdivision. If the act which violated subdivision (b) caused great bodily injury or caused a substantial probability that death could result, the person convicted of violating subdivision (b) may be punished by imprisonment pursuant to subdivision (h) of Section 1170 of the Penal Code for one, two, or three years, in addition and consecutive to the term specified in subdivision (b), and may be fined up to two hundred fifty thousand dollars ($250,000) for each day of violation.

Health and Safety Code § 109925

(MAUCRSA, Effective June 27, 2017.)

(a) "Drug" means any of the following:

(1) An article recognized in an official compendium.

(2) An article used or intended for use in the diagnosis, cure, mitigation, treatment, or prevention of disease in human beings or any other animal.

(3) An article other than food, that is used or intended to affect the structure or any function of the body of human beings or any other animal.

(4) An article used or intended for use as a component of an article designated in paragraphs (1) to (3), inclusive.

(b) The term "drug" does not include any device.

(c) Any food for which a claim (as described in Sections 403(r)(1)(B) (21 U.S.C. Sec. 343(r)(1)(B)) and 403(r)(3) (21 U.S.C. Sec. 343(r)(3)) or Sections 403(r)(1)(B) (21 U.S.C. Sec. 343(r)(1)(B)) and 403(r)(5)(D) (21 U.S.C. Sec. 343(r)(5)(D)) of the federal act), is made in accordance with the requirements set forth in Section 403(r) (21 U.S.C. Sec. 343(r)) of the federal act, is not a drug under subdivision (b) solely because the label or labeling contains such a claim.

(d) Cannabis product, including any cannabis product intended for external use, is not a drug.

VIII. Labor Code Sections

Labor Code § 147.5

(MCRSA- AB 266, Effective January 1, 2016)

(a) By January 1, 2017, the Division of Occupational Safety and Health shall convene an advisory committee to evaluate whether there is a need to develop industry-specific regulations related to the activities of facilities issued a license pursuant to Chapter 3.5 (commencing with Section 19300) of Division 8 of the Business and Professions Code.

(b) By July 1, 2017, the advisory committee shall present to the board its findings and recommendations for consideration by the board. By July 1, 2017, the board shall render a decision regarding the adoption of industry-specific regulations pursuant to this section.

Labor Code § 147.6

(AUMA, Effective November 9, 2016.)

(a) By March 1, 2018, the Division of Occupational Safety and Health shall convene an advisory committee to evaluate whether there is a need to develop industry-specific regulations related to the activities of licensees under Division 10 of the Business and Professions Code, including but not limited to, whether specific requirements are needed to address exposure to second-hand marijuana smoke by employees at facilities where on-site consumption of marijuana is permitted under subdivision (d) of Section 26200 of the Business and Professions Code, and whether specific requirements are needed to address the potential risks of combustion, inhalation, armed robberies or repetitive strain injuries.

(b) By October 1, 2018, the advisory committee shall present to the board its findings and recommendations for consideration by the board. By October 1, 2018, the board shall render a decision regarding the adoption of industry-specific regulations pursuant to this section.

Labor Code § 432.8

(Added by Statute, Effective 1976.)

The limitations on employers and the penalties provided for in Section 432.7 shall apply to a conviction for violation of subdivision (b) or (c) of Section 11357 of the Health and Safety Code or a statutory predecessor thereof, or subdivision (c) of Section 11360 of the Health and Safety Code, or Section 11364, 11365, or 11550 of the Health and Safety Code as they related to marijuana prior to January 1, 1976, or a statutory predecessor thereof, two years from the date of such a conviction.

Labor Code § 1140

(Added by Statute, Effective 1975.)

This part shall be known and may be referred to as the Alatorre-Zenovich-Dunlap-Berman Agricultural Labor Relations Act of 1975.

Labor Code § 1140.2

(Added by Statute, Effective 1975.)

It is hereby stated to be the policy of the State of California to encourage and protect the right of agricultural employees to full freedom of association, self-organization, and designation of representatives of their own choosing, to negotiate the terms and conditions of their employment, and to be free from the interference, restraint, or coercion of employers of labor, or their agents, in the designation of such representatives or in self-organization or in other concerted activities for the purpose of collective bargaining or other mutual aid or protection. For this purpose this part is adopted to provide for collective-bargaining rights for agricultural employees.

Labor Code § 1140.4

(Amended by Statute, Effective January 1, 1995.)

As used in this part:

(a) The term "agriculture" includes farming in all its branches, and, among other things, includes the cultivation and tillage of the soil, dairying, the production, cultivation, growing, and harvesting of any agricultural or horticultural commodities (including commodities defined as agricultural commodities in Section 1141j(g) of Title 12 of the United States Code), the raising of livestock, bees, furbearing animals, or poultry, and any practices (including any forestry or lumbering operations) performed by a farmer or on a farm as an incident to or in conjunction with such farming operations, including preparation for market and delivery to storage or to market or to carriers for transportation to market.

(b) The term "agricultural employee" or "employee" shall mean one engaged in agriculture, as such term is defined in subdivision (a). However, nothing in this subdivision shall be construed to include any person other than those employees excluded from the coverage of the National Labor Relations Act, as amended, as agricultural employees, pursuant to Section 2(3) of the Labor Management Relations Act (Section 152(3), Title 29, United States Code), and Section 3(f) of the Fair Labor Standards Act (Section 203(f), Title 29, United States Code).

Further, nothing in this part shall apply, or be construed to apply, to any employee who performs work to be done at the site of the construction, alteration, painting, or repair of a building, structure, or other work (as these terms have been construed under Section 8(e) of the Labor Management Relations Act, 29 U.S.C. Sec. 158(e)) or logging or timber-clearing operations in initial preparation of land for farming, or who does land leveling or only land surveying for any of the above.

As used in this subdivision, "land leveling" shall include only major land moving operations changing the contour of the land, but shall not include annual or seasonal tillage or preparation of land for cultivation.

(c) The term "agricultural employer" shall be liberally construed to include any person acting directly or indirectly in the interest of an employer in relation to an agricultural employee, any individual grower, corporate grower, cooperative grower, harvesting association, hiring association, land management group, any association of persons or cooperatives engaged in agriculture, and shall include any person who owns or leases or manages land used for agricultural purposes, but shall exclude any person supplying agricultural workers to an employer, any farm labor contractor as defined by Section 1682, and any person functioning in the capacity of a labor contractor. The employer engaging such labor contractor or person shall be deemed the employer for all purposes under this part.

(d) The term "person" shall mean one or more individuals, corporations, partnerships, limited liability companies, associations, legal representatives, trustees in bankruptcy, receivers, or any other legal entity, employer, or labor organization having an interest in the outcome of a proceeding under this part.

(e) The term "representatives" includes any individual or labor organization.

(f) The term "labor organization" means any organization of any kind, or any agency or employee representation committee or plan, in which employees participate and which exists, in whole or in part, for the purpose of dealing with employers concerning grievances, labor disputes, wages, rates of pay, hours of employment, or conditions of work for agricultural employees.

(g) The term "unfair labor practice" means any unfair labor practice specified in Chapter 4 (commencing with Section 1153) of this part.

(h) The term "labor dispute" includes any controversy concerning terms, tenure, or conditions of employment, or concerning the association or representation of persons in negotiating, fixing, maintaining, changing, or seeking to arrange terms or conditions of employment, regardless of whether the disputants stand in the proximate relation of employer and employee.

(i) The term "board" means Agricultural Labor Relations Board.

(j) The term "supervisor" means any individual having the authority, in the interest of the employer, to hire, transfer, suspend, lay off, recall, promote, discharge, assign, reward, or discipline other employees, or the responsibility to direct them, or to adjust their grievances, or effectively to recommend such action, if, in connection with the foregoing, the exercise of such authority is not of a merely routine or clerical nature, but requires the use of independent judgment.

IX. Penal Code Sections

Penal Code § 182

(Amended by Statute, Effective April 4, 2011, and Operative October 1, 2011.)

(a) If two or more persons conspire:

(1) To commit any crime.

(2) Falsely and maliciously to indict another for any crime, or to procure another to be charged or arrested for any crime.

(3) Falsely to move or maintain any suit, action, or proceeding.

(4) To cheat and defraud any person of any property, by any means which are in themselves criminal, or to obtain money or property by false pretenses or by false promises with fraudulent intent not to perform those promises.

(5) To commit any act injurious to the public health, to public morals, or to pervert or obstruct justice, or the due administration of the laws.

(6) To commit any crime against the person of the President or Vice President of the United States, the Governor of any state or territory, any United States justice or judge, or the secretary of any of the executive departments of the United States.

They are punishable as follows:

When they conspire to commit any crime against the person of any official specified in paragraph (6), they are guilty of a felony and are punishable by imprisonment pursuant to subdivision (h) of Section 1170 for five, seven, or nine years.

When they conspire to commit any other felony, they shall be punishable in the same manner and to the same extent as is provided for the punishment of that felony. If the felony is one for which different punishments are prescribed for different degrees, the jury or court which finds the defendant guilty thereof shall determine the degree of the felony the defendant conspired to commit. If the degree is not so determined, the punishment for conspiracy to commit the felony shall be that prescribed for the lesser degree, except in the case of conspiracy to commit murder, in which case the punishment shall be that prescribed for murder in the first degree.

If the felony is conspiracy to commit two or more felonies which have different punishments and the commission of those felonies constitute but one offense of conspiracy, the penalty shall be that prescribed for the felony which has the greater maximum term.

When they conspire to do an act described in paragraph (4), they shall be punishable by imprisonment in a county jail for not more than one year, or by imprisonment pursuant to subdivision (h) of Section 1170, or by a fine not exceeding ten thousand dollars ($10,000), or by both that imprisonment and fine.

When they conspire to do any of the other acts described in this section, they shall be punishable by imprisonment in a county jail for not more than one year, or pursuant to subdivision (h) of Section 1170, or by a fine not exceeding ten thousand dollars ($10,000), or by both that imprisonment and fine. When they receive a felony conviction for conspiring to commit identity theft, as defined in Section 530.5, the court may impose a fine of up to twenty-five thousand dollars ($25,000).

All cases of conspiracy may be prosecuted and tried in the superior court of any county in which any overt act tending to effect the conspiracy shall be done.

(b) Upon a trial for conspiracy, in a case where an overt act is necessary to constitute the offense, the defendant cannot be convicted unless one or more overt acts are expressly alleged in the indictment or information, nor unless one of the acts alleged is proved; but other overt acts not alleged may be given in evidence.

Penal Code § 290

(Amended by Proposition 35, Effective November 6, 2012.)

(a) Sections 290 to 290.024, inclusive, shall be known and may be cited as the Sex Offender Registration Act. All references to "the Act" in those sections are to the Sex Offender Registration Act.

(b) Every person described in subdivision (c), for the rest of his or her life while residing in California, or while attending school or working in

California, as described in Sections 290.002 and 290.01, shall be required to register with the chief of police of the city in which he or she is residing, or the sheriff of the county if he or she is residing in an unincorporated area or city that has no police department, and, additionally, with the chief of police of a campus of the University of California, the California State University, or community college if he or she is residing upon the campus or in any of its facilities, within five working days of coming into, or changing his or her residence within, any city, county, or city and county, or campus in which he or she temporarily resides, and shall be required to register thereafter in accordance with the Act.

(c) The following persons shall be required to register:

Any person who, since July 1, 1944, has been or is hereafter convicted in any court in this state or in any federal or military court of a violation of Section 187 committed in the perpetration, or an attempt to perpetrate, rape or any act punishable under Section 286, 288, 288a, or 289, Section 207 or 209 committed with intent to violate Section 261, 286, 288, 288a, or 289, Section 220, except assault to commit mayhem, subdivision (b) and (c) of Section 236.1, Section 243.4, paragraph (1), (2), (3), (4), or (6) of subdivision (a) of Section 261, paragraph (1) of subdivision (a) of Section 262 involving the use of force or violence for which the person is sentenced to the state prison, Section 264.1, 266, or 266c, subdivision (b) of Section 266h, subdivision (b) of Section 266i, Section 266j, 267, 269, 285, 286, 288, 288a, 288.3, 288.4, 288.5, 288.7, 289, or 311.1, subdivision (b), (c), or (d) of Section 311.2, Section 311.3, 311.4, 311.10, 311.11, or 647.6, former Section 647a, subdivision (c) of Section 653f, subdivision 1 or 2 of Section 314, any offense involving lewd or lascivious conduct under Section 272, or any felony violation of Section 288.2; any statutory predecessor that includes all elements of one of the above-mentioned offenses; or any person who since that date has been or is hereafter convicted of the attempt or conspiracy to commit any of the above-mentioned offenses.

Penal Code § 374.8

(Amended by Statute, Effective April 4, 2011, and Operative October 1, 2011.)

(a) In any prosecution under this section, proof of the elements of the offense shall not be dependent upon the requirements of Title 22 of the California Code of Regulations.

(b) Any person who knowingly causes any hazardous substance to be deposited into or upon any road, street, highway, alley, or railroad right-of-way, or upon the land of another, without the permission of the owner, or into the waters of this state is punishable by imprisonment in the county jail for not more than one year or by imprisonment pursuant to subdivision (h) of Section 1170 for a term of 16 months, two years, or three years, or by a fine of not less than fifty dollars ($50) nor more than ten thousand dollars ($10,000), or by both the fine and imprisonment, unless the deposit occurred as a result of an emergency that the person promptly reported to the appropriate regulatory authority.

(c) For purposes of this section, "hazardous substance" means either of the following:

(1) Any material that, because of its quantity, concentration, or physical or chemical characteristics, poses a significant present or potential hazard to human health and safety or to the environment if released into the environment, including, but not limited to, hazardous waste and any material that the administering agency or a handler, as defined in Chapter 6.91 (commencing with Section 25410) of Division 20 of the Health and Safety Code, has a reasonable basis for believing would be injurious to the health and safety of persons or harmful to the environment if released into the environment.

(2) Any substance or chemical product for which one of the following applies:

(A) The manufacturer or producer is required to prepare a MSDS, as defined in Section 6374 of the Labor Code, for the substance or product pursuant to the Hazardous Substances Information Training Act (Chapter 2.5 (commencing with Section 6360) of Part 1 of Division 5 of the Labor Code) or pursuant to any applicable federal law or regulation.

(B) The substance is described as a radioactive material in Chapter 1 of Title 10 of the Code of Federal Regulations maintained and updated by the Nuclear Regulatory Commission.

(C) The substance is designated by the Secretary of Transportation in Chapter 27 (commencing with Section 1801) of the appendix to Title 49 of the United States Code and taxed as a radioactive substance or material.

(D) The materials listed in subdivision (b) of Section 6382 of the Labor Code.

Penal Code § 667

(Amended by Proposition 36, November 6, 2012. This section was added by Prop. 8, June 8, 1982.)

(a) (1) In compliance with subdivision (b) of Section 1385, any person convicted of a serious felony who previously has been convicted of a serious felony in this state or of any offense committed in another jurisdiction which includes all of the elements of any serious felony, shall receive, in addition to the sentence imposed by the court for the present offense, a five-year enhancement for each such prior conviction on charges brought and tried separately. The terms of the present offense and each enhancement shall run consecutively.

(2) This subdivision shall not be applied when the punishment imposed under other provisions of law would result in a longer term of imprisonment. There is no requirement of prior incarceration or commitment for this subdivision to apply.

(3) The Legislature may increase the length of the enhancement of sentence provided in this subdivision by a statute passed by majority vote of each house thereof.

(4) As used in this subdivision, "serious felony" means a serious felony listed in subdivision (c) of Section 1192.7.

(5) This subdivision shall not apply to a person convicted of selling, furnishing, administering, or giving, or offering to sell, furnish, administer, or give to a minor any methamphetamine-related drug or any precursors of methamphetamine unless the prior conviction was for a serious felony described in subparagraph (24) of subdivision (c) of Section 1192.7.

(b) It is the intent of the Legislature in enacting subdivisions (b) to (i), inclusive, to ensure longer prison sentences and greater punishment for those who commit a felony and have been previously convicted of one or more serious and/or violent felony offenses.

(c) Notwithstanding any other law, if a defendant has been convicted of a felony and it has been pled and proved that the defendant has one or more prior serious and/or violent felony convictions as defined in subdivision (d), the court shall adhere to each of the following:

(1) There shall not be an aggregate term limitation for purposes of consecutive sentencing for any subsequent felony conviction.

(2) Probation for the current offense shall not be granted, nor shall execution or imposition of the sentence be suspended for any prior offense.

(3) The length of time between the prior serious and/or violent felony conviction and the current felony conviction shall not affect the imposition of sentence.

(4) There shall not be a commitment to any other facility other than the state prison. Diversion shall not be granted nor shall the defendant be eligible for commitment to the California Rehabilitation Center as provided in Article 2 (commencing with Section 3050) of Chapter 1 of Division 3 of the Welfare and Institutions Code.

(5) The total amount of credits awarded pursuant to Article 2.5 (commencing with Section 2930) of Chapter 7 of Title 1 of Part 3 shall not exceed one-fifth of the total term of imprisonment imposed and shall not accrue until the defendant is physically placed in the state prison.

(6) If there is a current conviction for more than one felony count not committed on the same occasion, and not arising from the same set of operative facts, the court shall sentence the defendant consecutively on each count pursuant to subdivision (e).

(7) If there is a current conviction for more than one serious or violent felony as described in paragraph (6), the court shall impose the sentence for each conviction consecutive to the sentence for any other conviction for which the defendant may be consecutively sentenced in the manner prescribed by law.

(8) Any sentence imposed pursuant to subdivision (e) will be imposed consecutive to any other sentence which the defendant is already serving, unless otherwise provided by law.

(d) Notwithstanding any other law and for the purposes of subdivisions (b) to (i), inclusive, a prior conviction of a serious and/or violent felony shall be defined as:

(1) Any offense defined in subdivision (c) of Section 667.5 as a violent felony or any offense defined in subdivision (c) of Section 1192.7 as a serious felony in this state. The determination of whether a prior conviction is a prior felony conviction for purposes of subdivisions (b) to (i), inclusive, shall be made upon the date of that prior conviction and is not affected by the sentence imposed unless the sentence automatically, upon the initial sentencing, converts the felony to a misdemeanor. None of the following dispositions shall affect the determination that a prior conviction is a prior felony for purposes of subdivisions (b) to (i), inclusive:

(A) The suspension of imposition of judgment or sentence.

(B) The stay of execution of sentence.

(C) The commitment to the State Department of Health Services as a mentally disordered sex offender following a conviction of a felony.

(D) The commitment to the California Rehabilitation Center or any other facility whose function is rehabilitative diversion from the state prison.

(2) A prior conviction in another jurisdiction for an offense that, if committed in California, is punishable by imprisonment in the state prison shall constitute a prior conviction of a particular serious and/or violent felony if the prior conviction in the other jurisdiction is for an offense that includes all of the elements of a particular violent felony as defined in subdivision (c) of Section 667.5 or serious felony as defined in subdivision (c) of Section 1192.7.

(3) A prior juvenile adjudication shall constitute a prior serious and/or violent felony conviction for purposes of sentence enhancement if:

(A) The juvenile was 16 years of age or older at the time he or she committed the prior offense.

(B) The prior offense is listed in subdivision (b) of Section 707 of the Welfare and Institutions Code or described in paragraph (1) or (2) as a serious and/or violent felony.

(C) The juvenile was found to be a fit and proper subject to be dealt with under the juvenile court law.

(D) The juvenile was adjudged a ward of the juvenile court within the meaning of Section 602 of the Welfare and Institutions Code because the person committed an offense listed in subdivision (b) of Section 707 of the Welfare and Institutions Code.

(e) For purposes of subdivisions (b) to (i), inclusive, and in addition to any other enhancement or punishment provisions which may apply, the following shall apply where a defendant has one or more prior serious and/or violent felony convictions:

(1) If a defendant has one prior serious and/or violent felony conviction as defined in subdivision (d) that has been pled and proved, the determinate term or minimum term for an indeterminate term shall be twice the term otherwise provided as punishment for the current felony conviction.

(2) (A) Except as provided in subparagraph (C), if a defendant has two or more prior serious and/or violent felony convictions as defined in subdivision (d) that have been pled and proved, the term for the current felony conviction shall be an indeterminate term of life imprisonment with a minimum term of the indeterminate sentence calculated as the greatest of:

(i) Three times the term otherwise provided as punishment for each current felony conviction subsequent to the two or more prior serious and/or violent felony convictions.

(ii) Imprisonment in the state prison for 25 years.

(iii) The term determined by the court pursuant to Section 1170 for the underlying conviction, including any enhancement applicable under Chapter 4.5 (commencing with Section 1170) of Title 7 of Part 2, or any period prescribed by Section 190 or 3046.

(B) The indeterminate term described in subparagraph (A) shall be served consecutive to any other term of imprisonment for which a consecutive term may be imposed by law. Any other term imposed subsequent to any indeterminateterm described in subparagraph (A) shall not be merged therein but shall commence at the time the person would otherwise have been released from prison.

(C) If a defendant has two or more prior serious and/or violent felony convictions as defined in subdivision (c) of Section 667.5 or subdivision

(c) of Section 1192.7 that have been pled and proved, and the current offense is not a serious or violent felony as defined in subdivision (d), the defendant shall be sentenced pursuant to paragraph (1) of subdivision (e) unless the prosecution pleads and proves any of the following:

> (i) The current offense is a controlled substance charge, in which an allegation under Section 11370.4 or 11379.8 of the Health and Safety Code was admitted or found true.

> (ii) The current offense is a felony sex offense, defined in subdivision (d) of Section 261.5 or Section 262, or any felony offense that results in mandatory registration as a sex offender pursuant to subdivision (c) of Section 290 except for violations of Sections 266 and 285, paragraph (1) of subdivision (b) and subdivision (e) of Section 286, paragraph (1) of subdivision (b) and subdivision (e) of Section 288a, Section 311.11, and Section 314.

> (iii) During the commission of the current offense, the defendant used a firearm, was armed with a firearm or deadly weapon, or intended to cause great bodily injury to another person.

> (iv) The defendant suffered a prior serious and/or violent felony conviction, as defined in subdivision (d) of this section, for any of the following felonies:

> > (I) A "sexually violent offense" as defined in subdivision (b) of Section 6600 of the Welfare and Institutions Code.

> > (II) Oral copulation with a child who is under 14 years of age, and who is more than 10 years younger than he or she as defined by Section 288a, sodomy with another person who is under 14 years of age and more than 10 years younger than he or she as defined by Section 286, or sexual penetration with another person who is under 14 years of age, and who is more than 10 years younger than he or she, as defined by Section 289.

> > (III) A lewd or lascivious act involving a child under 14 years of age, in violation of Section 288.

(IV) Any homicide offense, including any attempted homicide offense, defined in Sections 187 to 191.5, inclusive.

(V) Solicitation to commit murder as defined in Section 653f.

(VI) Assault with a machine gun on a peace officer or firefighter, as defined in paragraph (3) of subdivision (d) of Section 245.

(VII) Possession of a weapon of mass destruction, as defined in paragraph (1) of subdivision (a) of Section 11418.

(VIII) Any serious and/or violent felony offense punishable in California by life imprisonment or death.

(f) (1) Notwithstanding any other law, subdivisions (b) to (i), inclusive, shall be applied in every case in which a defendant has one or more prior serious and/or violent felony convictions as defined in subdivision (d). The prosecuting attorney shall plead and prove each prior serious and/or violent felony conviction except as provided in paragraph (2).

(2) The prosecuting attorney may move to dismiss or strike a prior serious and/or violent felony conviction allegation in the furtherance of justice pursuant to Section 1385, or if there is insufficient evidence to prove the prior serious and/or violent felony conviction. If upon the satisfaction of the court that there is insufficient evidence to prove the prior serious and/or violent felony conviction, the court may dismiss or strike the allegation. Nothing in this section shall be read to alter a court's authority under Section 1385.

(g) Prior serious and/or violent felony convictions shall not be used in plea bargaining as defined in subdivision (b) of Section 1192.7. The prosecution shall plead and prove all known prior felony serious and/or violent convictions and shall not enter into any agreement to strike or seek the dismissal of any prior serious and/or violent felony conviction allegation except as provided in paragraph (2) of subdivision (f).

(h) All references to existing statutes in subdivisions (c) to (g), inclusive, are to statutes as they existed on November 7, 2012.

(i) If any provision of subdivisions (b) to (h), inclusive, or the application thereof to any person or circumstance is held invalid, that invalidity shall not affect other provisions or applications of those subdivisions which can be given effect without the invalid provision or application, and to this end the provisions of those subdivisions are severable.

(j) The provisions of this section shall not be amended by the Legislature except by statute passed in each house by rollcall vote entered in the journal, two-thirds of the membership concurring, or by a statute that becomes effective only when approved by the electors.

Penal Code § 1000

(Amended by Statute, Effective January 1, 2015.)

(a) This chapter shall apply whenever a case is before any court upon an accusatory pleading for a violation of Section 11350, 11357, 11364, or 11365, paragraph (2) of subdivision (b) of Section 11375, Section 11377, or Section 11550 of the Health and Safety Code, or subdivision (b) of Section 23222 of the Vehicle Code, or Section 11358 of the Health and Safety Code if the marijuana planted, cultivated, harvested, dried, or processed is for personal use, or Section 11368 of the Health and Safety Code if the narcotic drug was secured by a fictitious prescription and is for the personal use of the defendant and was not sold or furnished to another, or subdivision (d) of Section 653f if the solicitation was for acts directed to personal use only, or Section 381 or subdivision (f) of Section 647 of the Penal Code, if for being under the influence of a controlled substance, or Section 4060 of the Business and Professions Code, and it appears to the prosecuting attorney that, except as provided in subdivision (b) of Section 11357 of the Health and Safety Code, all of the following apply to the defendant:

(1) The defendant has no conviction for any offense involving controlled substances prior to the alleged commission of the charged offense.

(2) The offense charged did not involve a crime of violence or threatened violence.

(3) There is no evidence of a violation relating to narcotics or restricted dangerous drugs other than a violation of the sections listed in this subdivision.

(4) The defendant's record does not indicate that probation or parole has ever been revoked without thereafter being completed.

(5) The defendant's record does not indicate that he or she has successfully completed or been terminated from diversion or deferred entry of judgment pursuant to this chapter within five years prior to the alleged commission of the charged offense.

(6) The defendant has no prior felony conviction within five years prior to the alleged commission of the charged offense.

(b) The prosecuting attorney shall review his or her file to determine whether or not paragraphs (1) to (6), inclusive, of subdivision (a) apply to the defendant. Upon the agreement of the prosecuting attorney, law enforcement, the public defender, and the presiding judge of the criminal division of the superior court, or a judge designated by the presiding judge, this procedure shall be completed as soon as possible after the initial filing of the charges. If the defendant is found eligible, the prosecuting attorney shall file with the court a declaration in writing or state for the record the grounds upon which the determination is based, and shall make this information available to the defendant and his or her attorney. This procedure is intended to allow the court to set the hearing for deferred entry of judgment at the arraignment. If the defendant is found ineligible for deferred entry of judgment, the prosecuting attorney shall file with the court a declaration in writing or state for the record the grounds upon which the determination is based, and shall make this information available to the defendant and his or her attorney. The sole remedy of a defendant who is found ineligible for deferred entry of judgment is a postconviction appeal.

(c) All referrals for deferred entry of judgment granted by the court pursuant to this chapter shall be made only to programs that have been certified by the county drug program administrator pursuant to Chapter 1.5 (commencing with Section 1211) of Title 8, or to programs that provide services at no cost to the participant and have been deemed by the court and the county drug program administrator to be credible and effective. The defendant may request to be referred to a program in any county, as long as that program meets the criteria set forth in this subdivision.

(d) Deferred entry of judgment for a violation of Section 11368 of the Health and Safety Code shall not prohibit any administrative agency from taking disciplinary action against a licensee or from denying a license. Nothing in this subdivision shall be construed to expand or restrict the provisions of Section 1000.4.

(e) Any defendant who is participating in a program referred to in this section may be required to undergo analysis of his or her urine for the purpose of testing for the presence of any drug as part of the program. However, urine analysis results shall not be admissible as a basis for any new criminal prosecution or proceeding.

Penal Code § 1170(h)

(Added by Statute, Effective 1982.)

(h) (1) Except as provided in paragraph (3), a felony punishable pursuant to this subdivision where the term is not specified in the underlying offense shall be punishable by a term of imprisonment in a county jail for 16 months, or two or three years.

(2) Except as provided in paragraph (3), a felony punishable pursuant to this subdivision shall be punishable by imprisonment in a county jail for the term described in the underlying offense.

(3) Notwithstanding paragraphs (1) and (2), where the defendant (A) has a prior or current felony conviction for a serious felony described in subdivision (c) of Section 1192.7 or a prior or current conviction for a violent felony described in subdivision (c) of Section 667.5, (B) has a prior felony conviction in another jurisdiction for an offense that has all the elements of a serious felony described in subdivision (c) of Section 1192.7 or a violent felony described in subdivision (c) of Section 667.5, (C) is required to register as a sex offender pursuant to Chapter 5.5 (commencing with Section 290) of Title 9 of Part 1, or (D) is convicted of a crime and as part of the sentence an enhancement pursuant to Section 186.11 is imposed, an executed sentence for a felony punishable pursuant to this subdivision shall be served in state prison.

(4) Nothing in this subdivision shall be construed to prevent other dispositions authorized by law, including pretrial diversion, deferred entry of judgment, or an order granting probation pursuant to Section 1203.1.

(5) (A) Unless the court finds that, in the interests of justice, it is not appropriate in a particular case, the court, when imposing a sentence pursuant to paragraph (1) or (2), shall suspend execution of a concluding portion of the term for a period selected at the court's discretion.

(B) The portion of a defendant's sentenced term that is suspended pursuant to this paragraph shall be known as mandatory supervision, and, unless otherwise ordered by the court, shall commence upon release from physical custody or an alternative custody program, whichever is later. During the period of mandatory supervision, the defendant shall be supervised by the county probation officer in accordance with the terms, conditions, and procedures generally applicable to persons placed on probation, for the remaining unserved portion of the sentence imposed by the court. The period of supervision shall be mandatory, and may not be earlier terminated except by court order. Any proceeding to revoke or modify mandatory supervision under this subparagraph shall be conducted pursuant to either subdivisions (a) and (b) of Section 1203.2 or Section 1203.3. During the period when the defendant is under that supervision, unless in actual custody related to the sentence imposed by the court, the defendant shall be entitled to only actual time credit against the term of imprisonment imposed by the court. Any time period which is suspended because a person has absconded shall not be credited toward the period of supervision.

(6) The sentencing changes made by the act that added this subdivision shall be applied prospectively to any person sentenced on or after October 1, 2011.

(7) The sentencing changes made to paragraph (5) by the act that added this paragraph shall become effective and operative on January 1, 2015, and shall be applied prospectively to any person sentenced on or after January 1, 2015.

Penal Code § 12022

(Amended by Statute, Effective January 1, 2014.)

(a) (1) Except as provided in subdivisions (c) and (d), a person who is armed with a firearm in the commission of a felony or attempted felony shall be punished by an additional and consecutive term of imprisonment pursuant to subdivision (h) of Section 1170 for one year, unless the arming is an element of that offense. This additional term shall apply to a person who is a principal in the commission of a felony or attempted felony if one or more of the principals is armed with a firearm, whether or not the person is personally armed with a firearm.

(2) Except as provided in subdivision (c), and notwithstanding subdivision (d), if the firearm is an assault weapon, as defined in Section 30510 or 30515, or a machinegun, as defined in Section 16880, or a .50 BMG rifle, as defined in Section 30530, the additional and consecutive term described in this subdivision shall be three years imprisonment pursuant to subdivision (h) of Section 1170 whether or not the arming is an element of the offense of which

the person was convicted. The additional term provided in this paragraph shall apply to any person who is a principal in the commission of a felony or attempted felony if one or more of the principals is armed with an assault weapon, machinegun, or a .50 BMG rifle, whether or not the person is personally armed with an assault weapon, machinegun, or a .50 BMG rifle.

(b) (1) A person who personally uses a deadly or dangerous weapon in the commission of a felony or attempted felony shall be punished by an additional and consecutive term of imprisonment in the state prison for one year, unless use of a deadly or dangerous weapon is an element of that offense.

(2) If the person described in paragraph (1) has been convicted of carjacking or attempted carjacking, the additional term shall be in the state prison for one, two, or three years.

(3) When a person is found to have personally used a deadly or dangerous weapon in the commission of a felony or attempted felony as provided in this subdivision and the weapon is owned by that person, the court shall order that the weapon be deemed a nuisance and disposed of in the manner provided in Sections 18000 and 18005.

(c) Notwithstanding the enhancement set forth in subdivision (a), a person who is personally armed with a firearm in the commission of a violation or attempted violation of Section 11351, 11351.5, 11352, 11366.5, 11366.6, 11378, 11378.5, 11379, 11379.5, or 11379.6 of the Health and Safety Code shall be punished by an additional and consecutive term of imprisonment pursuant to subdivision (h) of Section 1170 for three, four, or five years.

(d) Notwithstanding the enhancement set forth in subdivision (a), a person who is not personally armed with a firearm who, knowing that another principal is personally armed with a firearm, is a principal in the commission of an offense or attempted offense specified in subdivision (c), shall be punished by an additional and consecutive term of imprisonment pursuant to subdivision (h) of Section 1170 for one, two, or three years.

(e) For purposes of imposing an enhancement under Section 1170.1, the enhancements under this section shall count as a single enhancement.

(f) Notwithstanding any other provision of law, the court may strike the additional punishment for the enhancements provided in subdivision (c) or (d) in an unusual case where the interests of justice would best be served, if the court specifies on the record and enters into the minutes the circumstances indicating that the interests of justice would best be served by that disposition.

X. Revenue and Taxation Code Sections

Revenue and Taxation Code § 34010

(Amended by AB 133, Effective September 16, 2017.)

For purposes of this part:

(a) "Arm's length transaction" shall mean a sale entered into in good faith and for valuable consideration that reflects the fair market value in the open market between two informed and willing parties, neither under any compulsion to participate in the transaction.

(b) "Average market price" shall mean:

> (1) In an arm's length transaction, the average market price means the average retail price determined by the wholesale cost of the cannabis or cannabis products sold or transferred to a cannabis retailer, plus a mark-up, as determined by the department on a biannual basis in six-month intervals.

> (2) In a nonarm's length transaction, the average market price means the cannabis retailer's gross receipts from the retail sale of the cannabis or cannabis products.

(c) "Department" shall mean the California Department of Tax and Fee Administration or its successor agency.

(d) "Bureau" shall mean the Bureau of Cannabis Control within the Department of Consumer Affairs.

(e) "Tax Fund" means the California Cannabis Tax Fund created by Section 34018.

(f) "Cannabis" shall have the same meaning as set forth in Section 11018 of the Health and Safety Code and shall also mean medicinal cannabis.

(g) "Cannabis products" shall have the same meaning as set forth in Section 11018.1 of the Health and Safety Code and shall also mean medicinal concentrates and medicinal cannabis products.

(h) "Cannabis flowers" shall mean the dried flowers of the cannabis plant as defined by the board.

(i) "Cannabis leaves" shall mean all parts of the cannabis plant other than cannabis flowers that are sold or consumed.

(j) "Cannabis retailer" shall mean a person required to be licensed as a retailer, microbusiness, or nonprofit pursuant to Division 10 (commencing with Section 26000) of the Business and Professions Code.

(k) "Cultivator" shall mean all persons required to be licensed to cultivate cannabis pursuant to Division 10 (commencing with Section 26000) of the Business and Professions Code.

(l) "Distributor" shall mean a person required to be licensed as a distributor pursuant to Division 10 (commencing with Section 26000) of the Business and Professions Code.

(m) "Enters the commercial market" shall mean cannabis or cannabis product, except for immature cannabis plants and seeds, that complete and comply with a quality assurance review and testing, as described in Section 26110 of the Business and Professions Code.

(n) "Gross receipts" shall have the same meaning as set forth in Section 6012.

(o) "Microbusiness" shall have the same meaning as set forth in paragraph (3) of subdivision (a) of Section 26070 of the Business and Professions Code.

(p) "Nonprofit" shall have the same meaning as set forth in Section 26070.5 of the Business and Professions Code.

(q) "Person" shall have the same meaning as set forth in Section 6005.

(r) "Retail sale" shall have the same meaning as set forth in Section 6007.

(s) "Sale" and "purchase" shall mean any change of title or possession, exchange, or barter, conditional or otherwise, in any manner or by any means whatsoever, for consideration.

(t) "Transfer" shall mean to grant, convey, hand over, assign, sell, exchange, or barter, in any manner or by any means, with or without consideration.

(u) "Unprocessed cannabis" shall include cannabis flowers, cannabis leaves, or other categories of harvested cannabis, categories for unprocessed or frozen cannabis or immature plants, or cannabis that is shipped directly to manufacturers.

(v) "Manufacturer" shall mean a person required to be licensed as a manufacturer pursuant to Division 10 (commencing with Section 26000) of the Business and Professions Code.

Revenue and Taxation Code § 34011

(Amended by AB 133, Effective September 16, 2017.)

(a) (1) Effective January 1, 2018, a cannabis excise tax shall be imposed upon purchasers of cannabis or cannabis products sold in this state at the rate of 15 percent of the average market price of any retail sale by a cannabis retailer. A purchaser's liability for the cannabis excise tax is not extinguished until the cannabis excise tax has been paid to this state except that an invoice, receipt, or other document from a cannabis retailer given to the purchaser pursuant to this subdivision is sufficient to relieve the purchaser from further liability for the tax to which the invoice, receipt, or other document refers.

(2) Each cannabis retailer shall provide a purchaser with an invoice, receipt, or other document that includes a statement that reads: "The cannabis excise taxes are included in the total amount of this invoice."

(3) The department may prescribe other means to display the cannabis excise tax on an invoice, receipt, or other document from a cannabis retailer given to the purchaser.

(b) (1) A distributor in an arm's length transaction shall collect the cannabis excise tax from the cannabis retailer on or before 90 days after the sale or transfer of cannabis or cannabis product to the cannabis retailer. A distributor in a nonarm's length transaction shall collect the cannabis excise tax from the cannabis retailer on or before 90 days after the sale or transfer of cannabis or cannabis product to the cannabis retailer, or at the time of retail sale by the cannabis retailer, whichever is earlier. A distributor shall report and remit the cannabis excise tax to the department pursuant to Section 34015. A cannabis retailer shall be responsible for collecting the cannabis excise tax from the purchaser and remitting the cannabis excise tax to the distributor in accordance with rules and procedures established under law and any regulations adopted by the department.

(2) A distributor shall provide an invoice, receipt, or other similar document to the cannabis retailer that identifies the licensee receiving the product, the distributor from which the product originates, including the associated unique identifier, the amount of cannabis excise tax, and any other information deemed necessary by the department. The department may authorize other forms of documentation under this paragraph.

(c) The excise tax imposed by this section shall be in addition to the sales and use tax imposed by the state and local governments.

(d) Gross receipts from the sale of cannabis or cannabis products for purposes of assessing the sales and use tax under Part 1 (commencing with Section 6001) shall include the tax levied pursuant to this section.

(e) Cannabis or cannabis products shall not be sold to a purchaser unless the excise tax required by law has been paid by the purchaser at the time of sale.

(f) The sales and use taxes imposed by Part 1 (commencing with Section 6001) shall not apply to retail sales of medicinal cannabis, medicinal cannabis concentrate, edible medicinal cannabis products, or topical cannabis as those terms are defined in Division 10 (commencing with Section 26000) of the Business and Professions Code when a qualified patient or primary caregiver for a qualified patient provides his or her card issued under Section 11362.71 of the Health and Safety Code and a valid government-issued identification card.

Revenue and Taxation Code § 34012

(Amended by AB 133, Effective September 16, 2017.)

(a) Effective January 1, 2018, there is hereby imposed a cultivation tax on all harvested cannabis that enters the commercial market upon all cultivators. The tax shall be due after the cannabis is harvested and enters the commercial market.

(1) The tax for cannabis flowers shall be nine dollars and twenty-five cents ($9.25) per dry-weight ounce.

(2) The tax for cannabis leaves shall be set at two dollars and seventy-five cents ($2.75) per dry-weight ounce.

(b) The department may adjust the tax rate for cannabis leaves annually to reflect fluctuations in the relative price of cannabis flowers to cannabis leaves.

(c) The department may from time to time establish other categories of harvested cannabis, categories for unprocessed or frozen cannabis or immature plants, or cannabis that is shipped directly to manufacturers. These categories shall be taxed at their relative value compared with cannabis flowers.

(d) The department may prescribe by regulation a method and manner for payment of the cultivation tax that utilizes tax stamps or state-issued product bags that indicate that all required tax has been paid on the product to which the tax stamp is affixed or in which the cannabis is packaged.

(e) The tax stamps and product bags shall be of the designs, specifications, and denominations as may be prescribed by the department and may be purchased by any licensee under Division 10 (commencing with Section 26000) of the Business and Professions Code.

(f) Subsequent to the establishment of a tax stamp program, the department may by regulation provide that cannabis shall not be removed from a licensed cultivation facility or transported on a public highway unless in a state-issued product bag bearing a tax stamp in the proper denomination.

(g) The tax stamps and product bags shall be capable of being read by a scanning or similar device and must be traceable utilizing the track and trace system pursuant to Section 26068 of the Business and Professions Code.

(h) Cultivators shall be responsible for payment of the tax pursuant to regulations adopted by the department. A cultivator's liability for the tax is not extinguished until the tax has been paid to this state except that an invoice, receipt, or other document from a distributor or manufacturer given to the cultivator pursuant to paragraph (3) is sufficient to relieve the cultivator from further liability for the tax to which the invoice, receipt, or other document refers. Cannabis shall not be sold unless the tax has been paid as provided in this part.

> (1) A distributor shall collect the cultivation tax from a cultivator on all harvested cannabis that enters the commercial market. This paragraph shall not apply where a cultivator is not required to send, and does not send, the harvested cannabis to a distributor.

> (2) (A) A manufacturer shall collect the cultivation tax from a cultivator on the first sale or transfer of unprocessed cannabis by a cultivator to a manufacturer. The manufacturer shall remit the cultivation tax collected on the cannabis product sold or transferred to a distributor for quality

assurance, inspection, and testing, as described in Section 26110 of the Business and Professions Code. This paragraph shall not apply where a distributor collects the cultivation tax from a cultivator pursuant to paragraph (1).

(B) Notwithstanding subparagraph (A), the department may prescribe a substitute method and manner for collection and remittance of the cultivation tax under this paragraph, including a method and manner for collection of the cultivation tax by a distributor.

(3) A distributor or manufacturer shall provide to the cultivator, and a distributor that collects the cultivation tax from a manufacturer pursuant to paragraph (2) shall provide to the manufacturer, an invoice, receipt, or other similar document that identifies the licensee receiving the product, the cultivator from which the product originates, including the associated unique identifier, the amount of cultivation tax, and any other information deemed necessary by the department. The department may authorize other forms of documentation under this paragraph.

(4) The department may adopt regulations prescribing procedures for the refund of cultivation tax collected on cannabis or cannabis product that fails quality assurance, inspection, and testing as described in Section 26110 of the Business and Professions Code.

(i) All cannabis removed from a cultivator's premises, except for plant waste, shall be presumed to be sold and thereby taxable under this section.

(j) The tax imposed by this section shall be imposed on all cannabis cultivated in the state pursuant to rules and regulations promulgated by the department, but shall not apply to cannabis cultivated for personal use under Section 11362.1 of the Health and Safety Code or cultivated by a qualified patient or primary caregiver in accordance with the Compassionate Use Act of 1996 (Section 11362.5 of the Health and Safety Code).

(k) Beginning January 1, 2020, the rates set forth in subdivisions (a), (b), and (c) shall be adjusted by the department annually thereafter for inflation.

(l) The Department of Food and Agriculture is not responsible for enforcing any provisions of the cultivation tax.

Revenue and Taxation Code § 34012.5

(Amended by AB 133, Effective September 16, 2017.)

(a) The cultivation tax and cannabis excise tax required to be collected by the distributor, or required to be collected by the manufacturer pursuant to paragraph (2) of subdivision (h) of Section 34012, and any amount unreturned to the cultivator or cannabis retailer that is not tax but was collected from the cultivator or cannabis retailer under the representation by the distributor or the manufacturer that it was tax constitute debts owed by the distributor or the manufacturer to this state.

(b) A distributor or manufacturer that has collected any amount of tax in excess of the amount of tax imposed by this part and actually due from a cultivator or cannabis retailer, may refund such amount to the cultivator or cannabis retailer, even though such tax amount has already been paid over to the department and no corresponding credit or refund has yet been secured. The distributor or manufacturer may claim credit for that overpayment against the amount of tax imposed by this part that is due upon any other quarterly return, providing that credit is claimed in a return dated no later than three years from the date of overpayment.

(c) Any tax collected from a cultivator or cannabis retailer that has not been remitted to the department shall be deemed a debt owed to the State of California by the person required to collect and remit the tax.

Revenue and Taxation Code § 34013

(MAUCRSA, Effective June 27, 2017.)

(a) The board shall administer and collect the taxes imposed by this part pursuant to the Fee Collection Procedures Law (Part 30 (commencing with Section 55001)). For purposes of this part, the references in the Fee Collection Procedures Law to "fee" shall include the taxes imposed by this part, and references to "feepayer" shall include a person required to pay or collect the taxes imposed by this part.

(b) The board may prescribe, adopt, and enforce regulations relating to the administration and enforcement of this part, including, but not limited to, collections, reporting, refunds, and appeals.

(c) The board shall adopt necessary rules and regulations to administer the taxes in this part. Such rules and regulations may include methods or procedures to tag cannabis or cannabis products, or the packages thereof, to designate prior tax payment.

(d) Until January 1, 2019, the board may prescribe, adopt, and enforce any emergency regulations as necessary to implement, administer, and enforce its duties under this division. Any emergency regulation prescribed, adopted, or enforced pursuant to this section shall be adopted in accordance with Chapter 3.5 (commencing with Section 11340) of Part 1 of Division 3 of Title 2 of the Government Code, and, for purposes of that chapter, including Section 11349.6 of the Government Code, the adoption of the regulation is an emergency and shall be considered by the Office of Administrative Law as necessary for the immediate preservation of the public peace, health and safety, and general welfare. Notwithstanding any other provision of law, the emergency regulations adopted by the board may remain in effect for two years from adoption.

(e) Any person required to be licensed pursuant to Division 10 (commencing with Section 26000) of the Business and Professions Code who fails to pay the taxes imposed under this part shall, in addition to owing the taxes not paid, be subject to a penalty of at least one-half the amount of the taxes not paid, and shall be subject to having its license revoked pursuant to Section 26031 of the Business and Professions Code.

(f) The board may bring such legal actions as are necessary to collect any deficiency in the tax required to be paid, and, upon the board's request, the Attorney General shall bring the actions.

Revenue and Taxation Code § 34014

(MAUCRSA, Effective June 27, 2017.)

(a) All distributors must obtain a separate permit from the board pursuant to regulations adopted by the board. No fee shall be charged to any person for issuance of the permit. Any person required to obtain a permit who engages in business as a distributor without a permit or after a permit has been canceled, suspended, or revoked, and each officer of any corporation which so engages in business, is guilty of a misdemeanor.

(b) The board may require every licensed distributor, retailer, cultivator, microbusiness, nonprofit, or other person required to be licensed, to provide security to cover the liability for taxes imposed by state law on cannabis produced or received by the retailer, cultivator, microbusiness, nonprofit, or other person required to be licensed in accordance with procedures to be established by the board. Notwithstanding anything herein to the contrary, the board may waive any security requirement it imposes for good cause, as determined by the board. "Good cause" includes, but is not limited to, the inability of a distributor, retailer, cultivator, microbusiness, nonprofit, or other person required to be licensed to obtain security due to a lack of service providers or the policies of service providers that prohibit service to a cannabis business. A person may not commence or continue any business or operation relating to cannabis cultivation until any surety required by the board with respect to the business or operation has been properly prepared, executed, and submitted under this part.

(c) In fixing the amount of any security required by the board, the board shall give consideration to the financial hardship that may be imposed on licensees as a result of any shortage of available surety providers.

Revenue and Taxation Code § 34015

(MAUCRSA, Effective June 27, 2017.)

(a) Unless otherwise prescribed by the board pursuant to subdivision (c), the excise tax and cultivation tax imposed by this part is due and payable to the board quarterly on or before the last day of the month following each quarterly period of three months. On or before the last day of the month following each quarterly period, a return for the preceding quarterly period shall be filed with the board by each distributor using electronic media. Returns shall be authenticated in a form or pursuant to methods as may be prescribed by the board. If the cultivation tax is paid by stamp pursuant to subdivision (d) of Section 34012 the board may by regulation determine when and how the tax shall be paid.

(b) The board may require every person engaged in the cultivation, distribution, manufacturing, retail sale of cannabis or cannabis products, or any other person required to be licensed pursuant to Division 10 (commencing with Section 26000) of the Business and Professions Code to file, on or before the 25th day of each month, a report using electronic media respecting the person's inventory, purchases, and sales during the preceding month and any other information as the board may require to carry out the purposes of this part. Reports shall be authenticated in a form or pursuant to methods as may be prescribed by the board.

(c) The board may adopt regulations prescribing the due date for returns and remittances of excise tax collected by a distributor in an arm's length transaction pursuant to subdivision (b) of Section 34011.

(d) The board may make examinations of the books and records of any person licensed, or required to be licensed, pursuant to Division 10 (commencing with Section 26000) of the Business and Professions Code, as it may deem necessary in carrying out this part.

Revenue and Taxation Code § 34016

(MAUCRSA, Effective June 27, 2017.)

(a) Any peace officer or board employee granted limited peace officer status pursuant to paragraph (6) of subdivision (a) of Section 830.11 of the Penal Code, upon presenting appropriate credentials, is authorized to enter any place as described in paragraph (3) and to conduct inspections in accordance with the following paragraphs, inclusive.

> (1) Inspections shall be performed in a reasonable manner and at times that are reasonable under the circumstances, taking into consideration the normal business hours of the place to be entered.

> (2) Inspections may be at any place at which cannabis or cannabis products are sold to purchasers, cultivated, or stored, or at any site where evidence of activities involving evasion of tax may be discovered.

> (3) Inspections shall be conducted no more than once in a 24-hour period.

(b) Any person who fails or refuses to allow an inspection shall be guilty of a misdemeanor. Each offense shall be punished by a fine not to exceed five thousand dollars ($5,000), or imprisonment not exceeding one year in a county jail, or both the fine and imprisonment. The court shall order any fines assessed be deposited in the California Cannabis Tax Fund.

(c) Upon discovery by the board or a law enforcement agency that a licensee or any other person possesses, stores, owns, or has made a retail sale of cannabis or cannabis products, without evidence of tax payment or not contained in secure packaging, the board or the law enforcement agency shall be authorized to seize the cannabis or cannabis products. Any cannabis or cannabis products seized by a law enforcement agency or the board shall within seven days be deemed forfeited and the board shall comply with the procedures set forth in Sections 30436 through 30449, inclusive.

(d) Any person who renders a false or fraudulent report is guilty of a misdemeanor and subject to a fine not to exceed one thousand dollars ($1,000) for each offense.

(e) Any violation of any provisions of this part, except as otherwise provided, is a misdemeanor and is punishable as such.

(f) All moneys remitted to the board under this part shall be credited to the California Cannabis Tax Fund.

Revenue and Taxation Code § 34017

(AUMA, Effective November 9, 2016.)

The Legislative Analyst's Office shall submit a report to the Legislature by January 1, 2020, with recommendations to the Legislature for adjustments to the tax rate to achieve the goals of undercutting illicit market prices and discouraging use by persons younger than 21 years of age while ensuring sufficient revenues are generated for the programs identified in Section 34019.

Revenue and Taxation Code § 34018

(MAUCRSA, Effective June 27, 2017.)

(a) The California Cannabis Tax Fund is hereby created in the State Treasury. The Tax Fund shall consist of all taxes, interest, penalties, and other amounts collected and paid to the board pursuant to this part, less payment of refunds.

(b) Notwithstanding any other law, the California Cannabis Tax Fund is a special trust fund established solely to carry out the purposes of the Control, Regulate and Tax Adult Use of Marijuana Act and all revenues deposited into the Tax Fund, together with interest or dividends earned by the fund, are hereby continuously appropriated for the purposes of the Control, Regulate and Tax Adult Use of Marijuana Act without regard to fiscal year and shall be expended only in accordance with the provisions of this part and its purposes.

(c) Notwithstanding any other law, the taxes imposed by this part and the revenue derived therefrom, including investment interest, shall not be considered to be part of the General Fund, as that term is used in Chapter 1 (commencing with Section 16300) of Part 2 of Division 4 of the Government Code, shall not be considered General Fund revenue for purposes of Section

8 of Article XVI of the California Constitution and its implementing statutes, and shall not be considered "moneys" for purposes of subdivisions (a) and (b) of Section 8 of Article XVI of the California Constitution and its implementing statutes.

Revenue and Taxation Code § 34019

(MAUCRSA, Effective June 27, 2017.)

(a) Beginning with the 2017–18 fiscal year, the Department of Finance shall estimate revenues to be received pursuant to Sections 34011 and 34012 and provide those estimates to the Controller no later than June 15 of each year. The Controller shall use these estimates when disbursing funds pursuant to this section. Before any funds are disbursed pursuant to subdivisions (b), (c), (d), and (e) of this section, the Controller shall disburse from the Tax Fund to the appropriate account, without regard to fiscal year, the following:

> (1) Reasonable costs incurred by the board for administering and collecting the taxes imposed by this part; provided, however, such costs shall not exceed 4 percent of tax revenues received.

> (2) Reasonable costs incurred by the bureau, the Department of Consumer Affairs, the Department of Food and Agriculture, and the State Department of Public Health for implementing, administering, and enforcing Division 10 (commencing with Section 26000) of the Business and Professions Code to the extent those costs are not reimbursed pursuant to Section 26180 of the Business and Professions Code. This paragraph shall remain operative through the 2022–23 fiscal year.

> (3) Reasonable costs incurred by the Department of Fish and Wildlife, the State Water Resources Control Board, and the Department of Pesticide Regulation for carrying out their respective duties under Division 10 (commencing with Section 26000) of the Business and Professions Code to the extent those costs are not otherwise reimbursed.

> (4) Reasonable costs incurred by the Controller for performing duties imposed by the Control, Regulate and Tax Adult Use of Marijuana Act, including the audit required by Section 34020.

> (5) Reasonable costs incurred by the Department of Finance for conducting the performance audit pursuant to Section 26191 of the Business and Professions Code.

(6) Reasonable costs incurred by the Legislative Analyst's Office for performing duties imposed by Section 34017.

(7) Sufficient funds to reimburse the Division of Labor Standards Enforcement and the Division of Occupational Safety and Health within the Department of Industrial Relations and the Employment Development Department for the costs of applying and enforcing state labor laws to licensees under Division 10 (commencing with Section 26000) of the Business and Professions Code.

(b) The Controller shall next disburse the sum of ten million dollars ($10,000,000) to a public university or universities in California annually beginning with the 2018–19 fiscal year until the 2028–29 fiscal year to research and evaluate the implementation and effect of the Control, Regulate and Tax Adult Use of Marijuana Act, and shall, if appropriate, make recommendations to the Legislature and Governor regarding possible amendments to the Control, Regulate and Tax Adult Use of Marijuana Act. The recipients of these funds shall publish reports on their findings at a minimum of every two years and shall make the reports available to the public. The bureau shall select the universities to be funded. The research funded pursuant to this subdivision shall include but not necessarily be limited to:

(1) Impacts on public health, including health costs associated with cannabis use, as well as whether cannabis use is associated with an increase or decrease in use of alcohol or other drugs.

(2) The impact of treatment for maladaptive cannabis use and the effectiveness of different treatment programs.

(3) Public safety issues related to cannabis use, including studying the effectiveness of the packaging and labeling requirements and advertising and marketing restrictions contained in the act at preventing underage access to and use of cannabis and cannabis products, and studying the health-related effects among users of varying potency levels of cannabis and cannabis products.

(4) Cannabis use rates, maladaptive use rates for adults and youth, and diagnosis rates of cannabis-related substance use disorders.

(5) Cannabis market prices, illicit market prices, tax structures and rates, including an evaluation of how to best tax cannabis based on potency, and the structure and function of licensed cannabis businesses.

(6) Whether additional protections are needed to prevent unlawful monopolies or anti-competitive behavior from occurring in the adult-use cannabis industry and, if so, recommendations as to the most effective measures for preventing such behavior.

(7) The economic impacts in the private and public sectors, including, but not necessarily limited to, job creation, workplace safety, revenues, taxes generated for state and local budgets, and criminal justice impacts, including, but not necessarily limited to, impacts on law enforcement and public resources, short and long term consequences of involvement in the criminal justice system, and state and local government agency administrative costs and revenue.

(8) Whether the regulatory agencies tasked with implementing and enforcing the Control, Regulate and Tax Adult Use of Marijuana Act are doing so consistent with the purposes of the act, and whether different agencies might do so more effectively.

(9) Environmental issues related to cannabis production and the criminal prohibition of cannabis production.

(10) The geographic location, structure, and function of licensed cannabis businesses, and demographic data, including race, ethnicity, and gender, of license holders.

(11) The outcomes achieved by the changes in criminal penalties made under the Control, Regulate and Tax Adult Use of Marijuana Act for cannabis-related offenses, and the outcomes of the juvenile justice system, in particular, probation-based treatments and the frequency of up-charging illegal possession of cannabis or cannabis products to a more serious offense.

(c) The Controller shall next disburse the sum of three million dollars ($3,000,000) annually to the Department of the California Highway Patrol beginning with the 2018–19 fiscal year until the 2022–23 fiscal year to establish and adopt protocols to determine whether a driver is operating a vehicle while impaired, including impairment by the use of cannabis or cannabis products, and to establish and adopt protocols setting forth best practices to assist law enforcement agencies. The department may hire personnel to establish the protocols specified in this subdivision. In addition, the department may make grants to public and private research institutions for the purpose of developing technology for determining when a driver is operating a vehicle while impaired, including impairment by the use of cannabis or cannabis products.

(d) The Controller shall next disburse the sum of ten million dollars ($10,000,000) beginning with the 2018–19 fiscal year and increasing ten million dollars ($10,000,000) each fiscal year thereafter until the 2022–23 fiscal year, at which time the disbursement shall be fifty million dollars ($50,000,000) each year thereafter, to the Governor's Office of Business and Economic Development, in consultation with the Labor and Workforce Development Agency and the State Department of Social Services, to administer a community reinvestments grants program to local health departments and at least 50 percent to qualified community-based nonprofit organizations to support job placement, mental health treatment, substance use disorder treatment, system navigation services, legal services to address barriers to reentry, and linkages to medical care for communities disproportionately affected by past federal and state drug policies. The office shall solicit input from community-based job skills, job placement, and legal service providers with relevant expertise as to the administration of the grants program. In addition, the office shall periodically evaluate the programs it is funding to determine the effectiveness of the programs, shall not spend more than 4 percent for administrative costs related to implementation, evaluation, and oversight of the programs, and shall award grants annually, beginning no later than January 1, 2020.

(e) The Controller shall next disburse the sum of two million dollars ($2,000,000) annually to the University of California San Diego Center for Medicinal Cannabis Research to further the objectives of the center, including the enhanced understanding of the efficacy and adverse effects of cannabis as a pharmacological agent.

(f) By July 15 of each fiscal year beginning in the 2018–19 fiscal year, the Controller shall, after disbursing funds pursuant to subdivisions (a), (b), (c), (d), and (e), disburse funds deposited in the Tax Fund during the prior fiscal year into sub-trust accounts, which are hereby created, as follows:

(1) Sixty percent shall be deposited in the Youth Education, Prevention, Early Intervention and Treatment Account, and disbursed by the Controller to the State Department of Health Care Services for programs for youth that are designed to educate about and to prevent substance use disorders and to prevent harm from substance use. The State Department of Health Care Services shall enter into interagency agreements with the State Department of Public Health and the State

Department of Education to implement and administer these programs. The programs shall emphasize accurate education, effective prevention, early intervention, school retention, and timely treatment services for youth, their families and caregivers. The programs may include, but are not limited to, the following components:

(A) Prevention and early intervention services including outreach, risk survey and education to youth, families, caregivers, schools, primary care health providers, behavioral health and substance use disorder service providers, community and faith-based organizations, fostercare providers, juvenile and family courts, and others to recognize and reduce risks related to substance use, and the early signs of problematic use and of substance use disorders.

(B) Grants to schools to develop and support student assistance programs, or other similar programs, designed to prevent and reduce substance use, and improve school retention and performance, by supporting students who are at risk of dropping out of school and promoting alternatives to suspension or expulsion that focus on school retention, remediation, and professional care. Schools with higher than average dropout rates should be prioritized for grants.

(C) Grants to programs for outreach, education, and treatment for homeless youth and out-of-school youth with substance use disorders.

(D) Access and linkage to care provided by county behavioral health programs for youth, and their families and caregivers, who have a substance use disorder or who are at risk for developing a substance use disorder.

(E) Youth-focused substance use disorder treatment programs that are culturally and gender competent, trauma-informed, evidence-based and provide a continuum of care that includes screening and assessment (substance use disorder as well as mental health), early intervention, active treatment, family involvement, case management, overdose prevention, prevention of communicable diseases related to substance use, relapse management for substance use and other cooccurring behavioral health disorders, vocational services, literacy services, parenting classes, family therapy and counseling services, medication-assisted treatments, psychiatric medication and psychotherapy. When indicated, referrals must be made to other providers.

(F) To the extent permitted by law and where indicated, interventions shall utilize a two-generation approach to addressing substance use disorders with the capacity to treat youth and adults together. This would include supporting the development of family-based interventions that address substance use disorders and related problems within the context of families, including parents, foster parents, caregivers and all their children.

(G) Programs to assist individuals, as well as families and friends of drug using young people, to reduce the stigma associated with substance use including being diagnosed with a substance use disorder or seeking substance use disorder services. This includes peer-run outreach and education to reduce stigma, anti-stigma campaigns, and community recovery networks.

(H) Workforce training and wage structures that increase the hiring pool of behavioral health staff with substance use disorder prevention and treatment expertise. Provide ongoing education and coaching that increases substance use treatment providers' core competencies and trains providers on promising and evidenced-based practices.

(I) Construction of community-based youth treatment facilities.

(J) The departments may contract with each county behavioral health program for the provision of services.

(K) Funds shall be allocated to counties based on demonstrated need, including the number of youth in the county, the prevalence of substance use disorders among adults, and confirmed through statistical data, validated assessments, or submitted reports prepared by the applicable county to demonstrate and validate need.

(L) The departments shall periodically evaluate the programs they are funding to determine the effectiveness of the programs.

(M) The departments may use up to 4 percent of the moneys allocated to the Youth Education, Prevention, Early Intervention and Treatment Account for administrative costs related to implementation, evaluation, and oversight of the programs.

(N) If the Department of Finance ever determines that funding pursuant to cannabis taxation exceeds demand for youth prevention and treatment services in the state, the departments shall provide a plan to the Department of Finance to provide treatment services to adults as well as youth using these funds.

(O) The departments shall solicit input from volunteer health organizations, physicians who treat addiction, treatment researchers, family therapy and counseling providers, and professional education associations with relevant expertise as to the administration of any grants made pursuant to this paragraph.

(2) Twenty percent shall be deposited in the Environmental Restoration and Protection Account, and disbursed by the Controller as follows:

(A) To the Department of Fish and Wildlife and the Department of Parks and Recreation for the cleanup, remediation, and restoration of environmental damage in watersheds affected by cannabis cultivation and related activities including, but not limited to, damage that occurred prior to enactment of this part, and to support local partnerships for this purpose. The Department of Fish and Wildlife and the Department of Parks and Recreation may distribute a portion of the funds they receive from the Environmental Restoration and Protection Account through grants for purposes specified in this paragraph.

(B) To the Department of Fish and Wildlife and the Department of Parks and Recreation for the stewardship and operation of state-owned wildlife habitat areas and state park units in a manner that discourages and prevents the illegal cultivation, production, sale, and use of cannabis and cannabis products on public lands, and to facilitate the investigation, enforcement, and prosecution of illegal cultivation, production, sale, and use of cannabis or cannabis products on public lands.

(C) To the Department of Fish and Wildlife to assist in funding the watershed enforcement program and multiagency taskforce established pursuant to subdivisions (b) and (c) of Section 12029 of the Fish and Game Code to facilitate the investigation, enforcement, and prosecution of these offenses and to ensure the reduction of adverse impacts of cannabis cultivation, production, sale, and use on fish and wildlife habitats throughout the state.

(D) For purposes of this paragraph, the Secretary of the Natural Resources Agency shall determine the allocation of revenues between the departments. During the first five years of implementation, first consideration should be given to funding purposes specified in subparagraph (A).

(E) Funds allocated pursuant to this paragraph shall be used to increase and enhance activities described in subparagraphs (A), (B), and (C), and not replace allocation of other funding for these purposes. Accordingly, annual General Fund appropriations to the Department of Fish and Wildlife and the Department of Parks and Recreation shall not be reduced below the levels provided in the Budget Act of 2014 (Chapter 25 of the Statutes of 2014).

(3) Twenty percent shall be deposited into the State and Local Government Law Enforcement Account and disbursed by the Controller as follows:

(A) To the Department of the California Highway Patrol for conducting training programs for detecting, testing and enforcing laws against driving under the influence of alcohol and other drugs, including driving under the influence of cannabis. The department may hire personnel to conduct the training programs specified in this subparagraph.

(B) To the Department of the California Highway Patrol to fund internal California Highway Patrol programs and grants to qualified nonprofit organizations and local governments for education, prevention, and enforcement of laws related to driving under the influence of alcohol and other drugs, including cannabis; programs that help enforce traffic laws, educate the public in traffic safety, provide varied and effective means of reducing fatalities, injuries, and economic losses from collisions; and for the purchase of equipment related to enforcement of laws related to driving under the influence of alcohol and other drugs, including cannabis.

(C) To the Board of State and Community Corrections for making grants to local governments to assist with law enforcement, fire protection, or other local programs addressing public health and safety associated with the implementation of the Control, Regulate and Tax Adult Use of Marijuana Act. The board shall not make any grants to local governments which have banned the cultivation, including personal cultivation under paragraph (3) of subdivision (b) of Section 11362.2 of the Health and Safety Code, or retail sale of cannabis or cannabis products pursuant to Section 26200 of the Business and Professions Code or as otherwise provided by law.

(D) For purposes of this paragraph, the Department of Finance shall determine the allocation of revenues between the agencies; provided, however, beginning in the 2022–23 fiscal year the amount allocated pursuant to subparagraph (A) shall not be less than ten million dollars ($10,000,000) annually and the amount allocated pursuant to subparagraph (B) shall not be less than forty million dollars ($40,000,000) annually. In determining the amount to be allocated before the 2022–23 fiscal year pursuant to this paragraph, the Department of Finance shall give initial priority to subparagraph (A).

(g) Funds allocated pursuant to subdivision (f) shall be used to increase the funding of programs and purposes identified and shall not be used to replace allocation of other funding for these purposes.

(h) Effective July 1, 2028, the Legislature may amend this section by majority vote to further the purposes of the Control, Regulate and Tax Adult Use of Marijuana Act, including allocating funds to programs other than those specified in subdivisions (d) and (f). Any revisions pursuant to this subdivision shall not result in a reduction of funds to accounts established pursuant to subdivisions (d) and (f) in any subsequent year from the amount allocated to each account in the 2027–28 fiscal year. Prior to July 1, 2028, the Legislature may not change the allocations to programs specified in subdivisions (d) and (f).

Revenue and Taxation Code § 34020

(AUMA, Effective November 9, 2016.)

The Controller shall periodically audit the Tax Fund to ensure that those funds are used and accounted for in a manner consistent with this part and as otherwise required by law.

Revenue and Taxation Code § 34021

(AUMA, Effective November 9, 2016.)

(a) The taxes imposed by this Part shall be in addition to any other tax imposed by a city, county, or city and county.

Revenue and Taxation Code § 34021.5

(MAUCRSA, Effective June 27, 2017.)

(a) (1) A county may impose a tax on the privilege of cultivating, manufacturing, producing, processing, preparing, storing, providing, donating, selling, or distributing cannabis or cannabis products by a licensee operating under Division 10 (commencing with Section 26000) of the Business and Professions Code.

(2) The board of supervisors shall specify in the ordinance proposing the tax the activities subject to the tax, the applicable rate or rates, the method of apportionment, if necessary, and the manner of collection of the tax. The tax may be imposed for general governmental purposes or for purposes specified in the ordinance by the board of supervisors.

(3) In addition to any other method of collection authorized by law, the board of supervisors may provide for the collection of the tax imposed pursuant to this section in the same manner, and subject to the same penalties and priority of lien, as other charges and taxes fixed and collected by the county. A tax imposed pursuant to this section is a tax and not a fee or special assessment. The board of supervisors shall specify whether the tax applies throughout the entire county or within the unincorporated area of the county.

(4) The tax authorized by this section may be imposed upon any or all of the activities set forth in paragraph (1), as specified in the ordinance, regardless of whether the activity is undertaken individually, collectively, or cooperatively, and regardless of whether the activity is for compensation or gratuitous, as determined by the board of supervisors.

(b) A tax imposed pursuant to this section shall be subject to applicable voter approval requirements imposed by law.

(c) This section is declaratory of existing law and does not limit or prohibit the levy or collection of any other fee, charge, or tax, or a license or service fee or charge upon, or related to, the activities set forth in subdivision (a) as otherwise provided by law. This section shall not be construed as a limitation upon the taxing authority of a county as provided by law.

(d) This section shall not be construed to authorize a county to impose a sales or use tax in addition to the sales and use taxes imposed under an ordinance conforming to the provisions of Sections 7202 and 7203 of this code.

Revenue and Taxation Code § 55044

(Amended by AB 133, Effective September 16, 2017.)

(a) If the department finds that a person's failure to make a timely return or payment is due to reasonable cause and circumstances beyond the person's control, and occurred notwithstanding the exercise of ordinary care and the absence of willful neglect, the person may be relieved of the penalty provided by Sections 34013, 55042, 55050, and 55086.

(b) Except as provided in subdivision (c), any person seeking to be relieved of the penalty shall file with the department a statement, under penalty of perjury, setting forth the facts upon which he or she bases his or her claim for relief.

(c) The department shall establish criteria that provide for efficient resolution of requests for relief pursuant to this section.

XI. Vehicle Code Sections

Vehicle Code § 2429.7

(MAUCRSA, Effective June 27, 2017.)

(a) The commissioner shall appoint an impaired driving task force to develop recommendations for best practices, protocols, proposed legislation, and other policies that will address the issue of impaired driving, including driving under the influence of cannabis and controlled substances. The task force shall also examine the use of technology, including field testing technologies and validated field sobriety tests, to identify drivers under the influence of prescription drugs, cannabis, and controlled substances. The task force shall include, but is not limited to, the commissioner, who shall serve as chairperson, and at least one member from each of the following:

(1) The Office of Traffic Safety.

(2) The National Highway Traffic Safety Administration.

(3) Local law enforcement.

(4) District attorneys.

(5) Public defenders.

(6) California Association of Crime Laboratory Directors.

(7) California Attorneys for Criminal Justice.

(8) The California Cannabis Research Program, known as the Center for Medicinal Cannabis Research, authorized pursuant to Section 11362.9 of the Health and Safety Code.

(9) An organization that represents medicinal cannabis patients.

(10) Licensed physicians with expertise in substance abuse disorder treatment.

(11) Researchers with expertise in identifying impairment caused by prescription medications and controlled substances.

(12) Nongovernmental organizations committed to social justice issues.

(13) A nongovernmental organization that focuses on improving roadway safety.

(b) The members of the task force shall serve at the pleasure of the commissioner and without compensation.

(c) The task force members shall be free of economic relationships with any company that profits from the sale of technologies or equipment that is intended to identify impairment. Members and their organizations shall not receive pay from, grants from, or any form of financial support from companies or entities that sell such technologies or equipment.

(d) The task force shall make recommendations regarding prevention of impaired driving, means of identifying impaired driving, and responses to impaired driving that reduce reoccurrence, including, but not limited to, evidence-based approaches that do not rely on incarceration.

(e) The task force shall make recommendations regarding how to best capture data to evaluate the impact that cannabis legalization is having on roadway safety.

(f) By January 1, 2021, the task force shall report to the Legislature its policy recommendations and the steps state agencies are taking regarding impaired driving. The report shall be submitted in compliance with Section 9795 of the Government Code.

Vehicle Code § 23152

(Amended by Statute, Operative January 1, 2014.)

(a) It is unlawful for a person who is under the influence of any alcoholic beverage to drive a vehicle.

(b) It is unlawful for a person who has 0.08 percent or more, by weight, of alcohol in his or her blood to drive a vehicle.

For purposes of this article and Section 34501.16, percent, by weight, of alcohol in a person's blood is based upon grams of alcohol per 100 milliliters of blood or grams of alcohol per 210 liters of breath.

In any prosecution under this subdivision, it is a rebuttable presumption that the person had 0.08 percent or more, by weight, of alcohol in his or her blood at the time of driving the vehicle if the person had 0.08 percent or more, by weight, of alcohol in his or her blood at the time of the performance of a chemical test within three hours after the driving.

(c) It is unlawful for a person who is addicted to the use of any drug to drive a vehicle. This subdivision shall not apply to a person who is participating in a narcotic treatment program approved pursuant to Article 3 (commencing with Section 11875) of Chapter 1 of Part 3 of Division 10.5 of the Health and Safety Code.

(d) It is unlawful for a person who has 0.04 percent or more, by weight, of alcohol in his or her blood to drive a commercial motor vehicle, as defined in Section 15210.

In any prosecution under this subdivision, it is a rebuttable presumption that the person had 0.04 percent or more, by weight, of alcohol in his or her blood at the time of driving the vehicle if the person had 0.04 percent or more, by weight, of alcohol in his or her blood at the time of the performance of a chemical test within three hours after the driving.

(e) It is unlawful for a person who is under the influence of any drug to drive a vehicle.

(f) It is unlawful for a person who is under the combined influence of any alcoholic beverage and drug to drive a vehicle.

(g) This section shall become operative on January 1, 2014.

Vehicle Code § 23220

(Amended by SB 65, Effective January 1, 2018.)

(a) A person shall not drink any alcoholic beverage or smoke or ingest marijuana or any marijuana product while driving a motor vehicle on any lands described in subdivision (c).

(b) A person shall not drink any alcoholic beverage or smoke or ingest marijuana or any marijuana product while riding as a passenger in any motor vehicle being driven on any lands described in subdivision (c).

(c) As used in this section, "lands" means those lands to which the Chappie-Z'berg Off-Highway Motor Vehicle Law of 1971 (Division 16.5 (commencing with Section 38000)) applies as to off-highway motor vehicles, as described in Section 38001.

(d) A violation of subdivision (a) or (b) shall be punished as an infraction.

Vehicle Code § 23221

(Amended by SB 65, Effective January 1, 2018.)

(a) A driver shall not drink any alcoholic beverage or smoke or ingest marijuana or any marijuana product while driving a motor vehicle upon a highway.

(b) A passenger shall not drink any alcoholic beverage or smoke or ingest marijuana or any marijuana product while in a motor vehicle being driven upon a highway.

(c) A violation of this section shall be punished as an infraction.

Vehicle Code § 23222

(MAUCRSA, Effective June 27, 2017.)

(a) No person shall have in his or her possession on his or her person, while driving a motor vehicle upon a highway or on lands, as described in subdivision (b) of Section 23220, any bottle, can, or other receptacle, containing any alcoholic beverage which has been opened, or a seal broken, or the contents of which have been partially removed.

(b) (1) Except as authorized by law, every person who has in his or her possession on his or her person, while driving a motor vehicle upon a highway or on lands, as described in subdivision (b) of Section 23220, any receptacle containing any cannabis or cannabis products, as defined by Section 11018.1 of the Health and Safety Code, which has been opened or has a seal broken, or loose cannabis flower not in a container, is guilty of an infraction punishable by a fine of not more than one hundred dollars ($100).

(2) Paragraph (1) does not apply to a person who has a receptacle containing cannabis or cannabis products that has been opened, has a seal broken, or the contents of which have been partially removed, or to a person who has loose cannabis flower not in a container, if the receptacle or loose cannabis flower not in a container is in the trunk of the vehicle.

(c) Subdivision (b) does not apply to a qualified patient or person with an identification card, as defined in Section 11362.7 of the Health and Safety Code, if both of the following apply:

(1) The person is carrying a current identification card or a physician's recommendation.

(2) The cannabis or cannabis product is contained in a container or receptacle that is either sealed, resealed, or closed.

Vehicle Code § 40000.15

(Amended by Statute, Effective January 1, 2007.)

A violation of any of the following provisions shall constitute a misdemeanor, and not an infraction:

Subdivision (g), (j), (k), (l), or (m) of Section 22658, relating to unlawfully towed or stored vehicles.

Sections 23103 and 23104, relating to reckless driving.

Section 23109, relating to speed contests or exhibitions.

Subdivision (a) of Section 23110, relating to throwing at vehicles.

Section 23152, relating to driving under the influence.

Subdivision (b) of Section 23222, relating to possession of marijuana.

Subdivision (a) or (b) of Section 23224, relating to persons under 21 years of age knowingly driving, or being a passenger in, a motor vehicle carrying any alcoholic beverage.

Section 23253, relating to directions on toll highways or vehicular crossings.

Section 23332, relating to trespassing.

Section 24002.5, relating to unlawful operation of a farm vehicle.

Section 24011.3, relating to vehicle bumper strength notices.

Section 27150.1, relating to sale of exhaust systems.

Section 27362, relating to child passenger seat restraints.

Section 28050, relating to true mileage driven.

Section 28050.5, relating to nonfunctional odometers.

Section 28051, relating to resetting odometers.

Section 28051.5, relating to devices to reset odometers.

Subdivision (d) of Section 28150, relating to possessing four or more jamming devices.

XII. Water Code Sections

Water Code § 25

(Added by Statute, Effective 1967.)

"Board," unless otherwise specified, means the State Water Resources Control Board.

Water Code § 1052

(Amended by Statute, Effective March 1, 2014.)

(a) The diversion or use of water subject to this division other than as authorized in this division is a trespass.

(b) The Attorney General, upon request of the board, shall institute in the superior court in and for any county where the diversion or use is threatened, is occurring, or has occurred an action for the issuance of injunctive relief as may be warranted by way of temporary restraining order, preliminary injunction, or permanent injunction.

(c) Any person or entity committing a trespass as defined in this section may be liable in an amount not to exceed the following:

(1) If the unauthorized diversion or use occurs in a critically dry year immediately preceded by two or more consecutive below normal, dry, or critically dry years or during a period for which the Governor has issued a proclamation of a state of emergency under the California Emergency Services Act (Chapter 7 (commencing with Section 8550) of Division 1 of Title 2 of the Government Code) based on drought conditions, the sum of the following:

(A) One thousand dollars ($1,000) for each day in which the trespass occurs.

(B) Two thousand five hundred dollars ($2,500) for each acre-foot of water diverted or used in excess of that diverter's water rights.

(2) If the unauthorized diversion or use is not described by paragraph (1), five hundred dollars ($500) for each day in which the unauthorized

diversion or use occurs.

(d) Civil liability for a violation of this section may be imposed by the superior court or the board as follows:

(1) The superior court may impose civil liability in an action brought by the Attorney General, upon request of the board, to impose, assess, and recover any sums pursuant to subdivision (c). In determining the appropriate amount, the court shall take into consideration all relevant circumstances, including, but not limited to, the extent of harm caused by the violation, the nature and persistence of the violation, the length of time over which the violation occurs, and the corrective action, if any, taken by the violator.

(2) The board may impose civil liability in accordance with Section 1055.

(e) All funds recovered pursuant to this section shall be deposited in the Water Rights Fund established pursuant to Section 1550.

(f) The remedies prescribed in this section are cumulative and not alternative.

Water Code § 1525

(SB 837, Effective June 27, 2016.)

(a) Each person or entity who holds a permit or license to appropriate water, and each lessor of water leased under Chapter 1.5 (commencing with Section 1020) of Part 1, shall pay an annual fee according to a fee schedule established by the board.

(b) Each person or entity who files any of the following shall pay a fee according to a fee schedule established by the board:

(1) An application for a permit to appropriate water.

(2) A registration of appropriation for a small domestic use, small irrigation use, or livestock stockpond use.

(3) A petition for an extension of time within which to begin construction, to complete construction, or to apply the water to full beneficial use under a permit.

(4) A petition to change the point of diversion, place of use, or purpose

of use, under a permit, license, or registration.

(5) A petition to change the conditions of a permit or license, requested by the permittee or licensee, that is not otherwise subject to paragraph (3) or (4).

(6) A petition to change the point of discharge, place of use, or purpose of use, of treated wastewater, requested pursuant to Section 1211.

(7) An application for approval of a water lease agreement.

(8) A request for release from priority pursuant to Section 10504.

(9) An application for an assignment of a state-filed application pursuant to Section 10504.

(10) A statement of water diversion and use pursuant to Part 5.1 (commencing with Section 5100) that reports that water was used for cannabis cultivation.

(c) The board shall set the fee schedule authorized by this section so that the total amount of fees collected pursuant to this section equals that amount necessary to recover costs incurred in connection with the issuance, administration, review, monitoring, and enforcement of permits, licenses, certificates, and registrations to appropriate water, water leases, statements of water diversion and use for cannabis cultivation, and orders approving changes in point of discharge, place of use, or purpose of use of treated wastewater. The board may include, as recoverable costs, but is not limited to including, the costs incurred in reviewing applications, registrations, statements of water diversion and use for cannabis cultivation, petitions and requests, prescribing terms of permits, licenses, registrations, and change orders, enforcing and evaluating compliance with permits, licenses, certificates, registrations, change orders, and water leases, inspection, monitoring, planning, modeling, reviewing documents prepared for the purpose of regulating the diversion and use of water, applying and enforcing the prohibition set forth in Section 1052 against the unauthorized diversion or use of water subject to this division and the water diversion related provisions of Article 6 (commencing with Section 19331) of Chapter 3.5 of Division 8 of the Business and Professions Code, and the administrative costs incurred in connection with carrying out these actions.

(d) (1) The board shall adopt the schedule of fees authorized under this section as emergency regulations in accordance with Section 1530.

(2) For filings subject to subdivision (b), the schedule may provide for a single filing fee or for an initial filing fee followed by an annual fee, as appropriate to the type of filing involved, and may include supplemental fees for filings that have already been made but have not yet been acted upon by the board at the time the schedule of fees takes effect.

(3) The board shall set the amount of total revenue collected each year through the fees authorized by this section at an amount equal to the amounts appropriated by the Legislature for expenditure for support of water rights program activities from the Water Rights Fund established under Section 1550, taking into account the reserves in the Water Rights Fund. The board shall review and revise the fees each fiscal year as necessary to conform with the amounts appropriated. If the board determines that the revenue collected during the preceding year was greater than, or less than, the amounts appropriated, the board may further adjust the annual fees to compensate for the over or under collection of revenue.

(e) Annual fees imposed pursuant to this section for the 2003–04 fiscal year shall be assessed for the entire 2003–04 fiscal year.

Water Code § 1535

(SB 837, Effective June 27, 2016.)

(a) Any fee subject to this chapter that is required in connection with the filing of an application, registration, request, statement, or proof of claim, other than an annual fee required after the period covered by the initial filing fee, shall be paid to the board.

(b) If a fee established under subdivision (b) of Section 1525, Section 1528, or Section 13160.1 is not paid when due, the board may cancel the application, registration, petition, request, statement, or claim, or may refer the matter to the State Board of Equalization for collection of the unpaid fee.

Water Code § 1831

(MAUCRSA, Effective June 27, 2017.)

(a) When the board determines that any person is violating, or threatening to violate, any requirement described in subdivision (d), the board may issue an order to that person to cease and desist from that violation.

(b) The cease and desist order shall require that person to comply forthwith or in accordance with a time schedule set by the board.

(c) The board may issue a cease and desist order only after notice and an opportunity for hearing pursuant to Section 1834.

(d) The board may issue a cease and desist order in response to a violation or threatened violation of any of the following:

(1) The prohibition set forth in Section 1052 against the unauthorized diversion or use of water subject to this division.

(2) Any term or condition of a permit, license, certification, or registration issued under this division.

(3) Any decision or order of the board issued under this part, Section 275, Chapter 11 (commencing with Section 10735) of Part 2.74 of Division 6, or Article 7 (commencing with Section 13550) of Chapter 7 of Division 7, in which decision or order the person to whom the cease and desist order will be issued, or a predecessor in interest to that person, was named as a party directly affected by the decision or order.

(4) A regulation adopted under Section 1058.5.

(5) Any extraction restriction, limitation, order, or regulation adopted or issued under Chapter 11 (commencing with Section 10735) of Part 2.74 of Division 6.

(6) Any diversion or use of water for cannabis cultivation if any of paragraphs (1) to (5), inclusive, or any of the following applies:

(A) A license is required, but has not been obtained, under Chapter 6 (commencing with Section 26060) or Chapter 7 (commencing with Section 26070) of Division 10 of the Business and Professions Code.

(B) The diversion is not in compliance with an applicable limitation or requirement established by the board or the Department of Fish and Wildlife under Section 13149.

(C) The diversion or use is not in compliance with a requirement imposed under paragraphs (1) and (2) of subdivision (b) of Section 26060.1 of, and paragraph (3) of subdivision (a) of Section 26070 of, the Business and Professions Code.

(e) This article does not alter the regulatory authority of the board under other provisions of law.

Water Code § 1840

(MCRSA- SB 837, Effective June 27, 2016.)

(a) (1) Except as provided in subdivision (b), a person who, on or after January 1, 2016, diverts 10 acre-feet of water per year or more under a permit or license shall install and maintain a device or employ a method capable of measuring the rate of direct diversion, rate of collection to storage, and rate of withdrawal or release from storage. The measurements shall be made using the best available technologies and best professional practices, as defined in Section 5100, using a device or methods satisfactory to the board, as follows:

> (A) A device shall be capable of continuous monitoring of the rate and quantity of water diverted and shall be properly maintained. The permittee or licensee shall provide the board with evidence that the device has been installed with the first   report submitted after installation of the device. The permittee or licensee shall provide the board with evidence demonstrating that the device is functioning properly as part of the reports submitted at five-year intervals after the report documenting installation of the device, or upon request of the board.

> (B) In developing regulations pursuant to Section 1841, the board shall consider devices and methods that provide accurate measurement of the total amount diverted and the rate of diversion. The board shall consider devices and methods that provide accurate measurements within an acceptable range of error, including the following:

>> (i) Electricity records dedicated to a pump and recent pump test.

>> (ii) Staff gage calibrated with an acceptable streamflow rating curve.

>> (iii) Staff gage calibrated for a flume or weir.

>> (iv) Staff gage calibrated with an acceptable storage capacity curve.

>> (v) Pressure transducer and acceptable storage capacity curve.

(2) The permittee or licensee shall maintain a record of all diversion monitoring that includes the date, time, and diversion rate at time intervals of one hour or less, and the total amount of water diverted. These records shall be included with reports submitted under the permit or license, as required under subdivision (c), or upon request of the board.

(b) (1) The board may modify the requirements of subdivision (a) upon finding either of the following:

(A) That strict compliance is infeasible, is unreasonably expensive, would unreasonably affect public trust uses, or would result in the waste or unreasonable use of water.

(B) That the need for monitoring and reporting is adequately addressed by other conditions of the permit or license.

(2) The board may increase the 10-acre-foot reporting threshold of subdivision (a) in a watershed or subwatershed, after considering the diversion reporting threshold in relation to quantity of water within the watershed or subwatershed. The board may increase the 10-acre-foot reporting threshold to 25 acre-feet or above if it finds that the benefits of the additional information within the watershed or subwatershed are substantially outweighed by the cost of installing measuring devices or employing methods for measurement for diversions at the 10-acre-foot threshold.

(c) At least annually, a person who diverts water under a registration, permit, or license shall report to the board the following information:

(1) The quantity of water diverted by month.

(2) The maximum rate of diversion by months in the preceding calendar year.

(3) The information required by subdivision (a), if applicable.

(4) The amount of water used, if any, for cannabis cultivation.

(d) Compliance with the applicable requirements of this section is a condition of every registration, permit, or license.

Water Code § 1845

(SB 837, Effective June 27, 2016.)

(a) Upon the failure of any person to comply with a cease and desist order issued by the board pursuant to this chapter, the Attorney General, upon the request of the board, shall petition the superior court for the issuance of prohibitory or mandatory injunctive relief as appropriate, including a temporary restraining order, preliminary injunction, or permanent injunction.

(b) (1) A person or entity who violates a cease and desist order issued pursuant to this chapter may be liable in an amount not to exceed the following:

> (A) If the violation occurs in a critically dry year immediately preceded by two or more consecutive below normal, dry, or critically dry years or during a period for which the Governor has issued a proclamation of a state of emergency under the California Emergency Services Act (Chapter 7 (commencing with Section 8550) of Division 1 of Title 2 of the Government Code) based on drought conditions, ten thousand dollars ($10,000) for each day in which the violation occurs.

> (B) If the violation is not described by subparagraph (A), one thousand dollars ($1,000) for each day in which the violation occurs.

(2) Civil liability may be imposed by the superior court. The Attorney General, upon the request of the board, shall petition the superior court to impose, assess, and recover those sums.

(3) Civil liability may be imposed administratively by the board pursuant to Section 1055.

Water Code § 1846

(SB 837, Effective June 27, 2016.)

(a) A person or entity may be liable for a violation of any of the following in an amount not to exceed five hundred dollars ($500) for each day in which the violation occurs:

> (1) A term or condition of a permit, license, certificate, or registration issued under this division.

> (2) A regulation or order adopted by the board.

(b) Civil liability may be imposed by the superior court. The Attorney General, upon the request of the board, shall petition the superior court to impose, assess, and recover those sums.

(c) Civil liability may be imposed administratively by the board pursuant to Section 1055.

Water Code § 1847

(MAUCRSA, Effective June 27, 2017.)

(a) A person or entity may be liable for a violation of any of the requirements of subdivision (b) in an amount not to exceed the sum of the following:

(1) Five hundred dollars ($500), plus two hundred fifty dollars ($250) for each additional day on which the violation continues if the person fails to correct the violation within 30 days after the board has called the violation to the attention of that person.

(2) Two thousand five hundred dollars ($2,500) for each acre-foot of water diverted or used in violation of the applicable requirement.

(b) Liability may be imposed for any of the following violations:

(1) Violation of a principle, guideline, or requirement established by the board or the Department of Fish and Wildlife under Section 13149.

(2) Failure to submit information, or making a material misstatement in information submitted, under Section 26060.1 of the Business and Professions Code.

(3) Violation of any requirement imposed under subdivision (b) of Section 26060.1 of the Business and Professions Code.

(4) Diversion or use of water for cannabis cultivation for which a license is required, but has not been obtained, under Chapter 6 (commencing with Section 26060) or Chapter 7 (commencing with Section 26070) of Division 10 of the Business and Professions Code.

(c) Civil liability may be imposed by the superior court. The Attorney General, upon the request of the board, shall petition the superior court to impose, assess, and recover those sums.

(d) Civil liability may be imposed administratively by the board pursuant to Section 1055.

Water Code § 5100

(Amended by Statute, Effective February 3, 2010.)

As used in this part:

(a) "Best available technologies" means technologies at the highest technically practical level, using flow totaling devices, and if necessary, data loggers and telemetry.

(b) "Best professional practices" means practices attaining and maintaining the accuracy of measurement and reporting devices and methods.

(c) "Diversion" means taking water by gravity or pumping from a surface stream or subterranean stream flowing through a known and definite channel, or other body of surface water, into a canal, pipeline, or other conduit, and includes impoundment of water in a reservoir.

(d) "Person" means all persons whether natural or artificial, including the United States of America, State of California, and all political subdivisions, districts, municipalities, and public agencies.

Water Code § 5101

(Amended by Statute, Effective January 1, 2012.)

Each person who, after December 31, 1965, diverts water shall file with the board, prior to July 1 of the succeeding year, a statement of his or her diversion and use, except that a statement is not required to be filed if the diversion is any of the following:

(a) From a spring that does not flow off the property on which it is located and from which the person's aggregate diversions do not exceed 25 acre-feet in any year.

(b) Covered by a registration for small domestic use, small irrigation use, or livestock stockpond use, or permit or license to appropriate water on file with the board.

(c) Included in a notice filed pursuant to Part 5 (commencing with Section 4999).

(d) Regulated by a watermaster appointed by the department and included in annual reports filed with a court or the board by the watermaster, which reports identify the persons who have diverted water and describe the general purposes and the place, the use, and the quantity of water that has been diverted from each source.

(e) Included in annual reports filed with a court or the board by a watermaster appointed by a court or pursuant to statute to administer a final judgment determining rights to water, which reports identify the persons who have diverted water and give the general place of use and the quantity of water that has been diverted from each source.

(f) For use in compliance with Article 2.5 (commencing with Section 1226) or Article 2.7 (commencing with Section 1228) of Chapter 1 of Part 2.

(g) A diversion that occurs before January 1, 2009, if any of the following applies:

(1) The diversion is from a spring that does not flow off the property on which it is located, and the person's aggregate diversions do not exceed 25 acre-feet in any year.

(2) The diversion is covered by an application to appropriate water on file with the board.

(3) The diversion is reported by the department in its hydrologic data bulletins.

(4) The diversion is included in the consumptive use data for the Delta lowlands published by the department in its hydrologic data bulletins.

Water Code § 5102

(Amended by Statute, Effective 1967.)

The statement may be filed either by the person who is diverting water or, on his behalf, by an agency which he designates and which maintains a record of the water diverted. A separate statement shall be filed for each point of diversion.

Water Code § 5103

(SB 837, Effective June 27, 2016.)

Each statement shall be prepared on a form provided by the board. The statement shall include all of the following information:

(a) The name and address of the person who diverted water and of the person filing the statement.

(b) The name of the stream or other source from which water was diverted, and the name of the next major stream or other body of water to which the source is tributary.

(c) The place of diversion. The location of the diversion works shall be depicted on a specific United States Geological Survey topographic map, or shall be identified using the California Coordinate System, or latitude and longitude measurements. If assigned, the public land description to the nearest 40-acre subdivision and the assessor's parcel number shall also be provided.

(d) The capacity of the diversion works and of the storage reservoir, if any, and the months in which water was used during the preceding calendar year.

(e) (1) (A) At least monthly records of water diversions. The measurements of the diversion shall be made in accordance with Section 1840.

(B) (i) On and after July 1, 2016, the measurement of a diversion of 10 acre-feet or more per year shall comply with regulations adopted by the board pursuant to Article 3 (commencing with Section 1840) of Chapter 12 of Part 2.

(ii) The requirement of clause (i) is extended to January 1, 2017, for any statement filer that enters into a voluntary agreement that is acceptable to the board to reduce the statement filer's diversions during the 2015 irrigation season.

(2) (A) The terms of, and eligibility for, any grant or loan awarded or administered by the department, the board, or the California Bay-Delta Authority on behalf of a person that is subject to paragraph (1) shall be conditioned on compliance with that paragraph.

(B) Notwithstanding subparagraph (A), the board may determine that a person is eligible for a grant or loan even though the person is not complying with paragraph (1), if both of the following apply:

(i) The board determines that the grant or loan will assist the grantee or loan recipient in complying with paragraph (1).

(ii) The person has submitted to the board a one-year schedule for complying with paragraph (1).

(C) It is the intent of the Legislature that the requirements of this subdivision shall complement and not affect the scope of authority granted to the board by provisions of law other than this article.

(f) (1) The purpose of use.

(2) The amount of water used, if any, for cannabis cultivation.

(g) A general description of the area in which the water was used. The location of the place of use shall be depicted on a specific United States Geological Survey topographic map and on any other maps with identifiable landmarks. If assigned, the public land description to the nearest 40-acre subdivision and the assessor's parcel number shall also be provided.

(h) The year in which the diversion was commenced as near as is known.

Water Code § 13149

(MCRSA- SB 837, Effective June 27, 2016.)

(a) (1) (A) The board, in consultation with the Department of Fish and Wildlife, shall adopt principles and guidelines for diversion and use of water for cannabis cultivation in areas where cannabis cultivation may have the potential to substantially affect instream flows. The principles and guidelines adopted under this section may include, but are not limited to, instream flow objectives, limits on diversions, and requirements for screening of diversions and elimination of barriers to fish passage. The principles and guidelines may include requirements that apply to groundwater extractions where the board determines those requirements are reasonably necessary for purposes of this section.

(B) Prior to adopting principles and guidelines under this section, the board shall allow for public comment and hearing, pursuant to Section 13147. The board shall provide an opportunity for the public to review and comment on the proposal for at least 60 days and shall consider the public comments before adopting the principles and guidelines.

(2) The board, in consultation with the Department of Fish and Wildlife, shall adopt principles and guidelines pending the development of long-term principles and guidelines under paragraph (1). The principles and guidelines,

including the interim principles and guidelines, shall include measures to protect springs, wetlands, and aquatic habitats from negative impacts of cannabis cultivation. The board may update the interim principles and guidelines as it determines to be reasonably necessary for purposes of this section.

(3) The Department of Fish and Wildlife, in consultation with the board, may establish interim requirements to protect fish and wildlife from the impacts of diversions for cannabis cultivation pending the adoption of long-term principles and guidelines by the board under paragraph (1). The requirements may also include measures to protect springs, wetlands, and aquatic habitats from negative impacts of cannabis cultivation.

(b) (1) Notwithstanding Section 15300.2 of Title 14 of the California Code of Regulations, actions of the board and the Department of Fish and Wildlife under this section shall be deemed to be within Section 15308 of Title 14 of the California Code of regulations, provided that those actions do not involve relaxation of existing streamflow standards.

(2) The board shall adopt principles and guidelines under this section as part of state policy for water quality control adopted pursuant to Article 3 (commencing with Section 13140) of Chapter 3 of Division 7.

(3) If the Department of Fish and Wildlife establishes interim requirements under this section, it shall do so as emergency regulations in accordance with Chapter 3.5 (commencing with Section 11340) of Part 1 of Division 3 of Title 2 of the Government Code. The adoption of those interim requirements is an emergency and shall be considered by the Office of Administrative Law as necessary for the immediate preservation of the public peace, health, safety, and general welfare. Notwithstanding Chapter 3.5 (commencing with Section 11340) of Part 1 of Division 3 of Title 2 of the Government Code, the emergency regulations shall remain in effect until revised by the Department of Fish and Wildlife, provided that the emergency regulations shall not apply after long-term principles and guidelines adopted by the board under this section take effect for the stream or other body of water where the diversion is located.

(4) A diversion for cannabis cultivation is subject to both the interim principles and guidelines and the interim requirements in the period before final principles and guidelines are adopted by the board.

(5) The board shall have primary enforcement responsibility for principles

and guidelines adopted under this section, and shall notify the Department of Food and Agriculture of any enforcement action taken.

Water Code § 13260

(Amended by Statute, Effective March 24, 2011.)

(a) Each of the following persons shall file with the appropriate regional board a report of the discharge, containing the information that may be required by the regional board:

(1) A person discharging waste, or proposing to discharge waste, within any region that could affect the quality of the waters of the state, other than into a community sewer system.

(2) A person who is a citizen, domiciliary, or political agency or entity of this state discharging waste, or proposing to discharge waste, outside the boundaries of the state in a manner that could affect the quality of the waters of the state within any region.

(3) A person operating, or proposing to construct, an injection well.

(b) No report of waste discharge need be filed pursuant to subdivision (a) if the requirement is waived pursuant to Section 13269.

(c) Each person subject to subdivision (a) shall file with the appropriate regional board a report of waste discharge relative to any material change or proposed change in the character, location, or volume of the discharge.

(d) (1) (A) Each person who is subject to subdivision (a) or (c) shall submit an annual fee according to a fee schedule established by the state board.

(B) The total amount of annual fees collected pursuant to this section shall equal that amount necessary to recover costs incurred in connection with the issuance, administration, reviewing, monitoring, and enforcement of waste discharge requirements and waivers of waste discharge requirements.

(C) Recoverable costs may include, but are not limited to, costs incurred in reviewing waste discharge reports, prescribing terms of waste discharge requirements and monitoring requirements, enforcing and evaluating compliance with waste discharge requirements and waiver requirements, conducting surface water and groundwater monitoring and modeling, analyzing laboratory samples, adopting, reviewing, and revising water quality control plans and state policies for water quality control, and reviewing documents prepared for the purpose of regulating the discharge of waste, and administrative costs incurred in connection with carrying out these actions.

(D) In establishing the amount of a fee that may be imposed on a confined animal feeding and holding operation pursuant to this section, including, but not limited to, a dairy farm, the state board shall consider all of the following factors:

(i) The size of the operation.

(ii) Whether the operation has been issued a permit to operate pursuant to Section 1342 of Title 33 of the United States Code.

(iii) Any applicable waste discharge requirement or conditional waiver of a waste discharge requirement.

(iv) The type and amount of discharge from the operation.

(v) The pricing mechanism of the commodity produced.

(vi) Any compliance costs borne by the operation pursuant to state and federal water quality regulations.

(vii) Whether the operation participates in a quality assurance program certified by a regional water quality control board, the state board, or a federal water quality control agency.

(2) (A) Subject to subparagraph (B), the fees collected pursuant to this section shall be deposited in the Waste Discharge Permit Fund, which is hereby created. The money in the fund is available for expenditure by the state board, upon appropriation by the Legislature, solely for the purposes of carrying out this division.

(B) (i) Notwithstanding subparagraph (A), the fees collected pursuant to this section from stormwater dischargers that are subject to a general industrial or construction stormwater permit under the national pollutant discharge elimination system (NPDES) shall be separately accounted for in the Waste Discharge Permit Fund.

(ii) Not less than 50 percent of the money in the Waste Discharge Permit Fund that is separately accounted for pursuant to clause (i) is available, upon appropriation by the Legislature, for expenditure by the regional board with jurisdiction over the permitted industry or construction site that generated the fee to carry out stormwater programs in the region.

(iii) Each regional board that receives money pursuant to clause (ii) shall spend not less than 50 percent of that money solely on stormwater inspection and regulatory compliance issues associated with industrial and construction stormwater programs.

(3) A person who would be required to pay the annual fee prescribed by paragraph (1) for waste discharge requirements applicable to discharges of solid waste, as defined in Section 40191 of the Public Resources Code, at a waste management unit that is also regulated under Division 30 (commencing with Section 40000) of the Public Resources Code, shall be entitled to a waiver of the annual fee for the discharge of solid waste at the waste management unit imposed by paragraph (1) upon verification by the state board of payment of the fee imposed by Section 48000 of the Public Resources Code, and provided that the fee established pursuant to Section 48000 of the Public Resources Code generates revenues sufficient to fund the programs specified in Section 48004 of the Public Resources Code and the amount appropriated by the Legislature for those purposes is not reduced.

(e) Each person that discharges waste in a manner regulated by this section shall pay an annual fee to the state board. The state board shall establish, by regulation, a timetable for the payment of the annual fee. If the state board or a regional board determines that the discharge will not affect, or have the potential to affect, the quality of the waters of the state, all or part of the annual fee shall be refunded.

(f) (1) The state board shall adopt, by emergency regulations, a schedule of fees authorized under subdivision (d). The total revenue collected each year through annual fees shall be set at an amount equal to the revenue levels set forth in the Budget Act for this activity. The state board shall automatically adjust the annual fees each fiscal year to conform with the revenue levels set forth in the Budget Act for this activity. If the state board determines that the revenue collected during the preceding year was greater than, or less than, the revenue levels set forth in the Budget Act, the state board may further adjust the annual fees to compensate for the over and under collection of revenue.

(2) The emergency regulations adopted pursuant to this subdivision, any amendment thereto, or subsequent adjustments to the annual fees, shall be adopted by the state board in accordance with Chapter 3.5 (commencing with Section 11340) of Part 1 of Division 3 of Title 2 of the Government Code. The adoption of these regulations is an emergency and shall be

considered by the Office of Administrative Law as necessary for the immediate preservation of the public peace, health, safety, and general welfare. Notwithstanding Chapter 3.5 (commencing with Section 11340) of Part 1 of Division 3 of Title 2 of the Government Code, any emergency regulations adopted by the state board, or adjustments to the annual fees made by the state board pursuant to this section, shall not be subject to review by the Office of Administrative Law and shall remain in effect until revised by the state board.

(g) The state board shall adopt regulations setting forth reasonable time limits within which the regional board shall determine the adequacy of a report of waste discharge submitted under this section.

(h) Each report submitted under this section shall be sworn to, or submitted under penalty of perjury.

(i) The regulations adopted by the state board pursuant to subdivision (f) shall include a provision that annual fees shall not be imposed on those who pay fees under the national pollutant discharge elimination system until the time when those fees are again due, at which time the fees shall become due on an annual basis.

(j) A person operating or proposing to construct an oil, gas, or geothermal injection well subject to paragraph (3) of subdivision (a) shall not be required to pay a fee pursuant to subdivision (d) if the injection well is regulated by the Division of Oil and Gas of the Department of Conservation, in lieu of the appropriate California regional water quality control board, pursuant to the memorandum of understanding, entered into between the state board and the Department of Conservation on May 19, 1988. This subdivision shall remain operative until the memorandum of understanding is revoked by the state board or the Department of Conservation.

(k) In addition to the report required by subdivision (a), before a person discharges mining waste, the person shall first submit both of the following to the regional board:

> (1) A report on the physical and chemical characteristics of the waste that could affect its potential to cause pollution or contamination. The report shall include the results of all tests required by regulations adopted by the board, any test adopted by the Department of Toxic Substances Control pursuant to Section 25141 of the Health and Safety Code for extractable, persistent, and bioaccumulative toxic substances

in a waste or other material, and any other tests that the state board or regional board may require, including, but not limited to, tests needed to determine the acid-generating potential of the mining waste or the extent to which hazardous substances may persist in the waste after disposal.

(2) A report that evaluates the potential of the discharge of the mining waste to produce, over the long term, acid mine drainage, the discharge or leaching of heavy metals, or the release of other hazardous substances.

(l) Except upon the written request of the regional board, a report of waste discharge need not be filed pursuant to subdivision (a) or (c) by a user of recycled water that is being supplied by a supplier or distributor of recycled water for whom a master recycling permit has been issued pursuant to Section 13523.1.

Water Code § 13264

(Amended by Statute, Effective January 1, 2004.)

(a) No person shall initiate any new discharge of waste or make any material changes in any discharge, or initiate a discharge to, make any material changes in a discharge to, or construct, an injection well, prior to the filing of the report required by Section 13260 and no person shall take any of these actions after filing the report but before whichever of the following occurs first:

(1) The issuance of waste discharge requirements pursuant to Section 13263.

(2) The expiration of 140 days after compliance with Section 13260 if the waste to be discharged does not create or threaten to create a condition of pollution or nuisance and any of the following applies:

(A) The project is not subject to the California Environmental Quality Act (Division 13 (commencing with Section 21000) of the Public Resources Code).

(B) The regional board is the lead agency for purposes of the California Environmental Quality Act, a negative declaration is required, and at least 105 days have expired since the regional board assumed lead agency responsibility.

(C) The regional board is the lead agency for the purposes of the California Environmental Quality Act, and environmental impact report or written documentation prepared to meet the requirements of Section 21080.5 of the Public Resources Code is required, and at least one year has expired since the regional board assumed lead agency responsibility.

(D) The regional board is a responsible agency for purposes of the California Environmental Quality Act, and at least 90 days have expired since certification or approval of environmental documentation by the lead agency.

(3) The issuance of a waiver pursuant to Section 13269.

(b) The Attorney General, at the request of a regional board, shall petition the superior court for the issuance of a temporary restraining order, preliminary injunction, or permanent injunction, or combination thereof, as may be appropriate, prohibiting any person who is violating or threatening to violate this section from doing any of the following, whichever is applicable:

(1) Discharging the waste or fluid.

(2) Making any material change in the discharge.

(3) Constructing the injection well.

(c) (1) Notwithstanding any other provision of law, moneys collected under this division for a violation pursuant to paragraph (2) of subdivision (a) shall be deposited in the Waste Discharge Permit Fund and separately accounted for in that fund.

(2) The funds described in paragraph (1) shall be expended by the state board, upon appropriation by the Legislature, to assist regional boards, and other public agencies with authority to clean up waste or abate the effects of the waste, in cleaning up or abating the effects of the waste on waters of the state or for the purposes authorized in Section 13443.

Water Code § 13272

(Amended by Statute, Effective June 20, 2014.)

(a) Except as provided by subdivision (b), any person who, without regard to intent or negligence, causes or permits any oil or petroleum product to be discharged in or on any waters of the state, or discharged or deposited where it is, or probably will be, discharged in or on any waters of the state, shall, as soon as (1) that person has knowledge of the discharge, (2) notification is possible, and (3) notification can be provided without substantially impeding cleanup or other emergency measures, immediately notify the Office of Emergency Services of the discharge in accordance with the spill reporting provision of the California oil spill contingency plan adopted pursuant to Article 3.5 (commencing with Section 8574.1) of Chapter 7 of Division 1 of Title 2 of the Government Code.

(b) The notification required by this section shall not apply to a discharge in compliance with waste discharge requirements or other provisions of this division.

(c) Any person who fails to provide the notice required by this section is guilty of a misdemeanor and shall be punished by a fine of not less than five hundred dollars ($500) or more than five thousand dollars ($5,000) per day for each day of failure to notify, or imprisonment of not more than one year, or both. Except where a discharge to the waters of this state would have occurred but for cleanup or emergency response by a public agency, this subdivision shall not apply to any discharge to land that does not result in a discharge to the waters of this state. This subdivision shall not apply to any person who is fined by the federal government for a failure to report a discharge of oil.

(d) Notification received pursuant to this section or information obtained by use of that notification shall not be used against any person providing the notification in any criminal case, except in a prosecution for perjury or giving a false statement.

(e) Immediate notification to the appropriate regional board of the discharge, in accordance with reporting requirements set under Section 13267 or 13383, shall constitute compliance with the requirements of subdivision (a).

(f) The reportable quantity for oil or petroleum products shall be one barrel (42 gallons) or more, by direct discharge to the receiving waters, unless a more restrictive reporting standard for a particular body of water is adopted.

Water Code § 13276

(MAUCRSA, Effective June 27, 2017.)

(a) The multiagency task force, the Department of Fish and Wildlife and state board pilot project to address the Environmental Impacts of Cannabis Cultivation, assigned to respond to the damages caused by cannabis cultivation on public and private lands in California, shall continue its enforcement efforts on a permanent basis and expand them to a statewide level to ensure the reduction of adverse impacts of cannabis cultivation on water quality and on fish and wildlife throughout the state.

(b) The state board or the appropriate regional board shall address discharges of waste resulting from cannabis cultivation under Division 10 of the Business and Professions Code and associated activities, including by adopting a general permit, establishing waste discharge requirements, or taking action pursuant to Section 13269. In addressing these discharges, the state board or the regional board shall include conditions to address items that include, but are not limited to, all of the following:

(1) Site development and maintenance, erosion control, and drainage features.

(2) Stream crossing installation and maintenance.

(3) Riparian and wetland protection and management.

(4) Soil disposal.

(5) Water storage and use.

(6) Irrigation runoff.

(7) Fertilizers and soil.

(8) Pesticides and herbicides.

(9) Petroleum products and other chemicals.

(10) Cultivation-related waste.

(11) Refuse and human waste.

(12) Cleanup, restoration, and mitigation.

Water Code § 13387

(Amended by Statute, Effective April 4, 2011, and Operative October 1, 2011.)

(a) Any person who knowingly or negligently does any of the following is subject to criminal penalties as provided in subdivisions (b), (c), and (d):

(1) Violates Section 13375 or 13376.

(2) Violates any waste discharge requirements or dredged or fill material permit issued pursuant to this chapter or any water quality certification issued pursuant to Section 13160.

(3) Violates any order or prohibition issued pursuant to Section 13243 or 13301, if the activity subject to the order or prohibition is subject to regulation under this chapter.

(4) Violates any requirement of Section 301, 302, 306, 307, 308, 318, 401, or 405 of the Clean Water Act (33 U.S.C. Sec. 1311, 1312, 1316, 1317, 1318, 1328, 1341, or 1345), as amended.

(5) Introduces into a sewer system or into a publicly owned treatment works any pollutant or hazardous substances that the person knew or reasonably should have known could cause personal injury or property damage.

(6) Introduces any pollutant or hazardous substance into a sewer system or into a publicly owned treatment works, except in accordance with any applicable pretreatment requirements, which causes the treatment works to violate waste discharge requirements.

(b) Any person who negligently commits any of the violations set forth in subdivision (a) shall, upon conviction, be punished by a fine of not less than five thousand dollars ($5,000), nor more than twenty-five thousand dollars ($25,000), for each day in which the violation occurs, by imprisonment for not more than one year in a county jail, or by both that fine and imprisonment. If a conviction of a person is for a violation committed after a first conviction of the person under this subdivision, subdivision (c), or subdivision (d), punishment shall be by a fine of not more than fifty thousand dollars ($50,000) for each day in which the violation occurs, by imprisonment pursuant to subdivision (h) of Section 1170 of the Penal Code for 16, 20, or 24 months, or by both that fine and imprisonment.

(c) Any person who knowingly commits any of the violations set forth in subdivision (a) shall, upon conviction, be punished by a fine of not less than five thousand dollars ($5,000), nor more than fifty thousand dollars ($50,000), for each day in which the violation occurs, by imprisonment pursuant to subdivision (h) of Section 1170 of the Penal Code, or by both that fine and imprisonment. If a conviction of a person is for a violation committed after a first conviction of the person under this subdivision or subdivision (d), punishment shall be by a fine of not more than one hundred thousand dollars ($100,000) for each day in which the violation occurs, by imprisonment pursuant to subdivision (h) of Section 1170 of the Penal Code for two, four, or six years, or by both that fine and imprisonment.

(d) (1) Any person who knowingly commits any of the violations set forth in subdivision (a), and who knows at the time that the person thereby places another person in imminent danger of death or serious bodily injury, shall, upon conviction, be punished by a fine of not more than two hundred fifty thousand dollars ($250,000), imprisonment pursuant to subdivision (h) of Section 1170 of the Penal Code for 5, 10, or 15 years, or by both that fine and imprisonment. A person that is an organization shall, upon conviction under this subdivision, be subject to a fine of not more than one million dollars ($1,000,000). If a conviction of a person is for a violation committed after a first conviction of the person under this subdivision, the punishment shall be by a fine of not more than five hundred thousand dollars ($500,000), by imprisonment pursuant to subdivision (h) of Section 1170 of the Penal Code for 10, 20, or 30 years, or by both that fine and imprisonment. A person that is an organization shall, upon conviction for a violation committed after a first conviction of the person under this subdivision, be subject to a fine of not more than two million dollars ($2,000,000). Any fines imposed pursuant to this subdivision shall be in addition to any fines imposed pursuant to subdivision (c).

(2) In determining whether a defendant who is an individual knew that the defendant's conduct placed another person in imminent danger of death or serious bodily injury, the defendant is responsible only for actual awareness or actual belief that the defendant possessed, and knowledge possessed by a person other than the defendant, but not by the defendant personally, cannot be attributed to the defendant.

(e) Any person who knowingly makes any false statement, representation, or certification in any record, report, plan, notice to comply, or other document filed with a regional board or the state board, or who knowingly falsifies, tampers with, or renders inaccurate any monitoring device or method required under this division shall be punished by a fine of not more than twenty-five thousand dollars ($25,000), by imprisonment pursuant to subdivision (h) of Section 1170 of the Penal Code for 16, 20, or 24 months, or by both that fine and imprisonment. If a conviction of a person is for a violation committed after a first conviction of the person under this subdivision, punishment shall be by a fine of not more than twenty-five thousand dollars ($25,000) per day of violation, by imprisonment pursuant to subdivision (h) of Section 1170 of the Penal Code for two, three, or four years, or by both that fine and imprisonment.

(f) For purposes of this section, a single operational upset which leads to simultaneous violations of more than one pollutant parameter shall be treated as a single violation.

(g) For purposes of this section, "organization," "serious bodily injury," "person," and "hazardous substance" shall have the same meaning as in Section 309(c) of the Clean Water Act (33 U.S.C. Sec. 1319(c)), as amended.

(h) (1) Subject to paragraph (2), funds collected pursuant to this section shall be deposited in the State Water Pollution Cleanup and Abatement Account.

(2) (A) Notwithstanding any other provision of law, fines collected for a violation of a water quality certification in accordance with paragraph (2) of subdivision (a) or for a violation of Section 401 of the Clean Water Act (33 U.S.C. Sec. 1341) in accordance with paragraph (4) of subdivision (a) shall be deposited in the Water Discharge Permit Fund and separately accounted for in that fund.

(B) The funds described in subparagraph (A) shall be expended by the state board, upon appropriation by the Legislature, to assist regional boards, and other public agencies with authority to clean up waste or abate the effects of the waste, in cleaning up or abating the effects of the waste on waters of the state, or for the purposes authorized in Section 13443.

Water Code § 13575

(Amended by Statute, Effective January 1, 1999.)

(a) This chapter shall be known and may be cited as the Water Recycling Act of 1991.

(b) As used in this chapter, the following terms have the following meanings:

(1) "Customer" means a person or entity that purchases water from a retail water supplier.

(2) "Entity responsible for groundwater replenishment" means any

person or entity authorized by statute or court order to manage a groundwater basin and acquire water for groundwater replenishment.

(3) "Recycled water" has the same meaning as defined in subdivision (n) of Section 13050.

(4) "Recycled water producer" means any local public entity that produces recycled water.

(5) "Recycled water wholesaler" means any local public entity that distributes recycled water to retail water suppliers and which has constructed, or is constructing, a recycled water distribution system.

(6) "Retail water supplier" means any local entity, including a public agency, city, county, or private water company, that provides retail water service.

(7) "Retailer" means the retail water supplier in whose service area is located the property to which a customer requests the delivery of reycled water service.

XIII. Regulatory Agencies

State Licensing Agencies

Bureau of Cannabis Control - California Department of Consumer Affairs

2920 Kilgore Road, Rancho Cordova, CA 95670
Phone: (833) 768-5880
Website: http://www.bcc.ca.gov
Email: bcc@dca.ca.go

Regulates the licensing of cannabis testing laboratories, retailers, distributors, microbusinesses, and temporary cannabis events.

California Department of Food and Agriculture

1220 N Street, Sacramento, CA 95814
Phone: (833) 225-4769
Website: http://calcannabis.cdfa.ca.gov/
Email: calcannabis@cdfa.ca.gov

Responsible for licensing cultivation.
Establishes electronic database to track cannabis from seed to sale.
Assists other agencies in protecting the environment, public health, and safety.

California Department of Public Health - Manufactured Cannabis Safety Branch

PO Box 997377, MS 7606, Sacramento CA 95899-7377
Phone: (855) 421-7887
Website: http://www.cdph.ca.gov
Email: mcsb@cdph.ca.gov

Responsible for licensing manufacturers.

Additional Regulatory Agencies

California Department of Fish and Wildlife

830 S Street, Sacramento, CA 95811
Phone: (916) 445-8576
Website: http://www.wildlife.ca.gov/Conservation/Cannabis

Engaged in environmental review and permitting, enforcement, and coordination with other agencies developing and implementing programs.

California Department of Pesticide Regulation

1001 I Street, Sacramento, CA 95814
Phone: (916) 445-5010
Website: http://www.cdpr.ca.gov

Develops standards for the use of pesticides in cultivation and maximum tolerances for pesticides and other foreign object residue in harvested cannabis.

California Department of Tax and Fee Administration

450 N Street, Sacramento, CA 94279
Phone: (800) 400-7115
Website: https://www.cdtfa.ca.gov/industry/cannabis.htm

Businesses that sell cannabis and/or cannabis products must register with the CDTFA for a seller's permit and regularly file sales and use tax returns.

Distributors must register with the CDTFA for a cannabis tax permit and regularly file cannabis tax returns.

California State Water Resources Control Board

1001 I Street, Sacramento, CA 95814
Website:
http://www.waterboards.ca.gov/water_issues/programs/cannabis/index.shtml

Regulates potential water quality and quantity issues related to cultivation.

Reader's Notes

CPSIA information can be obtained
at www.ICGtesting.com
Printed in the USA
BVHW08*0046070618
518359BV00009B/219/P